T0211194

Lecture Notes in Business Information Processing 294

Series Editors

Wil M.P. van der Aalst
Eindhoven Technical University, Eindhoven, The Netherlands
John Mylopoulos
University of Trento, Trento, Italy
Michael Rosemann
Queensland University of Technology, Brisbane, QLD, Australia
Michael J. Shaw
University of Illinois, Urbana-Champaign, IL, USA
Clemens Szyperski
Microsoft Research, Redmond, WA, USA

More information about this series at http://www.springer.com/series/7911

Susanne Stigberg · Joakim Karlsen
Harald Holone · Cathrine Linnes (Eds.)

Nordic Contributions in IS Research

8th Scandinavian Conference
on Information Systems, SCIS 2017
Halden, Norway, August 6–8, 2017
Proceedings

 Springer

Editors
Susanne Stigberg
Østfold University College
Halden
Norway

Harald Holone
Østfold University College
Halden
Norway

Joakim Karlsen
Østfold University College
Halden
Norway

Cathrine Linnes
Østfold University College
Halden
Norway

ISSN 1865-1348   ISSN 1865-1356 (electronic)
Lecture Notes in Business Information Processing
ISBN 978-3-319-64694-7   ISBN 978-3-319-64695-4   (eBook)
DOI 10.1007/978-3-319-64695-4

Library of Congress Control Number: 2017948176

Printed on acid-free paper

This Springer imprint is published by Springer Nature
The registered company is Springer International Publishing AG
The registered company address is: Gewerbestrasse 11, 6330 Cham, Switzerland

Preface

The 8th Scandinavian Conference on Information Systems, SCIS 2017, was hosted by Østfold University College in Halden, Norway, during August 6–9, 2017.

Last year's theme for the conference was "Living in the Cloud," inviting papers that describe various aspects of the increased use of cloud-based systems, how this affects our lives, and how we as information systems scholars can design for this new paradigm. This year, we took this further by focusing on the so-called smart systems that prevail in many areas, from health systems to industry and education. As information systems scholars, we have a responsibility in the continued digitalization of our society. New technological innovations influence work processes, communication, leisure activities, and lifelong learning. To provide an arena for discussing larger questions in this context, we selected "Challenging Smart" for this year's conference. Not because we think "smart" systems are inherently problematic, but because the term "smart technology" is often used uncritically. Our community has a responsibility to ask these questions, in the design, implementation, and adaptation in organizations.

What does "smart technologies" mean in different contexts? For whom is the technology smart? In what way is it smart? What should we expect from the organizations and businesses involved in this development, and what does it mean to be a resident in a smart society?

We received 32 submissions and accepted 11 of these, leading to a final acceptance rate of 35%. Each submission was assigned a minimum of two external reviewers and a primary reviewer, who provided a meta-review; final decisions were taken using a combination of all of these reviews.

The keynote speakers at the conference were Hanne Cecilie Geirbo from the University of Oslo and Per-Anders Hillgren from Malmö University.

SCIS 2017 was held in conjunction with the 40th annual Information Systems Research Seminar in Scandinavia, IRIS 40.

We would like to thank all supporters and sponsors of this conference, the reviewers, organizers, Program Committee members, authors, and others who have helped make this possible.

June 2017

Susanne Stigberg
Joakim Karlsen
Cathrine Linnes
Harald Holone

The original version of this book was revised:
Contents were corrected throughout the chapter.
The erratum is available at http://link.springer.
com/10.1007/978-3-319-64695-4_12

Organization

Program Chairs

Susanne Stigberg   Østfold University College, Norway
Joakim Karlsen   Østfold University College, Norway

Program Committee

Mikko Ahonen   University of Tampere, Finland
Bendik Bygstad   University of Oslo, Norway
Klaudia Carcani   Østfold University College, Norway
Ricardo Colomo-Palàcios   Østfold University College, Norway
Abdolrasoul Habibipour   Luleå University of Technology, Finland
Louise Harder Fischer   University of Copenhagen, Denmark
Heidi Hartikainen   University of Oulu, Finland
Harald Holone   Østfold University College, Norway
Anna Sigridur Islind   Högskolan Väst, Sweden
Alexander Moltubakk   University of Oslo, Norway
    Kempton
Ditte Kolbæk   Aalborg Universitet, Denmark
Olli Korhonen   University of Oulu, Finland
Pentti Launonen   Aalto University, Finland
Susanne Lindberg   Högskolan i Halmstad, Sweden
Cathrine Linnes   Østfold University College, Norway
Christian Madsen   University of Copenhagen, Denmark
Amir Mohagheghzadeh   University of Gothenburg, Sweden
Petter Nielsen   University of Oslo, Norway
Arto Ojala   University of Jyväskylä, Finland
Daniel Rudmark   RISE Viktoria, Sweden
Markus Salo   University of Jyväskylä, Finland
Line Silsand   Norwegian Centre for E-health Research, Norway
Lise Tordrup Heeager   Aarhus University, Denmark
Polyxeni Vassilakopoulou   University of Agder, Norway
Parvaneh Westerlund   Luleå University of Technology, Finland
Egil Øvrelid   University of Oslo, Norway

Contents

Leading Digital Transformation:
The Scandinavian Way

Bendik Bygstad[1,2(✉)], Hans-Petter Aanby[3], and Jon Iden[2]

[1] University of Oslo, Gaustadalléen 23, 0373 Oslo, Norway
bendikby@ifi.uio.no
[2] NHH Norwegian School of Economics, Helleveien 30, 5045 Bergen, Norway
jon.iden@nhh.no
[3] OptimiseIT AS, Dillingtoppen 17, 1570 Dilling, Norway
hans-petter@optimiseit.no

Abstract. Digital transformation can be seen as the mutual reinforcement of process redesign and innovative use of IT. The literature on digital transformation focuses on digital business strategy and the transformational CIO. Stakeholder engagement in combination with leadership style is seldom discussed. Our research questions are (i) what characterises leadership in the digital transformation, and (ii) what does the Scandinavian workplace model add to the knowledge of digital transformation? Our empirical evidence is the digital transformation in a large airline, the SAS, during the years 2013–2016. The process was very turbulent but eventually quite successful. We identify two Scandinavian contributions to transformation research: firstly, the deep engagement with employees, including trade unions, supports a structured process with a focus on finding solutions, not conflicts. Second, a coaching leadership style, allowing space for autonomy, leverages the competence of highly-skilled employees.

Keywords: Digital transformation · Transformational leadership · Scandinavian workplace model · CIO · Case study

1 Introduction

It is one of the hard facts of management research that most managers do not get much done during their tenure, except keeping up with daily tasks and problems. This applies also to CIOs; many of them dream and talk about digital transformation, but the short-term challenges are so numerous and tough that even apparently successful CIOs seldom accomplish much more than keeping the lights on.

But some do. Some executives are credited with transformational leadership, and some CIOs have accomplished digital transformation of their organisations, or even sectors [1, 2]. For instance, in *Cases on IT Leadership,* Bjørn-Andersen [3] presented 16 cases, including some spectacular transformation successes, such as Maersk (shipping), Lego (toys) and NOVO (pharmaceutical). Researchers have identified two key success factors for digital transformation: competent strategic management and some specific capabilities of the acting CIO [2].

S. Stigberg et al. (Eds.): SCIS 2017, LNBIP 294, pp. 1–14, 2017.
DOI: 10.1007/978-3-319-64695-4_1

However, there are many unresolved questions about the role of the CIO in digital transformation. One of them is the role of the environments, such as the role of the transformation team, the vendors, the senior management and perhaps most importantly, the role of the entire focal organisation.

Our starting point is that digital transformation requires a transformational CIO, but a successful transformation is the result of a collective organisational effort, not the sole result of a heroic and charismatic CIO. Our research context is the Scandinavian work-place tradition, emphasising a broad and inclusive approach to organisational change. Our research questions are,

- What characterises leadership in the digital transformation?
- What does the Scandinavian workplace model add to the knowledge of digital transformation?

To develop our argument, we draw on insights from transformational leadership, the Scandinavian workplace model and an in-depth study of a turbulent transformation at the SAS airline. Our contribution is that the Scandinavian workplace model adds two elements: deep engagement with employees and a coaching leadership style, ensuring that the process leverages the competence of highly-skilled employees.

2   Relevant Research

2.1   Digital Transformation and the CIO

Bharadway et al. [4] presented influential ideas on digital transformation. Their key point is that firms no longer need an IT strategy (as one of several sub-strategies) but rather a digital business strategy, defined as an organisational strategy formulated and executed by leveraging digital resources to create differential value. The digital business strategy is described as different than the IT strategy in four aspects: *scope* (transcends traditional functional silos), *scale* (rapid digital scale-up and down), *speed* (of product launches and decisions) and *source of value creation* (multi-sided business models and information). This also requires a different type of CIO.

In *The Transformational CIO* [2], Muller builds on established insights from strategic management for the transformational CIO:

- *Define a vision:* the people carrying out the transformation project must have a clear vision
- *Build an executive team*: this includes usually bringing in new managers and moving people to different positions
- *Lead and inspire:* this means to changing the IT organisation from a reactive to a proactive mode, and getting people to believe in your ideas
- *Change the way people think and behave:* the three essentials (people, business processes and technology) must be orchestrated together to accomplish the transformation

Muller points to the fact that most CIOs are not transformational, and that the successful CIO must be able to convince the business that the IT unit is a real business partner, with the necessary insight and means to transform the organisation.

A successful transformation is also context sensitive. In his classic HBR article [5], Kotter argued that most transformation efforts failed because in a normal business-as-usual situation, there are simply too many forces that resist change. Only in a crisis are these forces are weakened, and a window of opportunity emerges, where real transformation is possible.

Which attributes, then, are important for the transformational CIO?

2.2 Transformational Leadership

Leadership is described as 'a stream of evolving interrelationships in which leaders are continuously evoking motivational responses from followers and modifying their behaviour as they meet responsiveness or resistance, in a ceaseless process of flow and counter flow' [6]. Masood et al. [7] argued that in a global and changing business world, leaders must be able to respond to continuous changes in markets, customer needs, resources and technologies. Consequently, transformational leadership, first introduced by Burns [6], has received a tremendous amount of attention and has emerged as one of the most dominant leadership theories [8]. The essence of trans-formational leadership, as postulated by Boehnke et al. [9], is that superior performance is possible only by transforming followers' values, attitudes and motives from a lower to a higher plane of arousal and maturity. Research by Krishnan [10] suggests that superior performance is possible only through stimulating and motivating followers to higher levels of performance through transformational leadership.

According to Bass [11], transformational leaders possess good visioning, rhetorical and impression management skills, and they use these skills to develop strong emotional bonds with followers. Transformational leaders offer a purpose that transcends short-term goals and focuses on higher-order intrinsic needs [6]. Four dimensions of transformational leadership have been proposed [8, 12]. Firstly, *idealised influence* characterises the extent to which a leader behaves in admirable ways that encourage followers to identify with him or her. Second, *inspirational motivation* describes the extent to which a leader puts forth a vision which is appealing and inspiring to followers. Third, *intellectual stimulation* characterises the extent to which a leader challenge existing assumptions and takes risks that stimulate and encourage creativity in followers. Finally, *individual consideration* describes the extent to which a leader listens to followers' concerns and seeks to meet their individual needs.

2.3 The Scandinavian Workplace Model and Scandinavian Leadership

The three Scandinavian countries (Sweden, Denmark and Norway) form a rather tight cluster [13, 14]. They share a common history, their languages are similar, they share the same Lutheran religion, and politically, they share the social-democratic ideology responsible for what is known as 'the Scandinavian workplace model'. The Scandinavian model is a relatively loose term. At a macro level, the model refers to a highly educated and relatively homogeneous workforce, stable labour relations, a high level of unionisation, small wage differentials, high productivity and strong governments committed to an extensive welfare and social security system with full employment as an absolute objective [15, 16]. At a micro level, the term refers to a relatively high degree of workplace democracy based on co-operation, consensus, participation and power-sharing [15]. The classic survey by Hofstede [17] typifies a rather distinctive Scandinavian workplace culture, categorised as very low on power distance and with a preference for good working relations.

Research has revealed that leadership in Scandinavia differs in many ways from that of other supranational entities [15], and Scandinavian leadership is suggested as a distinctive management concept. Scandinavian leaders favour coaching rather than directing [18], frequently ask subordinates for opinions [19], are more willing to delegate decisions to subordinates than in many other nations [20] and tend to favour team integration and team collaboration [21].

3   Method

The chosen approach was *engaged scholarship* [22], defined as a form of inquiry where researchers involve practitioners and leverage their different perspectives to learn about a problem domain. The basic idea of engaged scholarship is that when researchers interact and learn with practitioners, it is more likely to produce significant knowledge advances than doing either basic or applied research. A key point is that any lack of agreement may provide particular illumination when addressing complex research questions. Engaged scholarship is based on a critical realist philosophy of science.

3.1   Research Setting

The setting was unusual. In 2013 a new CIO, Mr Aanby, was hired by the Scandinavian airline SAS, first to deal with an immediate crisis and later to transform the airline's IT structure and services. Aanby had previously been an IT manager at SAS but had spent the past decade as CIO and director of business development at SAS's main competitor Norwegian Air Shuttle. At Norwegian, Aanby had built a modern, SOA-type IT architecture and an agile IT organisation, which had been a key element in Norwegian's spectacular success [23] during the decade the start-up airline had grown to a billion-dollar international airline, carrying 25 million passengers in 2015. In 2012 Aanby quit Norwegian and started a consulting business. Shortly after, SAS called on his services, asking him to do the same as he had accomplished in Norwegian, i.e. to establish a low-cost IT-platform to support business agility (or almost the same but from an opposite position). At Norwegian, the challenge had been to build a new solution from scratch; at SAS, the challenge was to reduce the complexity of a mature but siloed IT structure.

3.2   Data Collection and Analysis

In line with van de Ven's method for *engaged scholarship* [22], the study was conducted in co-operation with Aanby and with other key actors in SAS.

The main steps were:

(i) *Ground problem/question in reality up close and from afar*
Mr. Aanby and the first researcher had co-researched the Norwegian case and co-published results [24]. Building on Aanby's experience in SAS, we wished to assess the digital transformation in SAS, with a particular focus on the role of the Scandinavian workplace model and Scandinavian leadership.

(ii) *Develop alternative theories to address the question*
In particular, we wished to investigate the *environments* of the transitional CIO, in order to theorise on which factors that might support digital transformation. Our assumption was that this aspect was central but under-researched.

(iii) *Collect evidence to compare models or theories*
A case description was crafted, building on in-depth interviews with seven key informants from the SAS case, and supplemented with written records, such as project documentation, technical descriptions and evaluations. The analysis focused on identifying specific patterns of the change process, in order to understand the transformational CIO and assess the Scandinavian contribution.

(iv) *Communicate and apply findings to address the problem/question*
Preliminary results were discussed with the key informants. The same applied to draft versions of this paper.

4   The Case

SAS is an international airline, based in Scandinavia, partly owned by the governments of Sweden, Denmark and Norway. Founded in 1946, the company operated relatively protected by privileged routes inside Scandinavia and regulated international connections. After the European airlines were deregulated in 2000, competition became much stronger; air ticket prices fell, and SAS revenues plummeted. The company were used to being rich and protected, and struggled to adjust the new situation. Although SAS had been losing money since 2002, the sense of crisis was weak, and programmes and projects had continued. Instead of a turnaround strategy and operations, the company chose to solve the problems financially, by selling assets and by asking for more money from government shareholders.

4.1   An International Airline in Crisis in 2012

By November 2012, the crisis became acute because the company was running out of cash and not paying its bills. One of the actions was a short-term engagement of Hans-Petter Aanby, a former SAS IT executive who later had built a strong career as the CIO of SAS's main competitor, Norwegian Air Shuttle. Aanby had recently quit

Norwegian and was available as a consultant. His assignment was to ensure – in the case of SAS bankruptcy – that the IT systems would be in operation to allow aircraft from various destinations across the globe to return to Scandinavia.

By the end of December, the crisis had been temporarily solved by SAS's creditors, the banks, which granted the necessary cash. In practice, this meant that the banks were taking the main decisions during the coming period. The key short-term decision was to cut cost dramatically, and IT was not excluded; building on a report from PwC, the stated objective was to cut IT costs by 50% and IT personnel by 70%, without negative effects on operations. Aanby was asked to take the CIO position and accepted.

An overview of the chronology of the case is offered in Fig. 1.

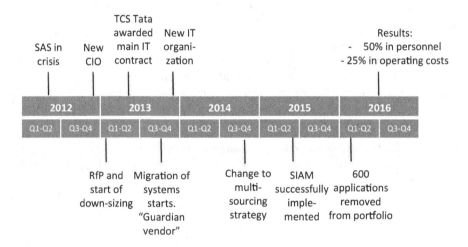

Fig. 1. Timeline.

4.2   A New CIO in 2013

Reducing IT costs by 50% (of an official budget of 1.3 billion SEK, which in reality turned out to be 1.7 billion) without affecting operations was extremely challenging. However, the IT function had not been well managed the past ten years, and there was some slack in several layers of the organisation. Aanby quickly initiated three initiatives, which were run in parallel:

- Establishing a new IT organisation and redesigning internal processes
- Reducing the number of systems and redesigning the IT architecture
- Negotiating and implementing a new sourcing model.

4.3 Establishing a New IT Organisation and Redesigning Internal Processes

The new IT organisation was established with seven units as shown in Fig. 2. All managers (five of them called "business CIO"), with one exception, were new; most of them came from other companies.

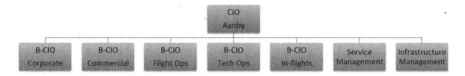

Fig. 2. The new IT organisation.

The business CIOs were given extensive decision rights. One commented:

> I spent my first month learning the business, and meeting as many stakeholders as possible, business managers, IT personnel, vendors and customers. I did not start with the existing IT resources, but began by trying to understand what was really important for our internal and external customers. Then I proceeded by designing how the business processes should work with IT and asking how we could deliver the services at much lower costs.

Over time, SAS had developed a high diversity of business processes and IT systems. In 2013, although development and operations had been outsourced, the IT staff included 211 personnel. The goal was to reduce this number to 60. Many IT employees were assigned to departmental systems. When many of these systems were terminated, the consequence was usually lay-offs. This process is regulated extensively in Swedish law and was carefully executed. The CIO commented:

> Around any IT system, over time, a small ecology of owners, users, hardware and tools, developers and operation support, develops. So, reducing the number of business processes and systems also meant staff reduction. We dealt with this very carefully, involving the unions in every step. It took time and effort, but we found reasonable solutions with relatively low levels of conflict.

4.4 Reducing the Number of Systems and Redesigning the IT Architecture

The systems portfolio in SAS had grown since the early 1970s, and by 2013, it included around registered 1200 applications, large and small, which were run by CSC in the Copenhagen data centre. The average system age was 15–20 years. Some of them were central business systems in air planning and operations, marketing, booking and financials, and were crucial to the company. However, most applications were departmental solutions serving a useful purpose, but not all were really necessary. But which ones could be removed? Aanby and his management team had the advantage of deep knowledge of the business and IT sides of the matter and did not leave the decision to middle management. Instead, they went head-on, analysed every application and decided its importance: Was it really needed? Could other applications provide the same or equal functionality? Through this process, they decided that approximately 50% of the 1200 applications could be discarded.

The remaining applications needed better integration. The IT architecture was partly built on an enterprise bus solution (Tibco), and Aanby decided to keep this as the backbone. The major business systems were first integrated and later worked as a gravitational force on other applications. A service-oriented approach was chosen, where integrations were analysed, and in many cases rebuilt as services. Gradually, a more integrated and leaner portfolio emerged, and by 2015, the number of applications was reduced to 600, in 175 systems.

In parallel, the core systems were gradually renewed; in 2014 a new SAP platform and an e-commerce solution were implemented, and in 2015 new solutions for revenue management and aircraft maintenance were introduced. The speed of change was considerable; in the period 2013–2015 there were 238 new releases, i.e. more than one every week. There were no major disruptions of IT stability during the transformation period. One business CIO commented:

> We worked extremely hard in this period, to keep operations going whilst changing the whole infrastructure. First we had to define a new configuration; then roll it out at all bases. We established a command centre, where managers, IT staff, vendors and business people met and solved problems. Up to 50 people attended these sessions, where decisions were taken on the go. We had to co-ordinate the actions of support personnel and technicians at a large number of airports around the world, and the same time deal with technical and vendor issues.

4.5   Negotiating and Implementing a New Sourcing Model

IT development and operations had been outsourced to CSC in 2004, with the data centre in Copenhagen and development in Stockholm. The contract was expensive and the services unsatisfactory, and in February 2013 Aanby issued a Request for Proposal. The main contract was awarded to Tata Consultancy Services (TCS), an Indian IT service giant, at a much lower cost. Transitioning to a new data centre in Aarhus, from CSC to Tata, was complicated and ripe with conflicts. Each system was analysed in terms of services and dependencies, and then changed, moved and tested, before set into production. One manager commented:

> We realised from the start that we were not only changing the technology, but more importantly, changing the company's business processes. Our key challenge was to deliver better services to customers, at lower costs. In order to do this, we had to understand the inside of the processes, both the people and the technology. This could not be done in contracts; rather we had to work very closely with the vendors to design the right solutions. Even the CIO was very hands-on with these details.

Infrastructure was completely renewed; 4000 servers, 15.000 workstations, and various LAN/WAN networks were installed. In addition to Tata, large contracts were awarded to Amadeus, SITA and others; in total 300 IT vendors (many of which were local companies delivering services to airports around the world) were involved.

4.6   Moving from Guardian Vendor to SIAM in 2014

When Tata was implementing the new solution in autumn 2013, they assumed the role of *guardian vendor*, i.e. ensuring that all sub-vendors delivered according to contracts and Service Level Agreements. This arrangement turned out to be unsuccessful; it led to a number of conflicts, vendor responses to problems took a long time, and SAS lacked direct access to information on upcoming issues.

The solution was a different model, called Service Integration and Management (SIAM), which is a management approach to dealing with multi-sourcing [25]. Multi-sourcing deals with a blend of internal and external services, and offers the opportunity to select best-of-breed services from various vendors. The challenge is to integrate these, often interdependent, services into a seamless whole.

SAS decided in autumn 2014 to implement SIAM, and this element was taken out of the contract with Tata. The transition was demanding, because it involved technical redesign and new contracts with vendors, as well as orchestrating the services to the SAS organisation. Firstly, an ITIL consultant was hired to help structure the new SIAM process. Secondly, an internal unit was established to take responsibility for integration and services. In March 2015, the SIAM solution was working successfully; the incident and problem management processes were in place, users were satisfied, and vendor issues were dealt with at operational level. See Fig. 3.

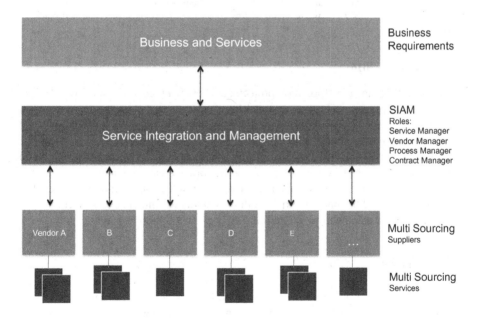

Fig. 3. Multi-sourcing with service integration and management.

As illustrated in Fig. 2, the SIAM unit integrated the services from the various vendors and served as a *facade* to the business.

4.7   CIO Leadership

Mr. Aanby turned out to be a very hands-on leader but also kept the vision clear. One of his business CIOs described his leadership in these terms:

> He was quite likeable, always in a good mood, joking and laughing. But he was very clear on the overall goals, and on the gravity of the situation. He explained in several large briefings what the mission was, and how we should deal with it. In negotiations, both with vendors and the unions, he was tough. It was evident that he knew what he was doing, and we knew he had the necessary experience. He was not hiding behind polished consulting language but used funny illustrations and stories to illustrate his thinking.

The overall focus was on changing the company's business processes. The restructuring of the processes was the responsibility of his "business CIOs", who were all quite experienced in this line of thinking. Restructuring often implied simplifying or automating sub-processes, in order to provide better services and reduce costs. For instance, marketing and sales processes were fragmented in different units and IT systems, and the new solutions were simpler and more efficient. Aanby had the advantage of extensive experience with the strategic and commercial issues, as well as the technical issues. A business CIO commented:

> He was very hands-on, knowing the critical details. For instance, if a middle manager argued that there were specific reasons for keeping things as they were, Aanby knew the details so well that he could intervene, and argue – correctly – that the business process should be changed, and describe why this was possible. Without this ability, we would have accomplished much less.

4.8   Results in 2016

By summer 2016, the transformation project had been completed, and the CIO left. The results were impressive; IT personnel had been reduced by 50%, and operative costs had been reduced by 25%. SAS had new and much more flexible solutions, and operations had been running smoothly during the whole transition.

However, this also meant that the objectives had not been fully reached. One reason was that new solutions had been added along the way, increasing available services but also costs. Another reason was that some old applications in the operative part were not changed, because of the operative risk. A third was that the initial cost was set too low; the total IT costs amounted to 1.7 billion SEK, not 1.3 billion.

5   Discussion

Considering the case, we think it is reasonable to conclude that it confirms the main assumptions of the strategic management and digital strategy. It was the sense of urgency and crisis that made the transformation possible [5], and the change from IT strategy to digital business strategy [4] is reflected in the depth of the transformation. In addition, the action pattern of the transformational CIO is in line with the research, for instance the need for strong senior management support. One top executive in SAS commented:

> Remember, a CIO can do only as much as the organisation allows him. In this kind of transformation, there are many forces that resist change. If not overridden by top management, they will obstruct the CIO; there are potentially an endless number of reasons to keep things as they are.

Regarding the personal attributes of the transformational CIO, this is a complex topic, but we believe that the leadership of Mr Aanby resonates with earlier research [8, 12], as shown in Table 1.

Table 1. Characteristics of the transformational leader.

Aspect	How the SAS CIO enacted this aspect
Idealised influence	The CIO established trust through open and truthful communication
Inspirational motivation	He put forth a clear mission and stayed with it, also in times of crisis
Intellectual stimulation	He worked with high risk throughout the process, and inspired and empowered his colleagues to find solutions
Individual consideration	He dealt individually with his managers and employees, empowering the able

This certainly does not mean that all employees appreciated the CIO's leadership. The transformation was quite turbulent, and some employees may have interpreted the CIO's behaviour not as good leadership but rather as a kind of soft manipulation to make people work extremely hard over a long period of time. It might have some significance that the importance of involving different people, with divergent perspectives, in multiple aspects of the research process, in order to create a richer process that can enable the complexity of important problems to be examined more fully.

Mr. Aanby chose to leave his position when the mission had been completed.

There is, however, one aspect that needs more discussion, namely the role of the environment and organisation in the transformations process. We will assess this in the following section, focusing on two issues of the digital transformation: the Scandinavian model for engagement and leadership.

5.1   The Scandinavian Approach I: Deep Participation

Whilst the CIO literature [2] and the transformational leadership research [8] emphasise the need for good communication, stakeholder relationships and stimulated and motivated followers, the SAS case goes beyond this in its continuous and deep engagement with employees.

The level of engagement was deep in the SAS case, and we can describe it on three levels. Firstly, at the top level the goals of the initiative (which were dramatic) were discussed with the trade unions (of which SAS had a large number), and an agreement on the change process was reached, which was extensively communicated. Secondly, the need for each system was assessed, and in the many cases of system termination, employees were deemed redundant. Each case was negotiated with the employee and his union, and flexible solutions were found. Thirdly, during the change process, managers (including Aanby himself) were heavily engaged, taking the time to listen, discuss and decide. One of the managers commented:

> Big changes require an *understanding* of the key issues from all stakeholders, and we spent time on this. It is much easier to conduct a transformation like this when employees are involved. We also spent some time explaining our foreign partners this; they clearly were not used to this kind of time-consuming process.

The Scandinavian approach to leadership recognises that transformation processes cannot be run solely top-down but are subject to negotiation and sharing of burdens and benefits. Research has shown that non-Scandinavian managers believe that this leads to slow and ineffective decision-making, whilst Scandinavian managers argue that the stronger commitment is more important [26].

5.2   The Scandinavian Approach II: Knowledge-Sharing

The deep level of engagement was important not only for employee commitment but also for knowledge-sharing. Research has shown that Scandinavians prefer leadership based on coaching, rather than direction [18], and the use of objectives and values, not to command and control [15]. This requires that employees are empowered with some space for autonomy, but also that knowledge workers engage heavily in problem solving.

Both of these conditions were present in the SAS case. The transformation included almost every business process and unit in the corporation, and every detail had to be right. This depended to a large degree on employees' local knowledge, and the change process (and culture) allowed for open discussions on these issues. One of the business CIOs commented:

> An important reason for the success was the leadership style. First, the managers were very relaxed in terms of authority, allowing employees to take decisions when needed, which was extremely important in a project like this. Second, we were able to leverage the competence of involved employees, since everybody were encouraged to express their opinion at meeting. In a more hierarchical culture, this seldom happens, because only the boss will speak.

Summing-Up the Scandinavian Contribution:
One of the key insights of Scandinavian leadership is that commitment requires meaningful and real engagement, and that the leadership style leverages the knowledge of employees. Both of these aspects were success factors in the SAS case.

6   Conclusion

In this paper, we analysed a digital transformation process in an international airline, in order to understand the role of the CIO. The research questions were (i) what characterises leadership in the digital transformation, and (ii) what does the Scandinavian workplace model add to the knowledge of digital transformation?

We find that the insights from extant research are valid also for Scandinavian transformation initiatives. However, we add to the knowledge of digital transformation two key elements from the Scandinavian workplace model; deep employee participation, and a leadership culture that leverages employee knowledge.

Acknowledgements. We thank the informants for their time and engagement.

References

1. Hess, T., Matt, C., Wiesböck, F., Benlian, A.: Options for formulating a digital transformation strategy. MIS Q. Exec. **15**, 103–119 (2016)
2. Hoehle, H., Venkatesh, V.: Mobile application usability: conceptualization and instrument development. MIS Q. **39**, 435–472 (2015)
3. Hansen, M.T.: The search-transfer problem: the role of weak ties in sharing knowledge across organization subunits. Adm. Sci. Q. **44**, 82–111 (1999)
4. Turkulainen, V., Aaltonen, K., Lohikoski, P.: Managing project stakeholder communication: the Qstock festival case. Proj. Manag. J. **46**, 74–91 (2015)
5. Thomas, M., Jacques, P.H., Adams, J.R., Kihneman-Wooten, J.: Developing an effective project: planning and team building combined. Proj. Manag. J. **39**, 105–113 (2008)
6. Manu, E., Ankrah, N., Chinyio, E., Proverbs, D.: Trust influencing factors in main contractor and subcontractor relationships during projects. Int. J. Proj. Manag. **33**, 1495–1508 (2015)
7. Buvik, M.P., Rolfsen, M.: Prior ties and trust development in project teams—a case study from the construction industry. Int. J. Proj. Manag. **33**, 1484–1494 (2015)
8. Pee, L.G., Kankanhalli, A., Kim, H.-W.: Knowledge sharing in information systems development: a social interdependence perspective. J. Assoc. Inf. Syst. **11**, 550 (2010)
9. Nooteboom, B., Van Haverbeke, W., Duysters, G., Gilsing, V., van den Oord, A.: Optimal cognitive distance and absorptive capacity. Res. Policy **36**, 1016–1034 (2007)
10. Lee, L., Reinicke, B., Sarkar, R., Anderson, R.: Learning through interactions: improving project management through communities of practice. Proj. Manag. J. **46**, 40–52 (2015)
11. Mueller, J.: Formal and informal practices of knowledge sharing between project teams and enacted cultural characteristics. Proj. Manag. J. **46**, 53–68 (2015)
12. Solli-Sæther, H., Karlsen, J.T., van Oorschot, K.: Strategic and cultural misalignment: knowledge sharing barriers in project networks. Proj. Manag. J. **46**, 49–60 (2015)
13. Ronen, S., Shenkar, O.: Clustering countries on attitudinal dimensions: a review and synthesis. Acad. Manag. Rev. **10**, 435–454 (1985)
14. Hoppe, M.H.: The effects of national culture on the theory and practice of managing R&D professionals abroad. R&D Manag. **23**, 313–325 (1993)
15. McLeod, L., Doolin, B.: Information systems development as situated socio-technical change: a process approach. Eur. J. Inf. Syst. **21**, 176–191 (2012)
16. Ghobadi, S., Mathiassen, L.: Perceived barriers to effective knowledge sharing in agile software teams. Inf. Syst. J. **26**, 95–125 (2016)
17. Hofstede, G.: Culture's Consequences. Sage, Beverly Hills (1980)
18. Zander, L.: The Licence to Lead, An 18-Country Study of the Relationship Between Employees' Preferences Regarding Interpersonal Leadership and National Culture. Institute of International Business, Stockholm School of Economics, Stockholm (1997)
19. Avison, D., Malaurent, J.: Qualitative research in three is journals: unequal emphasis but common rigour, depth and richness. Syst. D'inf. Manag. **18**, 75–123 (2013)

20. Kim, G., Behr, K., Spafford, G.: The Phoenix Project: A Novel About IT, DevOps, and Helping Your Business Win. IT Revolution, Portland (2014)
21. Bass, L., Weber, I., Zhu, L.: DevOps: A Software Architect's Perspective. Addison-Wesley Professional, New York (2015)
22. Amabile, T.M., Conti, R., Coon, H., Lazenby, J., Herron, M.: Assessing the work environment for creativity. Acad. Manag. J. **39**, 1154–1184 (1996)
23. Henfridsson, O., Bygstad, B.: The generative mechanisms of digital infrastructure evolution. MIS Q. **37**, 907–931 (2013)
24. Bygstad, B., Aanby, H.P.: ICT infrastructure for innovation: a case study of the enterprise service bus approach. Inf. Syst. Front. **12**, 257–265 (2010)
25. Dibrell, C., Davis, P.S., Craig, J.: Fueling innovation through information technology in SMEs. J. Small Bus. Manag. **46**, 203–218 (2008)
26. Das, S.R., Zahra, S.A., Warkentin, M.E.: Integrating the content and process of strategic MIS planning with competitive strategy. Dec. Sci. **22**, 953–984 (1991)

Software Complexity and Organization of Firms' Offshoring Activities

Arto Ojala[1]([✉]), Eriikka Paavilainen-Mäntymäki[2], Ning Su[3], and Kalle Lyytinen[4]

[1] University of Jyväskylä, Jyväskylä, Finland
arto.k.ojala@jyu.fi
[2] University of Turku, Turku, Finland
[3] Ivey Business School, London, Canada
[4] Case Western Reserve University, Cleveland, USA

Abstract. How does software complexity shape software providers' offshoring tasks, and how do such firms organize their offshoring activity? These questions are important, since the global software development market is growing rapidly, offering new opportunities for software managers and entrepreneurs to distribute their activities geographically. Based on a multi-site case study of 12 software firms, we study connections between software complexity and the offshoring strategies selected. Our findings suggest that software firms select a variety of organizational structures for their offshoring activity, and that the selection is shaped by the complexity of the software in question.

Keywords: Software complexity · Offshoring · Outsourcing · Software firms

1 Introduction

Global software markets are growing rapidly [1, 2], highlighting the growing strategic importance of the software industry in the global economy. At the same time the development and distribution of software has become a global activity, and customers and software suppliers are often located in entirely different geographical locations [3, 4]. For the most part, the geographical distribution of the software poses no great problems, as the software can be delivered to customers at low cost and high speed over the Internet [5, 6]. In contrast, multiple challenges can arise from identifying requirements that are sensitive to the local context, developing software across multiple geographical sites, or providing services to maintain and run the software globally. These challenges are often related to the fact that software complexity[1] [7, 8] increases as the expansion of global operations grows [9].

When software firms specify requirements for multiple foreign customers, they must usually customize the software according to the customers' preferences and local needs, and integrate it with the customers' existing complex IT infrastructure; in accordance with this, the complexity of the software increases [8–10]. The phenomenon overall is linked to the growing heterogeneity of the client base as the global

---

[1] In line with Jarke and Lyytinen [8] we refer here to external software complexity.

© Springer International Publishing AG 2017
S. Stigberg et al. (Eds.): SCIS 2017, LNBIP 294, pp. 15–27, 2017.
DOI: 10.1007/978-3-319-64695-4_2

reach expands [11]. This increases variance in requirements, gives rise to new dependencies between technology components, and generates unexpected interactions in software solutions [8, 12]. Within these interdependencies, the software complexity can vary considerably, depending on the nature and context of the software use, and the software development strategy selected. When a firm seeks to develop software for "mass-markets" it will deliberately seek to keep the complexity lower and to exercise strict control over variance in local adaptations and services, so that the software can suit a maximally wide (and preferably homogenous) customer segment [13–15]. In contrast, some software firms seek to develop "tailored" software solutions [14–16] which cater for customers' specific local requirements. This increases the complexity of the software underlying the delivered service [7, 8].

As firms develop software and related services for a growing body of foreign customers the firm's operations expand internationally [3, 11]. The international operations can be carried out using a variety of offshoring strategies, whereby the firm relocates its activities on a global scale [17, 18]. For instance, a firm may offshore-outsource its development activities to third-parties in a foreign country, or alternatively it may offshore-insource development tasks to its own foreign units [19–22].

The existing offshoring literature has focused on a number of questions, in particular (i) why software organizations offshore their operations, (ii) what activities they should offshore and where, (iii) what related rationale they follow, including the structure of the decision-making process, and (iv) how the organization implements, monitors, and manages offshored activities [3, 17]. There has been less research on how software complexity, plus related operations, aligns with firms' management of offshoring operations. Hence, the aim of the research is to indicate how software complexity [8, 23] shapes the organization of software offshoring. We specifically wished to examine how offshoring firms choose alternative organizational structures as a way to manage the complexity caused by software complexity [24].

2   Literature Review

2.1   Offshoring

Two different terms, namely offshoring and outsourcing have been applied to describe how firms move their tasks and processes to other organizations. Because the usage of the terminology is sometimes vague, these terms are defined in this study as follows: Offshoring refers to moving certain activities to another country, either to a firm's own foreign unit or to a third-party located abroad. By contrast, outsourcing refers to moving some of the firm's activities to another organization, located either in the same country or in a foreign country (see e.g. [25]). In practice, offshoring can be implemented using two different options. The first option is to offshore-outsource some of the firm's activities to third parties, e.g. to foreign distributors. The use of foreign distributors offers a low-cost access to local knowledge in a foreign country [26]. For instance, software firms can utilize distributors' knowledge of different activities (e.g. localization, customization, technical support, etc.) to better serve their foreign customers [6, 19]. Another option is offshore-insourcing, in other words, the establishment of one's own subsidiary in a foreign country; this will operate as a remote service site for the parent firm [19–22]. By using a foreign subsidiary, a software firm can use its own personnel to deal with customers and local distributors. In many cases, this requires the recruitment of personnel with relevant knowledge of the target industry and customers in the target country (e.g. [27]). This approach requires more resources and includes higher financial risk, but it also increases market control and lowers transaction-related risks [28]. A firm might apply one of these options solely, or else they can be used in parallel, depending on the software developed (cf. [19]).

The main idea behind offshoring is that a firm should focus on its core competences, and that it should offshore activities that are not related to its core business [20]. Offshoring has traditionally been seen as an activity in which an organization moves parts of its manufacturing or other activities to a low-cost country (e.g. [25, 29]). In the software industry, offshoring has usually been applied to software coding, in which the coding process is moved to a country such as India, which has substantially lower labor costs [19, 30–32]. However, offshoring is increasingly seen as a strategy to attain qualified personnel [17], technical expertise [5], and worthwhile innovations [33]. For instance, there might be a lack of expertise to develop software for customers' specific needs in a target country [16]. By offshoring software development activities to another country, a firm can get an access to local knowledge and special skills [5, 17, 29, 31]. This can help the firm to develop software that meets the requirements of the local market [11, 19]. Offshoring can also be a decision involving the language and the business culture, in that the offshoring partner's language and its local business culture skills are needed in order to deal with e.g. sales, support, and localization activities (cf. [20, 34]). Altogether, offshoring may help firms to create global markets by increasing the talent pool and innovation capability of the firm [20].

2.2 Software Complexity

In the software industry, the characteristics of software can vary greatly, from highly complex software to software with low complexity [23, 35]. The complexity can involve internal complexity, referring to the type and number of dependencies within the software code, which is largely a function of the size of the code base [23, 35]. Alternatively, it can involve external complexity [8], which relates to the dependencies of the software with its development and use environments, covering for example the scope and rate of change in customers' requirements [8, 10], or changes in the market environment [7, 9]. In the context of this study, we are interested in external complexity of software and how it shapes offshoring strategies.

If software is "tailored" or "customized" according the prior requirements set by the customers [15, 16], the software complexity increases [8, 23, 35]. This is mainly due to increases in the diversity and dependencies of the software, which in turn increase the number of versions and functionalities that need to be developed and managed [8, 23]. When a firm develops highly complex software for foreign customers, there may be a growing need to offshore some of the development activities to countries where the customers are located. The development of complex software thus requires close cooperation with customers [13], and this means that knowledge of customers' idiosyncrasies and specific software requirements becomes an important asset [14, 36]. By offshoring labor-intensive development tasks [10] to nearby customers, a firm can get a better understanding of a foreign customer's preferences.

Conversely, software can also be developed according to the aim of keeping the software complexity low. This kind of software involves "packaged" [14] or "mass-market" [15, 16] software which is generally developed for a wide market segment [35]. This is achieved by designing software on a broad basis, using general knowledge of customers' behavior and needs [37]. General requirements can thereafter be merged and grouped, while at the same time seeking to remove or minimize any context-specific elements [13, 14, 37]. In addition, one will seek to have fewer different versions of the software, and attempt to include the same functionalities of the software in each version [23, 35]. This kind of software is easier to install; it can be downloaded from the Internet, or it can be used as a cloud service.

In practice, it can be challenging to formulate a strict division of software firms into high-complexity software developers on the one hand, and low-complexity developers on the other. For this reason, we see it as more fruitful to approach software firms as operating on a continuum, with high-complexity and low-complexity software representing opposite ends. Hoch et al. [16] call firms operating on the middle of this continuum as "enterprise solution firms." Compared to software firms developing highly complex software, such firms use a more standard modular structure in their software. The modular structure makes it possible to reuse and recombine components of the software, thereby decreasing design complexity [23, 36]. The modular structure also makes it easier to customize and localize other components according to different customer requirements [16, 36].

3   Research Methodology

The aim of the study was to identify how software complexity shapes the organization of software offshoring, and consequently the management of organizational complexity. To gain an in-depth understanding of the phenomenon, we applied an exploratory case study method [38]. This method was chosen because it is capable of encompassing empirically rich and detailed data relating to a complex and understudied phenomenon [38–40].

3.1   Data Sampling

The case firms were selected by using purposeful, theoretical sampling, as recommended by Eisenhardt [41]. We thus deemed it important that the case selection should fit the research aim of understanding the relationship between software complexity and the offshoring strategy. The firms selected complied with the following criteria: (i) the firms had international operations; (ii) the firms provided software and related services (i.e. they were not pure service providers, as would be the case for software consulting firms); and (iii) the firms in the sample differed in the nature of their software and related service offerings; hence the sample covered a range of firms, from low-complexity to high-complexity software firms.

The firms were divided into three groups according to the complexity of the software they developed. The first group, the developers of low-complexity software, developed software aimed at mass-markets without any need for tailoring or customization. In addition, the software could be installed by the customer on a self-service basis. The second group, the developers of medium-complexity software, developed software that was broadly aimed at business users. The software had a modular software structure, and the modules were customized and/or localized in line with customer requirements. The third group, the developers of high-complexity software, developed software that was tailored according to the individual customer's requirements; thus, it called for close liaison with the customer during the requirement analysis and the installation phases. Table 1 provides detailed information on each case firm.

3.2   Data Collection

The data for this study were collected within three different projects conducted between 2004 and 2015. The final round of the interviews was conducted in 2014 and 2015, to ensure the continued applicability of the data obtained in previous years. This final round of interviews was undertaken with all the case companies, as a means of checking the comparability of cases. Although the data were collected over a 10-year period, there were only very slight changes in the firms' software offering. Altogether, 71 semi-structured interviews were conducted for this study, with each interview lasting 30–90 min. The first author of this study conducted all the interviews. Most of the interviews were conducted face-to-face. Nevertheless, eight telephone interviews and one Skype interview were undertaken because of difficulties in finding a suitable time for a face-to-face interview. Interviews with the CEO or the manager responsible for foreign operations were the main source of information. However, to avoid bias from individual opinions [42–44], other employees with a variety of positions in the case firms were also interviewed.

All the interviews were recorded and transcribed verbatim, using a word processing program. Thereafter, the complete transcripts were sent back to the interviewees for review. To avoid retrospective bias [43, 45], several different types of secondary data were collected and used to validate the interview data whenever possible. The secondary data included press releases, advertising material, annual reports, industrial reports, and news articles. The interview data were compared with early records. If there were inconsistencies, these were discussed with the persons interviewed.

3.3   Data Analysis

The analysis was conducted in line with the recommendations of Miles and Huberman [46], and it consisted of three parallel activities: (i) data reduction, (ii) data display, and (iii) conclusion-drawing/verification. In the data reduction phase, the complete transcripts from all the interviews were simplified and summarized by compiling a detailed document covering the history of each case firm. In addition, information from other sources (secondary data) was added to the written case documents. Thereafter, the case firms were categorized into three different groups according to the complexity of their

Table 1. Overview of the case firms

Firm	Year of establishment	Description of software	Target industry	Software complexity	Number of interviews
Firm A	1988	Data-security software	Consumers and diverse industries	Low-complexity software	2
Firm B	2000	Cloud gaming software	Network operators and consumers	Low-complexity software	16
Firm C	1998	Mobile gaming software	Mobile operators and consumers	Low-complexity software	3
Firm D	1995	Firewall software	Diverse industries	Medium-complexity software	3
Firm E	1990	Data-in-transit security software	Diverse industries	Medium-complexity software	3
Firm F	1966	3D modeling software	Building and construction industry	Medium-complexity software	5
Firm G	1991	Network analysis software	Mobile phone manufacturers and network operators	Medium-complexity software	4
Firm H	2006	3D modeling software	Furniture industry	High-complexity software	10
Firm I	2008	Identity and access management software	Diverse industries	High-complexity software	5
Firm J	1998	Virtual design and modeling software	Mobile phone manufacturers, mobile operators	High-complexity software	3
Firm K	2006	Risk management software	Financial sector	High-complexity software	7
Firm L	1992	Video codec software	Mobile phone manufacturers	High-complexity software	10

software. The general procedure followed the guidelines of Pettigrew [47], who argued that arranging incoherent aspects in chronological order is essential in understanding the causal links between different events.

In the data display phase, the most important data drawn from the categories were arranged in tables. These tables included quotes from the interview data illustrating the important events in the case firms' international operations. The most relevant quotes from the interviews are included later in this paper (see the "Findings" section). The tables facilitated comparison of the cases, making it possible to detect similarities and differences between the case firms' international behavior and offshoring strategies.

The phase of conclusion drawing and verification concentrated on identifying the aspects that appeared to have significance for this study. In this phase, the regularities, patterns, explanations, and causalities related to the phenomena were noted. From these, it was possible to develop the constructs and theoretical logic behind the use of different offshoring strategies.

4 Findings

In all cases, the firms kept their core competences (i.e. specific skills and techniques related to core software development) in-house. However, the case analysis indicates that the firms' offshoring focused on four different sets of activities, which were affected by software complexity. These activities were: (i) localization, which was needed in order to make the software appropriate to the target market, (ii) customization according to customer-specific needs, (iii) integration of the software within the customer's IT environment, and (iv) product support. All these activities[2] further influenced the ways in which the firms organized their international operations. The following subsections provide detailed descriptions of how these activities were organized by the case firms. Here is should be noted once again that the categorization in the table does not represent three totally separate groups; rather, these firms represent points on a continuum, with Firm A having the least complex software and Firm L the most complex software.

4.1   The Offshoring Strategies of Developers of Low-Complexity Software

The developers of low-complexity software (firms A, B, C, and D) conducted their software development in their headquarters. Because their software was aimed at a wide customer segment, the needs for localization or customization were low. In fact, the decrease in the need for offshoring was substantial, since no localization work was required except in relation to language. In the software provided by firms A and B, language support for various (widely-used) languages was already included in the software within the development process; by contrast, firms C and D localized the language separately for each target country if it was deemed necessary. Firm C conducted its localization activities at headquarters, whereas Firm D offshore-outsourced and/or insourced localization to foreign distributors or subsidiaries. The software that these firms provided was easy to install, and it integrated automatically with a customer's existing IT environment, with no need for external support. Thus, customers were able to handle these activities by themselves. The Sales Manager of Firm A explained this as follows:

---

[2] Activities (i)–(ii) were related to software development for foreign customers, whereas activities (iii)–(iv) were supporting services.

"Technically the software is very standard. It includes language support, which is important, especially for consumer markets. The language support is included in all versions of the software...customers can install the software by themselves and all the version updates are delivered automatically."

The only activity that all the providers of low-complexity software offshored was customer support. Because the software was easy to learn and to understand, requiring no specific knowledge of software development, the distributors were able to handle customer support. Consequently, these firms developing the least complex software organized their global service and support activities so that the distributors took care of customer relationships and support activities, while the subsidiaries had control over the distributors. Thus, the task of the subsidiaries was to supervise the distributors, to give training related to new products and features, and to support existing distributors if they had problems with the software. In some extreme cases, the subsidiaries gave support to end-users, if the problem was something that the distributors were not able to solve.

4.2   The Offshoring Strategies of Developers of Medium-Complexity Software

The firms developing medium-complexity software had a somewhat different strategy. Headquarters had the main responsibility for software development, but a substantial proportion of the development and support activities were offshored to foreign distributors and subsidiaries. The software development tasks that were offshored were mainly related to localization and/or customization work for customers in the target countries. This required local knowledge, since the localization included (in addition to the language) aspects such as the inclusion of local standards, regulations, and measurement units for the software. In addition, firms G and H customized software according to the customer's specific needs. The customization was done jointly between a foreign distributor or subsidiary and headquarters. The Executive Vice President of Firm G explained the customization needs of their network analysis software as follows:

"The customization that we do for the customers is related to their [network] controlling system; each customer has slightly different kinds of systems, protocols, and ways to stimulate networks."

The customers of firms E, F, and G were in fact able to integrate the software, since on the whole they were familiar with the technology and the software. However, Firm H did provide integration services for its customers; this was because the software was targeted at furniture manufacturers and furniture chains, where users were not so familiar with new technologies.

All the providers of medium-complexity software organized their global service and support activities so that the distributors supported their own customers, while the subsidiaries gave support to their direct customers. In more demanding cases, when the distributors or subsidiaries were not able to support their customers, the responsibility for product support moved to headquarters. Contrary to the situation among providers of low-complexity software, there was no foreign subsidiary supervising or controlling the distributor, since the distributors were directly responsible to headquarters for their activities. The Executive Vice President of Firm F explained this as follows:

"Each subsidiary and distributor has exactly the same tasks. Even if our R&D is in Finland, each foreign unit takes care of localization for its customers. They all have an employee who works as a product manager, so we have local product management in each target country. However, we use subsidiaries in the main markets, and distributors in smaller market areas."

4.3   The Offshoring Strategies of Developers of High-Complexity Software

The providers of high-complexity software (firms I, J, K, and L) used a strategy by which headquarters had the main responsibility for software development. This was mainly because the complexity of the software made offshore-outsourcing and insourcing more difficult. Even if these firms used distributors and/or subsidiaries for marketing and sales, the high complexity of the software decreased the possibilities for offshore development or for other support activities.

All the providers of high-complexity software localized and customized their software for customers. The localization work was truly customer-centric. It included localization of different kinds of reports, user interfaces, and so on, in contrast to other types of software providers, who mainly localized language, or who made some industry-specific changes to the software. In the case firms (I, J, K, and L), localization and customization were conducted at headquarters, since the processes required knowledge that was available only in R&D units. This kind of knowledge was related to, for example, the industry platforms in which the software would be integrated (Firm L), the customers' R&D processes (Firm J), and the specific function of the software (firms I and K). The Vice President of Firm K explained this as follows, commenting in relation to the firm's finance and risk management software:

"[Related to localization and customization] Even though banking and finance activities are similar from day to day, each bank is different, and they all have different kinds of systems, different kinds of processes, and their own requirements that they want to follow when using our software."

In all the cases in this group, technical support personnel from headquarters carried out the integration of the software with the customer's existing IT environment. This process was, in many cases, time consuming and required a thorough knowledge of the customer's IT environment. Because of the high complexity of the software, global support activities were organized so that headquarters had the main responsibility for product support. However, in less complex situations, subsidiaries or distributors were used to provide first-line support.

5   Discussion

According to our findings, the firms developing the less complex software offshored only a limited portion of their activities, because the software was easy to understand, install, and use with no need for localization or customization [11, 14, 16]. These features decreased the overall complexity of the software [7, 8, 23]. The only activity they typically offshored was product support. By using this strategy, the firms were able to focus on their core competence, i.e. product development in a single location.

In the case of firms E, F, G, and H, the software complexity increased as the customers indicated more requirements for localization and customization [23, 36]. Their demands generated variation in different versions of the software [8], each targeted for a certain market or customer segment. The increased complexity was dealt with by offshoring localization and customization activities to foreign subsidiaries or distributors. These units were better able to manage development tasks for local customers, as they had the local knowledge needed for the related development tasks (cf. [11]).

The firms developing the most complex software (I, J, K, and L), tailored their software for each customer separately. This required in-depth knowledge of the customers' business processes and of the system environment in which the software was integrated [11, 14, 36]. This specialized knowledge was available only at headquarters, and it was not easily offshored to a foreign unit. Hence, the high complexity of the software decreased the possibilities to offshore the firms' activities. Because of this, offshored activities were limited again to product-related support.

Altogether, the findings indicate that a low level of complexity decreases offshoring needs, whereas a high level of complexity inhibits offshoring possibilities. Firms developing medium-level complex software do the most offshoring, since (i) most of their localization and customization activities require local knowledge from the target countries, but (ii) the level of complexity of the software is not so high as to inhibit offshoring. Thus, the connection between software complexity and the need for offshoring is not linear.

Taken as a whole, the findings indicated that the level of software complexity had a significant effect on how the software firms organized their foreign operations. Figure 1 illustrates three different service and support models emerging from our analysis demonstrating how software complexity affects the organization of offshoring activities. The models are abstractions arrived at by analysis of the interviews. Within the figure, solid arrows represent strong support/control, and dotted arrows demonstrate weak support/control. In the first model, depicting providers of less complex software, firm headquarters focuses on product development, while subsidiaries are used to support and supervise existing distributors. The distributors take care of product support activities when there is a need for direct contact with the customers. Hence, direct control and support is organized vertically. In the second model, which is followed by the providers of medium-complex software, the subsidiaries and distributors have equal tasks, and they comprise the main actors in dealing with customers (solid arrows). As discussed above, these tasks are related to localization/customization, integration, installation, and customer support. In this model, the firm's headquarters supports/controls subsidiaries and distributors (solid arrows); however, headquarters has only indirect contact with the actual end-users, and provides second-line support for users (dotted arrow). In the third model, followed by the providers of most complex software, headquarters takes a substantial role in controlling development and use. It has direct contact with the customers (solid arrow); in this case, the subsidiaries and distributors give only indirect support (dotted arrows).

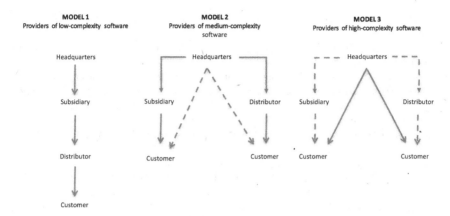

Fig. 1. Models for offshoring international service and support activities, based on software complexity.

6 Conclusions

This study examined software firms' offshoring strategies and the extent to which they are influenced by software complexity. Our results contribute to IS literature in several ways. First of all, the study shows how software complexity [7, 8, 23] shapes offshoring strategies. Low software complexity decreases offshoring needs, whereas high software complexity limits offshoring possibilities. However, the firms that do the most offshoring tend to be those that develop software which sits between the two extremes of the continuum. This highlights the fact that the connection between software complexity and the need for more complex offshoring solutions is not linear.

Secondly, the findings contribute to an understanding of the interplay between software complexity [8, 23] and software firms' approaches to managing and coordinating global software development and distribution activities [3, 6, 48]. We show that software firms can adjust their international operations according to the underlying software complexity in their efforts to better serve their foreign customers. Even though previous literature has shown that variations in software complexity are related to different approaches in managing requirements [7, 8] or in developing software [23, 35], less attention has been paid to the connection between software complexity and the strategies related to the offshoring and organizing foreign activities after the development phase.

References

1. Gartner: Gartner Says Worldwide Software Market Grew 4.8 Percent in 2013. Press release (2014). www.gartner.com/newsroom/id/2696317
2. Peltonen, J., Rönkkö, M., Mutanen, O.-P.: Growth Forum 2013 Summary Report. Ohjelmistoyrittäjätry, Helsinki (2014). http://www.kasvufoorumi.fi/wp-content/uploads/2013/12/Growth-forum-report-2013.pdf

3. Su, N.: Internationalization strategies of Chinese IT service suppliers. MIS Q. **37**(1), 175–200 (2013)
4. Su, N.: Cultural sensemaking in offshore information technology service suppliers. MIS Q. **39**(4), 959–983 (2015)
5. Metters, R.: A typology of offshoring and outsourcing in electronically transmitted services. J. Oper. Manag. **26**(2), 198–211 (2008)
6. Ojala, A., Tyrväinen, P.: Business models and market entry mode choice of small software firms. J. Int. Entrepreneurship **4**(2–3), 69–81 (2006)
7. Jarke, M., Loucopoulos, P., Lyytinen, K., Mylopoulos, J., Robinson, W.: The brave new world of design requirements. Inf. Syst. **36**(7), 992–1008 (2011)
8. Jarke, M., Lyytinen, K.: Complexity of systems evolution: requirements engineering perspective. ACM Trans. Manag. Inf. Syst. **5**(3), 11:1–11:7 (2015)
9. Sambamurthy, V., Zmud, R.W.: The organizing logic for an enterprise's IT activities in the digital era—a prognosis of practice and a call for research. Inf. Syst. Res. **11**(2), 105–114 (2000)
10. Pressman, R.S.: Software Engineering: A Practitioner's Approach. McGraw-Hill Higher Education, New York (2004)
11. Wareham, J., Fox, P.B., Cano Giner, J.L.: Technology ecosystem governance. Organ. Sci. **25**(4), 1195–1215 (2014)
12. Hanseth, O., Lyytinen, K.: Design theory for dynamic complexity in information infrastructures: the case of building internet. J. Inf. Technol. **25**(1), 1–19 (2010)
13. Alajoutsijärvi, K., Mannermaa, K., Tikkanen, H.: Customer relationships and the small software firm: a framework for understanding challenges faced in marketing. Inf. Manag. **37**(3), 153–159 (2000)
14. Nambisan, S.: Why service business are not product businesses. MIT Sloan Manag. Rev. **42**(4), 72–80 (2001)
15. Segelod, E., Jordan, G.: The use and importance of external sources of knowledge in the software development process. R&D Manag. **34**(3), 239–252 (2004)
16. Hoch, D.J., Roeding, C.R., Purkert, G., Lindner, S.K., Müller, R.: Secrets of Software Success. Harvard Business School Press, Boston (2000)
17. Levin, A.Y., Massini, S., Peeters, C.: Why are companies offshoring innovation? The emerging global race for talent. J. Int. Bus. Stud. **40**(6), 901–925 (2009)
18. Manning, S., Massini, S., Lewin, Y.A.: A dynamic perspective on next-generation offshoring: the global sourcing of science and engineering talent. Acad. Manag. Perspect. **22**(3), 35–54 (2008)
19. Aspray, W., Mayadas, F. & Vardi, M.Y.: Globalization and offshoring of software. Report of the ACM Job Migration Task Force, Association for Computing Machinery (2006)
20. Davis, G., Ein-Dor, P., King, W., Torkzadeh, R.: IT offshoring: history, prospects and challenges. J. Assoc. Inf. Syst. **7**(11), 770–795 (2006)
21. Jarvenpaa, S.L., Mao, J.-Y.: Operational capabilities development in mediated offshore software services models. J. Inf. Technol. **23**(1), 3–17 (2008)
22. Prikladnicki, R., Audy, J.L.N.: Comparing offshore outsourcing and the internal offshoring of software development: a qualitative study. In: AMCIS 2009 Proceedings (2009)
23. Mens, T.: On the complexity of software systems. Computer **45**(8), 79–81 (2012)
24. Anderson, P.: Perspective: complexity theory and organization science. Organ. Sci. **10**(3), 216–232 (1999)
25. Carmel, E., Tjia, P.: Offshoring Information Technology: Sourcing and Outsourcing to a Global Workforce. Cambridge University Press, Cambridge (2005)
26. Williams, C.: Client–vendor knowledge transfer in IS offshore outsourcing: insights from a survey of Indian software engineers. Inf. Syst. J. **21**(4), 335–356 (2011)

27. Luo, Y.: Dynamic capabilities in international expansion. J. World Bus. **35**(4), 355–378 (2000)
28. Lu, J.W., Beamish, P.W.: The internationalization and performance of SMEs. Strateg. Manag. J. **22**(6–7), 565–586 (2001)
29. Oshri, I., Kotlarsky, J., Willcocks, L.P.: The Handbook of Global Outsourcing and Offshoring, 3rd edn. Palgrave Macmillan, London (2015)
30. Carmel, E., Nicholson, B.: Small firms and offshore software outsourcing: high transaction costs and their mitigation. J. Glob. Inf. Manag. **13**(3), 33–54 (2005)
31. Lacity, M.C., Khan, S., Yan, A., Willcocks, L.P.: A review of the IT outsourcing empirical literature and future research directions. J. Inf. Technol. **25**(4), 395–433 (2010)
32. Lacity, M.C., Solomon, S., Yan, A., Willcocks, L.P.: Business process outsourcing studies: a critical review and research directions. J. Inf. Technol. **26**(4), 221–258 (2011)
33. Su, N., Levina, N., Ross, J.W.: The long-tail strategy of IT outsourcing. MIT Sloan Manag. Rev. **57**(2), 81–89 (2016)
34. Khan, S.U., Niazi, M., Rashid, A.: Barriers in the selection of offshore software development outsourcing vendors: an exploratory study using a systematic literature review. Inf. Softw. Technol. **53**(7), 693–706 (2011)
35. Banker, R.D., Davis, G.B., Slaughter, S.A.: Software development practices, software complexity, and software maintenance performance: a field study. Manag. Sci. **44**(4), 433–450 (1998)
36. Tauterat, T., Mautsch, L.O., Herzwurmm, G.: Strategic success factors in customization of business software. Lect. Notes Bus. Inf. Process. **114**, 267–272 (2012)
37. Kabbedijk, J., Brinkkemper, S., Jansen, S., van der Veldt, B.: Customer involvement in requirements management: lessons from mass market software development. In: 17th IEEE International Requirements Engineering Conference, pp. 281–286 (2009)
38. Yin, R.K.: Case Study Research: Design and Methods. Sage, Beverly Hills, CA (2009)
39. Benbasat, I., Goldstein, K.K., Mead, M.: The case research strategy in studies of information systems. MIS Q. **11**(3), 369–386 (1987)
40. Edmondson, A.C., McManus, S.E.: Methodological fit in management field research. Acad. Manag. Rev. **32**(4), 1155–1179 (2007)
41. Eisenhardt, K.M.: Building theories from case study research. Acad. Manag. Rev. **14**(4), 532–550 (1989)
42. Eisenhardt, K.M., Graebner, M.E.: Theory building from cases: opportunities and challenges. Acad. Manag. J. **50**(1), 25–32 (2007)
43. Huber, G.P., Power, D.J.: Retrospective reports of strategic-level managers: guidelines for increasing their accuracy. Strateg. Manag. J. **6**, 171–180 (1985)
44. Myers, M.D., Newman, M.: The qualitative interview in IS research: examining the craft. Inf. Organ. **17**(1), 2–26 (2007)
45. Miller, C.C., Cardinal, L.B., Glick, W.H.: Retrospective reports in organizational research: a reexamination of recent evidence. Acad. Manag. J. **40**(1), 189–204 (1997)
46. Miles, M.B., Huberman, A.M.: Qualitative Data Analysis: An Expanded Sourcebook. Sage, Beverly Hills (1994)
47. Pettigrew, A.M.: Longitudinal field research on change: theory and practice. Organ. Sci. **1** (3), 267–292 (1990)
48. Ojala, A., Tyrväinen, P.: Market entry and priority of small and medium-sized enterprises in the software industry: an empirical analysis of cultural distance, geographical distance, and market size. J. Int. Mark. **15**(3), 123–149 (2007)

Exploring Factors Influencing Participant Drop-Out Behavior in a Living Lab Environment

Abdolrasoul Habibipour[(✉)], Ali Padyab, Birgitta Bergvall-Kåreborn,
and Anna Ståhlbröst

Information Systems, Luleå University of Technology, Luleå, Sweden
{Abdolrasoul.Habibipour, Ali.Padyab,
Birgitta.Bergvall-Kareborn, Anna.Stahlbrost}@ltu.se

Abstract. The concept of "living lab" is a rather new phenomenon that facilitates user involvement in open innovation activities. The users' motivations to contribute to the living lab activities at the beginning of the project are usually higher than once the activities are underway. However, the literature still lacks an understanding of what actions are necessary to reduce the likelihood of user drop-out throughout the user engagement process. This study aims to explore key factors that are influential on user drop-out in a living lab setting by engaging users to test an innovation during the pilot phase of the application's development. The stability of the prototype, ease of use, privacy protection, flexibility of the prototype, effects of reminders, and timing issues are the key influential factors on user drop-out behavior. This paper summarizes the key lessons learned from the case study and points to avenues for future research.

Keywords: User engagement · Drop-out · Living lab · Case study · Field test

1 Introduction

Open innovation by involving individual users within the process of information systems development (ISD) contributes positively to new innovations [1] as well as system success, system acceptance, and user satisfaction [2, 3]. Open innovation assumes that "firms can and should use external ideas as well as internal ideas, and internal and external paths to market, as firms look to advance their technology" [4]. In this regard, a living lab is a way of managing open innovation in which individual users are involved in co-creating, testing, and evaluating an innovation in open, collaborative, multi-contextual, and real-world settings [5, 6]. In contrast with traditional information systems research where organizational leverage exists to secure user participation, within the living lab approach the participation is usually voluntary, and the participation of the end-users needs to be encouraged [7]. However, the participants tend to drop-out of living lab activities before the project has ended [8, 9]. Participant drop-out might be due to an internal decision to stop the activity or to external environmental factors that cause them to terminate their engagement before completing the

© Springer International Publishing AG 2017
S. Stigberg et al. (Eds.): SCIS 2017, LNBIP 294, pp. 28–40, 2017.
DOI: 10.1007/978-3-319-64695-4_3

assigned tasks [10]. Such drop-out can occur in all phases of the ISD process, from contextualization, to testing, and to evaluation [11].

Despite the fact that keeping participants motivated is more challenging than motivating them to start participating in a project [9, 12], the literature still lacks an understanding on how to keep participants motivated and what actions are necessary to reduce the likelihood of user drop-out throughout the user engagement process [1, 8]. Sustainable user engagement throughout the ISD process is deemed important due to factors such as time efficiency, cost efficiency, quality assurance, the value of an established mutual trust, and the participants' deep understanding about the project or activity [9, 13]. In this study, we aim to determine which key factors are influential on participant drop-out behavior during the testing of an innovation in a living lab environment. We carried out an exploratory case study within a living lab setting to elicit as many influential factors on participant drop-out behavior as possible. In this case study, the participants were engaged in testing an innovation during the pilot phase the application's development. The paper summarizes the key lessons learned from our case study for how to reduce the likelihood of participant drop-out throughout the innovation process in a living lab setting, and it concludes with several avenues for future research in this field.

2 Background

User involvement in the ISD process had already had a long tradition when the participatory design was first introduced [14, 15]. On the other hand, opening up the innovation process by involving different stakeholders such as individual users in different innovation activities is a key factor in ISD [16]. Open innovation research is strongly grounded in democratization and empowerment values, and it highlights the perspective of the users [6, 7]. Therefore, users should be motivated to contribute to the projects [7]. However, finding motivated participants for long-term engagement in a project is not an easy task because they might tend to drop-out before completing the project or activity [17, 18]. Habibipour et al. [11] carried out a comprehensive literature review and identified more than 30 influential factors on participant drop-out behavior that are associated with: (1) task design; (2) scheduling; (3) the participant selection process; (4) participant preparation; (5) implementation and testing processes; and (6) interactions with the participants. However, in the above-mentioned study, the authors did not focus on a specific phase or type of activity, and they extracted the drop-out reasons for all steps of the ISD process such as ideation, co-design or co-creation, and finally testing and evaluation. In this paper, we argue that this view is too general and that drop-out reasons need to be scrutinized at specific phases of the innovation process.

There have been attempts to present a user engagement process model that includes the variety of reasons for participant drop-out [18, 19]. For instance, Georges et al. [18] proposed the user engagement model for field trials, aiming to explain the factors that affect the engagement of end-users to test innovations in real-life environments. In this model, although they included some possible influential factors on user drop-out behavior in general terms such as perceived usefulness, perceived ease of use, uncertainty, and functional maturity, their analysis of these factors remained cursory, and this is something that current research needs to investigate in greater detail.

Although some studies have identified influential factors on participant drop-out behavior, there are contradictions among different research studies. For example, Kienle and Ritterskamp [20] recommend that the task should divided into subtasks with a fixed deadline per task, whereas Kobren et al. [21] claim that setting specific goals may be disadvantageous for user participation because participants immediately tend to drop-out upon finishing that goal. Therefore, the question is what the consequences are of a single deadline to complete all tasks compared to one deadline per task on participant drop-out behavior.

The main objective of this study, therefore, was to identify key influential factors on participant drop-out behavior during the testing of an innovation in a living lab environment, as well as the influence of fixed and flexible deadlines on participant drop-out behavior in the field test.

3   Methodology

In this study, we aimed to identify the factors influencing participant drop-out behavior throughout the process of testing an innovation in a living lab setting. An exploratory case study is the most suitable method for end-user studies because there is no contractual relationship between the subjects and the setting [22]. This approach enabled us to combine multiple sources of evidence as a means to ensure construct validity of the study. Triangulation of the data yielded stronger and more reliable conclusions compared with a single data source [22, 23].

Our case study research consisted of the four major steps as suggested by Yin [22]: designing the case study, preparing for data collection, collecting the evidence, and analyzing case study evidence.

3.1   Study Design

In this research, a user study was performed as part of an EU-FP 7 project called USEMP[1]. The project is aimed at developing tools to enhance privacy management in online social networks. The DataBait tool is the result of the USEMP project, and this tool makes predictions of users' privacy dimensions by inferring the online social network profile from the user's data. The project adopted Facebook as the case. Moreover, the tool gives an indication of what can be inferred from the user's profile and the effects of his/her Facebook friends on their own privacy.

Participants were invited to participate in the development process of the DataBait application. This phase of the application development consisted of five sub-activities that we called MicroTasks (MicroTask1 to MicroTask5). Within each MicroTask, the participants tested each feature of the DataBait tool and they filled in a questionnaire after completing the assigned task. The MicroTasks focused on application usability,

---

[1] For an overview of the project and list of deliverables, please refer to: www.usemp-project.eu.

and user's feedback acted as a formative evaluation approach to further improve the DataBait application.

3.2 Preparation for Data Collection

In the first step – the preparation phase – we developed a semi-structured online questionnaire (i.e., the drop-out questionnaire) to elicit open-ended responses from the participants who completely filled out the recruitment survey but did not complete all of the MicroTasks (i.e., "dropped out participants"). In the drop-out questionnaire, we were interested in knowing why those who signed up for the test dropped out before the activity or project ended. Thus, the questions were mainly focused on the participant's drop-out reason and other possible influential factors on their drop-out behavior such as their initial motivation to participate. The questionnaire was customized for two different groups of participants. The first group was the participants who filled out the recruitment survey but did not participate in the DataBait application test or dropped out after the first MicroTask. We categorized this group as "early dropped out participants" because the first MicroTask only involved general questions about the participants and their privacy preferences and were not related to the DataBait application. The second type of drop-out participants was the participants who had been involved in the DataBait test and who had completed two or more MicroTasks. We named this group "late dropped out participants" because they were truly involved in the DataBait application test before dropping out.

The majority of the test users were recruited through an invitation that was advertised twice on the university website. The second stage of user recruitment was to send an invitation to the users who had participated in the previous phase of the DataBait application testing and who had agreed to participate in later phases of the project. An advertisement was also posted on some of Swedish universities' public Facebook pages. A total of 118 participants showed interest and completely filled out the recruitment survey.

In order to investigate the influence of flexible timing on participant drop-out behavior, we classified participants into two main groups, both with 59 participants. Group1 were the participants who received all five MicroTasks together at one time with a single deadline. Group2 were the participants who received the tasks one at a time with a specific deadline per MicroTask. This categorization was done to enable us to investigate the influence of a single deadline compared to one deadline per task.

We also applied two different incentive structures [24]. In each of the above-mentioned groups, half of the participants were incentivized with an online voucher worth 300 SEK ($\simeq$30€) after completing all five MicroTasks. Thus, if the participant did not complete all five MicroTasks, they were not paid anything. The other half of the participants were incentivized by periodic micro-incentives, which means that the participants who completed the first three MicroTasks were paid 100 SEK ($\simeq$10€), those who completed the first four MicroTasks were paid 200 SEK ($\simeq$20 €), and those who completed all five MicroTasks were paid 300 SEK.

3.3   Collecting the Evidence

The case study started in late June 2016 with a total duration of 34 days. In our study, qualitative data were gathered from three different sources: (1) direct observation of participants and their behavior during the test phase; (2) email communication with participants during the test phase regarding information about how to carry out the test, technical problems that occurred during the test, and other problems they experienced; and (3) an online semi-structured questionnaire carried out after the user study had ended. The drop-out questionnaire was sent to all participants who filled out the recruitment survey but did not complete the test. If the participant did not complete the assigned MicroTask within the scheduled time, reminders were sent out. If we did not hear from them within 3–4 days after that reminder, we considered them to be "dropped out participants". A reminder also was sent out for the drop-out questionnaire. Figure 1 show the execution timeline of this user study.

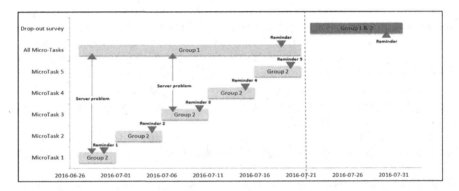

Fig. 1. Execution timeline of this user study.

3.4   Analyzing Case Study Evidence

The main analysis method employed in our study was qualitative data analysis of our direct observations, participant's feedback during their participation, and participants' responses to open-ended questions in the questionnaire. According to Yin [22], examining, categorizing, coding, and recombining evidence collected from multiple sources by different methods are the major steps of data analysis in a case study. To gain new insights about participant drop-out behavior, we started the data analysis in parallel with data collection by monitoring and documenting participants' behavior from the first day of the project. Thereafter, all participant feedback during the test was classified and coded by date and subject. We then combined these data with our observations of the project events such as reminders and server failures. Such observation were deemed important. For example, the server failures could potentially affect participants' motivation to remain or to drop-out of the user study. Finally, we classified and coded participants' answers to our questions related to their drop-out reasons and other influential factors on their participation behavior that were extracted from the qualitative questionnaire. In order to properly analyze the data and gain thorough insights, Microsoft Excel 2016 was used for coding and combining the collected information from the three waves of data collection.

4 Results

4.1 Participation and Drop-Out Rate

A total of 118 participants showed interest in participating in our user study and completely filled out the recruitment survey. Of these, 86 participants completed MicroTask1, 53 completed MircoTask2, 34 completed MicroTask3, 31 completed MicroTask4, and 27 completed MicroTask5 and reached the end of the user study. This resulted in 91 participants (77%) who dropped out of our user study. Figure 2 shows the participation and drop-out rate.

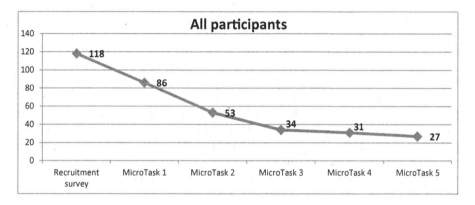

Fig. 2. Participation and drop-out rate

The drop-out rates were then compared between the two defined groups. The number of participants who reached the end of the test in Group1 was more than two times greater than in Group2. As it can be seen in Fig. 3, 19 participants in Group1 completed all five MicroTasks compared to only 8 participants in Group2 who fulfilled all the MicroTasks within the scheduled time.

Our results did not show any significant differences between participant behaviors with the two different method of receiving incentives.

4.2 Drop-Out Questionnaire Results

The drop-out questionnaire was sent to all 91 "dropped out participants" who filled out the recruitment survey but did not complete the test. In sum, we received 32 complete responses. Of these, 14 responses were from "late dropped out participants" and the other 18 responses were from the "early dropped out participants".

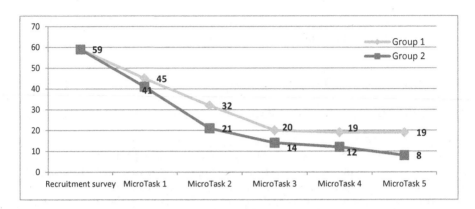

Fig. 3. Participant drop-out rate in the two groups

We first asked open questions about the initial motivation of participants to participate in the user study. The main motivation of half of the respondents (16 of 32) was curiosity about the research subject. Other motivations that were mentioned by the participants were financial reward, helping their university by contributing to research, learning something new, and having fun.

With regard to the "late dropped out participants", instability or non-functionality of the DataBait prototype was the most influential factor and was mentioned by six participants. They encountered many problems while trying to log in to the DataBait application. Some participants also complained that the MicroTasks were hard to understand, too long, exhausting, and the instructions difficult to follow. Inflexibility of the DataBait application due to incompatibility with the smartphone was the next affective factor on their drop-out decision. Limitation of access to the computer or Internet, insufficient number of reminders, too strict deadlines, summer holiday, and time limitations were other influential factors.

For "early dropped out participants", privacy concerns due to detailed personal questions and insecurity about the DataBait application were mentioned by seven participants. Similar to "late dropped out participants", the complexity of the Micro-Tasks besides the lack of clear instructions was also very influential in their motivation. The forgetfulness of the participants and their request to receive more than one reminder was another important factor. Summer holiday and the time intensity of the tasks were the next discouraging factors. Some participants also were dissatisfied with DataBait's incompatibility with the smartphone or non-functionality of the DataBait application when they tried to log in to the application. Table 1 shows the main drop-out reasons for both groups of dropped out participants.

5   Data Analysis

The results of our analysis show that there were many reasons for why participants dropped out of this user study. The analysis was conducted based on different sources of evidence, including direct observation, email communication, and the drop-out

Table 1. Content analysis of responses to the open-ended question: 'What were your main reasons for dropping out of the DataBait user study?' (number of survey respondents: 32)

Drop-out reason	Late dropped out participants	Early dropped out participants	Sum
Instability/non-functionality of the prototype	6	1	7
Too long tasks/exhausting	3	3	6
Prototype inflexibility/incompatibility with smartphones	3	1	4
Forgetfulness/insufficient reminders	2	5	7
Hard to understand/too complicated	2	3	5
Personal life problems	2	1	3
Limited access to the computer/internet	2	0	2
Strict deadlines/deadlines too close to each other	2	0	2
Summer break/vacation	1	4	5
Unclear instructions	1	3	4
Time limitation	1	2	3
Privacy concerns/personal questions	0	5	5
Unsure about the app's security	0	2	2
Other	2	1	3

questionnaire. By coding the results of all three data sources, six categories seem to us to be the most meaningful way of organizing the factors influencing participant drop-out behavior within a living lab setting. These include the stability of the prototype, ease of use and understandability, privacy and security protection, flexibility or compatibility of the prototype, the effects of reminders, and timing issues. In the following, we discuss each of the following factors.

Stability of the Prototype. Most of the drop-outs were due to the instability of the prototype. We faced two major server failures during the test phase (see Fig. 1). This issue was highlighted mostly by the late dropped out participants, and they became exhausted because they were not able to log in to the system. In response to the question of "what were your main reasons for dropping out of the DataBait user study", we got responses such as: "*Could not get the software to work, tried many times*" and "*The DataBait site did not work*". The results of email communication as well as the drop-out questionnaire showed that some participants were also confused about the problem: "*Do you have a server problems or do I have a bad memory? Did I do something wrong?*" Moreover, if the prototype does not work as promised, it can lead to participant frustration. As one of the late dropped out participants stated: "*It didn't work as planned*".

Ease of Use and Understandability. Regarding the ease of use and understandability, we obtained answers like "*Some things were hard to understand how they worked*", "*I did not understand what to do*", "*... exhausting! So many questions!*", "*Sometimes hard* to understand. A bit complicated", "Tests were too difficult with too much to read", "Surveys were too difficult, boring", and "Tasks were too complicated" from both early and late dropped out participants. Some of the dropped out participants also argued that they were discouraged due to the lack of clear instructions on how to perform the MicroTasks. They expressed their discouragement by saying: "Did not find any help or guidelines when my problems occurred", "After completing the first questionnaire, [I] did not find information on how to proceed", "Clarify instructions ...", and "I signed up late, did not find sufficient information (and did not have time to ask for clarifications)".

Privacy and Security Protection. Some dropped out participants, especially early dropped out participants, expressed their concerns about their privacy by commenting: "... questions that were too personal", "... [I] didn't want to share my data...", "Insecure about how much data the application will be able to get", and "Not feeling certain about installing something I know little about".

Flexibility or Compatibility of the Prototype. In this category, we got responses from dropped out participants such as "I had problems reading in the DataBait interface. It was not compatible with my iPhone. I had to twist and turn the phone to be able to get a whole view", "Could not use my smartphone instead of my computer when on a trip...", and "I could not do the test on my iPhone. DataBait didn't work on the screen". Besides the compatibility issues, some participants also complained about accessibility problems. Because the test users should have installed an extension to their browser, they usually needed to have access to their own computer. Therefore, some participants were discouraged from remaining in the field test by saying: "I don't have access to a computer regularly" and "I was on a trip and I didn't bring my computer. Then I tried to use my smartphone to solve the final task but it did not work. I tried to use the hotel computer, but it did not work either...".

The Effect of Reminders. Another influential factor on participant drop-out rate in our field test was related to the participants' forgetfulness. For instance, an early dropped out participant in response to his drop-out reason stated: "Forgetfulness. I regularly forgot that I had signed up, and I simply did not remember to finish the test." We tried to overcome the problem of participant forgetfulness by sending one reminder for each MicroTask to the participants who did not fulfill the task within the scheduled time. However, some participants still argued that they needed more reminders to complete the tasks. For example, an early dropped out participant stated: "... write one more reminder mail - I know there actually was one, but sometimes there are just too many other mails and other things to do...". This issue was also mentioned by some of the late dropped out participants, as one said: "Give more reminders. I understand that there are people that maybe don't want constant reminders, but I am one of those who really need to be reminded - I have a terrible memory and I keep prioritizing things that I probably shouldn't. Maybe give participants options for how often they should be reminded? (I could seriously use daily reminders, at least when the deadline is closing in)".

Timing Issues. Regarding the timing issues, the reasons for participants to drop-out of the field test were related to the inflexibility of the scheduling as well as an inappropriate time of the year. Some of the dropped out participants in Group2 mentioned that the tasks were too close together by stating: *"The surveys had numerous tasks that needed a lot of time [...]. Also give more time between surveys"*. The importance of flexibility in timing became more apparent to us when we received some comments from those who asked for longer time to complete the assigned tasks. We got responses such as: *"The timing was my biggest problem, if I had a few days extra it would have not been any problem"*, *"At the moment I don't have the time. But next week I do so if you could wait until then I will gladly be a participant"*, and *"The surveys were too close together and that in addition to a very stressful period at work, I didn't get the time to do it"*.

Concerning the time of the year, we got some responses such as *"I received one of the assignments while I was on vacation and couldn't access my computer. By the time I got home I was behind and couldn't continue"*, *"... Vacation. I went on vacation in the summer, which limited my access to computers and the Internet"*, and *"Bad idea having a test during the vacation months"*.

6   Discussion and Conclusion

Our study contributes to previous research by featuring key negative factors that influence the motivation of participants to stay engaged and that lead to participant drop-out when testing an innovation in a living lab setting.

A notable finding of our case study was related to the stability of the prototype, especially when the participants had access to all of the subtasks. For example, participants in Group1 started to test the application with the intention to complete all five MicroTasks as soon as possible. The rush to use the application caused the server to fail to respond to any request on two occasions both for two days. Therefore, it is of crucial importance to verify the stability of the prototype to prevent server overload behavior, especially when the number of test users is relatively high, otherwise it can lead to participant frustration. One way to overcome this type of problem is to make the participants aware and well informed that the prototype is not as stable and reliable as a commercial technology, which is in line with Taylor et al.'s [25] recommendation.

Our finding also supports Zheng et al.'s [26] finding that analyzability (i.e., the degree of task complexity as well as the availability of information about the tasks) is positively associated with the users' motivation. If the tasks are not simple enough, some participants are not able to understand the task [21] and consequently will not enthusiastically engage in the process. To avoid complexity, a clear and accessible guideline would minimize the risk of confusion and resulting discouragement. Although guidelines and instructions on how to perform the MicroTasks had been prepared for the participants, some of them were not able to find and use them. Therefore, the organizers of the field test need to make the participants aware of the whole engagement process and to create guidelines and instructions that in addition to being comprehensible are easily accessible and available.

When it comes to privacy and security concerns, our findings were consistent with previous studies that privacy protection is positively associated with sustainable user engagement [27, 28]. As Georgeos et al. [29] argue, users are concerned about the security of their information and they might drop-out of the project if they have to fill in their personal information in a system or an application, especially when the system is under development and thus is not highly stable. Another interesting observation about the privacy concerns was that a total of 205 participants started to fill out the recruitment survey, but only 118 of them completed this survey. Most of them stopped completing the survey when they were asked to give a link to their Facebook account in the recruitment survey. One plausible explanation is that they were concerned about their identity and preferred to be an anonymous contributor.

Regarding the flexibility of the timing, the number of participants who reached the end of the test in Group1 was almost two times greater than in Group2. This finding aligns with Wilson et al.'s [30] finding that users prefer to carry out the tasks at their own pace, especially when they are participating in a multi-task user study. Interestingly, despite the fact that the total time for carrying out all five MicroTasks was equal in both Group1 and Group2, we did not receive any comment from the dropped out participants in Group1 regarding the time limitation because they were able to complete the tasks at their own pace. However, as mentioned earlier, giving all tasks together might cause other problems in the field tests such as overload on the server, as we experienced in our case.

In consideration of the time of the year, we faced many drop-outs due to summer holiday and vacation time because the field test was conducted in the summer. Therefore, the organizers of a user study should consider that the test users might not have access to their computer or to the Internet during their vacation period. Moreover, in order to reduce the likelihood of participants' forgetfulness, a sufficient number of reminders must be set in the schedule of the field tests. As our direct observations showed, the participation rate immediately increased after sending a reminder to the test users, and thus the effects of sending reminders need to be further investigated.

Regarding different kinds of incentivization, although many of dropped out participants mentioned monetary reward as their main motivation to participate in the test, our results were contradictory to [24], and there were no significant differences in participant drop-out behavior with two different method of receiving incentives. One possible explanation for this is the duration of the user study, which was relatively short and thus the periodic micro-incentives might not have had an effect. Moreover, the amount of the financial reward in this case was very small and thus might not have made a difference in the drop-out rate.

One limitation of this study is that the factors extracted in our study might be case or project specific, and they need to be tested in other projects. For example, the issue of privacy was very crucial in our project because the developed application needed to get access to the user's Facebook data. Another limitation was that cultural factors were likely to be influential. Our sample participants included only Swedish participants, and employing a mixed panel might have led to different results. The relatively low number of responses to our drop-out questionnaire (32 of 91 dropped out participants) is also a limitation of this study.

This study also opens opportunities for future research. As O'Brien and Toms [10] have introduced re-engagement as one of the core concepts of their user engagement process model, an interesting topic for further research would be to clarify how and why user motivation for engaging and staying engaged differ. More specifically, it would be interesting to identify how the organizers of a user study can re-motivate the dropped out participants to re-engage in the study.

Acknowledgments. This work was funded by the European Commission in the context of the FP7 project USEMP (Grant Agreement No. 611596), the Horizon 2020 project PrivacyFlag (Grant Agreement No. 653426), and the Horizon 2020 project U4IoT (Grant Agreement No. 732078). We would also like to thank all participants who helped us with their feedback during the application test and the post-test survey.

References

1. Leonardi, C., Doppio, N., Lepri, B., Zancanaro, M., Caraviello, M., Pianesi, F.: Exploring long-term participation within a living lab: satisfaction, motivations and expectations. In: Proceedings of the 8th Nordic Conference on Human-Computer Interaction: Fun, Fast, Foundational, pp. 927–930. ACM, New York (2014)
2. Bano, M., Zowghi, D.: A systematic review on the relationship between user involvement and system success. Inf. Softw. Technol. **58**, 148–169 (2015)
3. Lin, W.T., Shao, B.B.: The relationship between user participation and system success: a simultaneous contingency approach. Inf. Manag. **37**, 283–295 (2000)
4. Chesbrough, H.: Open innovation: a new paradigm for understanding industrial innovation. In: Chesbrough, H., Vanhaverbeke, W., West, J. (eds.) Open Innovation: Researching a New Paradigm, pp. 1–12. Oxford University Press, Oxford (2006)
5. Ståhlbröst, A.: Forming future IT: the living lab way of user involvement (2008). http://epubl.ltu.se/1402-1544/2008/62/index-en.html
6. Bergvall-Kareborn, B., Holst, M., Stahlbrost, A.: Concept design with a living lab approach. In: 42nd Hawaii International Conference on System Sciences, 2009. HICSS 2009, pp. 1–10. IEEE (2009)
7. Ståhlbröst, A., Bergvall-Kåreborn, B.: Voluntary contributors in open innovation processes. In: Eriksson-Lundström, J.S.Z., Wiberg, M., Hrastinski, S., Edenius, M., Ågerfalk, P. J. (eds.) Managing Open Innovation Technologies, pp. 133–149. Springer, Berlin (2013)
8. Ogonowski, C., Ley, B., Hess, J., Wan, L., Wulf, V.: Designing for the living room: long-term user involvement in a living lab. In: Proceedings of the SIGCHI Conference on Human Factors in Computing Systems, pp. 1539–1548. ACM, New York (2013)
9. Ley, B., Ogonowski, C., Mu, M., Hess, J., Race, N., Randall, D., Rouncefield, M., Wulf, V.: At home with users: a comparative view of living labs. Interact. Comput. **27**, 21–35 (2015)
10. O'Brien, H.L., Toms, E.G.: What is user engagement? A conceptual framework for defining user engagement with technology. J. Am. Soc. Inf. Sci. Technol. **59**, 938–955 (2008)
11. Habibipour, A., Bergvall-Kåreborn, B., Ståhlbröst, A.: How to sustain user engagement over time: a research agenda. In: Proceedings of Twenty-Second Americas Conference on Information Systems (AMCIS). AIS, San Diego (2016)
12. Pedersen, J., Kocsis, D., Tripathi, A., Tarrell, A., Weerakoon, A., Tahmasbi, N., Xiong, J., Deng, W., Oh, O., De Vreede, G.-J.: Conceptual foundations of crowdsourcing: a review of IS research. In: 46th Hawaii International Conference on System Sciences (HICSS), pp. 579–588. IEEE (2013)
13. Sambamurthy, V., Kirsch, L.J.: An integrative framework of the information systems development process. Decis. Sci. **31**, 391–411 (2000)

14. Bansler, J.: Systems development research in Scandinavia: three theoretical schools. Scand. J. Inf. Syst. **1**, 3–20 (1989)
15. Iivari, J., Lyytinen, K.: Research on information systems development in Scandinavia—unity in plurality. Scand. J. Inf. Syst. **10**, 135–185 (1998)
16. Chesbrough, H., Crowther, A.K.: Beyond high tech: early adopters of open innovation in other industries. R&D Manag. **36**, 229–236 (2006)
17. Kaasinen, E., Koskela-Huotari, K., Ikonen, V., Niemelä, M., Näkki, P.: Three approaches to co-creating services with users. In: Spohrer, J.C., Freund, L.E. (eds.) Advances in the Human Side of Service Engineering, pp. 286–295. CRC Press, Boca Raton (2013)
18. Georges, A., Schuurman, D., Baccarne, B., Coorevits, L.: User engagement in living lab field trials. Info **17**, 26–39 (2015)
19. Habibipour, A., Bergvall-Kåreborn, B.: Towards a user engagement process model in open innovation. In: ISPIM Innovation Symposium. The International Society for Professional Innovation Management: Moving the Innovation Horizon. ISPIM (2016)
20. Kienle, A., Ritterskamp, C.: Facilitating asynchronous discussions in learning communities: the impact of moderation strategies. Behav. Inf. Technol. **26**, 73–80 (2007)
21. Kobren, A., Tan, C.H., Ipeirotis, P., Gabrilovich, E.: Getting more for less: optimized crowdsourcing with dynamic tasks and goals. In: Proceedings of the 24th International Conference on World Wide Web, pp. 592–602. International World Wide Web Conferences Steering Committee, Republic and Canton of Geneva, Switzerland (2015)
22. Yin, R.K.: Case Study Research: Design and Methods. SAGE, Los Angeles (2008)
23. Benbasat, I., Goldstein, D.K., Mead, M.: The case research strategy in studies of information systems. MIS Q. **11**, 369–386 (1987)
24. Musthag, M., Raij, A., Ganesan, D., Kumar, S., Shiffman, S.: Exploring micro-incentive strategies for participant compensation in high-burden studies. In: Proceedings of the 13th International Conference on Ubiquitous Computing, pp. 435–444. ACM, New York (2011)
25. Taylor, N., Cheverst, K., Wright, P., Olivier, P.: Leaving the wild: lessons from community technology handovers. In: CHI 2013 Proceedings of the SIGCHI Conference on Human Factors in Computing Systems, pp. 1549–1558. ACM, New York (2013)
26. Zheng, H., Li, D., Hou, W.: Task design, motivation, and participation in crowdsourcing contests. Int. J. Electron. Commer. **15**, 57–88 (2011)
27. Ståhlbröst, A., Padyab, A., Sällström, A., Hollosi, D.: Design of smart city systems from a privacy perspective. IADIS Int. J. WWW Internet **13**, 1–16 (2015)
28. Padyab, A.M.: Getting more explicit on genres of disclosure: towards better understanding of privacy in digital age (research in progress). In: Nor. Konf. Organ. Bruk Av IT. **22** (2014)
29. Georges, A., Schuurman, D., Baccarne, B.: An exploratory model of the willingness of end-users to participate in field tests: a living lab case-study analysis. In: Proceedings of Open Living Lab Days 2014, Amsterdam, The Netherlands (2014)
30. Wilson, S., Bekker, M., Johnson, P., Johnson, H.: Helping and hindering user involvement—a tale of everyday design. In: CHI 1997 Proceedings of the ACM SIGCHI Conference on Human factors in computing systems, pp. 178–185. ACM, New York (1997)

Technostress and Social Networking Services: Uncovering Strains and Their Underlying Stressors

Markus Salo[1](✉), Henri Pirkkalainen[2], and Tiina Koskelainen[1]

[1] University of Jyväskylä, Mattilanniemi 2, 40100 Jyväskylä, Finland
{markus.salo,tiina.koskelainen}@jyu.fi
[2] Tampere University of Technology,
Korkeakoulunkatu 8, 33720 Tampere, Finland
henri.pirkkalainen@tut.fi

Abstract. Numerous users of social networking sites and services (SNS) suffer from technostress and its various strains that hinder well-being. Despite a growing research interest on technostress, the extant studies have not explained what kinds of various strains can SNS use create and how can these strains be traced back to different stressors. To address this gap in research, we employed a qualitative approach by narrative interviews. As a contribution, our findings introduce four SNS strains (concentration problems, sleep problems, identity problems, and social relation problems) and explain how they link with different underlying SNS stressors. As practical implications, the findings of this study can help technostressed users to identify their SNS strains, understand how they are created, and increase their possibilities to avoid the strains in the future.

Keywords: Technostress · Social networking sites · Social networking services · Strains · Stressors

1 Introduction

Social networking sites and services (SNS) have gained mass popularity and been incorporated into nearly all activities of life [1–3]. SNS refer to online services that users employ to build and maintain social relations, for instance, by shared discussions, interests, and other activities [4]. In this study, we focus on the personal/leisure SNS that reflect non-organizational and non-work-related purposes. Examples of currently popular SNS include Facebook, Instagram, and Snapchat.

Despite their many benefits, researchers and practitioners have reported that the use of SNS derives also serious negative consequences for their users [2, 5–7]. One of the main negative consequences is technostress. Technostress refers to an individual user's experience of stress caused by the user's inability to deal with information technology (IT) in a healthy manner [8–11]. In the context of SNS, numerous users reportedly suffer from stress [5, 7] since SNS enable users, for example, to receive on-going push notifications and peek at the *"glossified lives reported by other users"* [12, 13].

© Springer International Publishing AG 2017
S. Stigberg et al. (Eds.): SCIS 2017, LNBIP 294, pp. 41–53, 2017.
DOI: 10.1007/978-3-319-64695-4_4

Studying technostress is deemed critical, since it has been found to cause personal burden, decrease individual well-being, and even contribute to burnout [8, 14, 15].

Technostress has recently gained research interest particularly in the field of information systems (IS). A majority of technostress studies have focused on work-related technostress in organizational contexts (e.g., [8, 11, 16–18]). Lately, technostress has been found relevant and important also in outside of work contexts and personal/leisure IT such as SNS [2, 4, 6]. Although these studies have offered first valuable insights about technostress in the personal/leisure IT and SNS contexts, they have not identified users' concrete SNS strains or explored how different types of strains can potentially emerge in different ways.

To address this void of knowledge, our study attempts to answer the following research questions: (1) What different types of strains do the SNS users suffer from? (2) How are the different types of SNS strains created by their underlying SNS stressors? To grasp these research questions, we employed a qualitative approach by narrative interviews since it enabled us first to identify the users' SNS strains and then to track down the reasons behind them. Such approach is deemed useful for generating context-specific insights about IT use in real-life situations [19, 20].

As a contribution, our findings introduce four different strains deriving from SNS use and explain how individual strains link with different underlying SNS stressors than social strains. Thus, we uncover two different ways with different sets of SNS stressors that contribute to different SNS strains. These new findings go beyond the prior studies on technostress in SNS and personal/leisure IT contexts, which have focused on rather abstract and general strains (e.g., [2, 4, 6, 21]). As practical implications, the findings of this study can assist technostressed users and their stakeholders (e.g., families, friends, employers, and health organizations) to identify their SNS strains, understand how they are created, and mitigate them. Since the widespread nature of users' SNS strains and problems have been highlighted in media and practitioner reports [5, 7, 12], our findings can potentially help numerous SNS users.

2   Theoretical Background

Many scholars across various disciplines such as psychology, sociology, and medicine have paid attention to stress over several decades. Thus, technostress researchers have applied theoretical knowledge from stress research (e.g., [22, 23]), which has led to a consensus about the two main concepts of technostress: stressors and strains. In general, stressors refer to demand conditions that create stress, while strains refer to the individual's responses and outcomes to them [8, 11, 18, 22, 23]. We summarize related research on technostress as follows.

2.1   Technostress Research

The term technostress dates back to the 1980s when it was first coined by a psychologist named Brod [9]. He noticed how this *"modern disease"* harmed individuals' well-being and, through computerization and digitalization in the society, it had come to stay both at workplaces and homes [10]. Technostress, however, did not gain prominent research attention until late 2000s when IS scholars started to pay attention to it.

A majority of the technostress studies has focused on the work and organizational context (e.g., [8, 11, 16–18, 24–27]). Studies have concluded that work-related IT can cause technostress due to stressors such as work/home conflicts and job insecurity [8]. They, in turn, can bring about strains such as reduced productivity, decreased organizational commitment, or even work burnout [11, 15, 28]. Work-related technostress literature has also showed that organizational support mechanisms such as help desk support can mitigate technostress [11, 17, 18, 29].

Recently, technostress has been found to be a relevant and important issue also with the use of personal/leisure IT [2, 4, 6]. The use of personal/leisure IT differs from the use of organizational/work IT because the former is fundamentally voluntary, and users' own perceptions, decisions, and responsibilities are highlighted [30, 31]. Within studies that focus on technostress outside of work, researchers have found general links between compulsive smartphone use and technostress [21] as well as excessive SNS use and technostress [4]. In the SNS context, social information consumption has been found to influence users' envy, which further hinders users' well-being [13]. Researchers have also demonstrated how general emotional exhaustion mediates the relationship between social overload and satisfaction as well as SNS use discontinuance intentions [32]. Further, two general types of exhaustion that affect SNS discontinuance include SNS and switching exhaustion [2]. Finally, usage amount, relationship amount, and relationship characteristics can contribute to social overload that increases exhaustion, dissatisfaction and discontinuance intentions [6].

Despite these recent advancements in technostress research, the extant literature is still missing (at least) two essential aspects regarding technostress in the personal/leisure IT or SNS contexts: First, prior studies have focused only on rather general and abstract SNS-related strains (e.g., emotional exhaustion and dissatisfaction) and neglected the more concrete problems that the individual users may face. Second, prior studies have not investigated how different types of strains can potentially emerge in different ways based on their linkages with different stressors. Studying these missing aspects is deemed crucial because users' different types of concrete strains and problems can be deliberately reduced only by identifying them and understanding their underlying stressors. Such knowledge can potentially help numerous SNS users to get rid of their strains and prevent them from becoming chronic.

2.2   Research Framework

To address the noted research gap, we employ the transaction theory of stress as a broad research framework [22, 23]. We chose the framework for the following reasons: First, it is based on the two main concepts of stress (stressors and strains) that have been established and found useful across various disciplines. Second, it has been stated to be particularly fitting for IS research and technostress [18]. Third, use of a such broad framework sensitizes us to the theoretically important concepts but, at the same time, allows us to pay attention to the specific aspects of SNS use [19].

Essentially, the theory depicts a linkage between stressors and strains (Fig. 1). Stressors refer to the stress-creating stimuli encountered by the user, while strains refer to the user's responses and outcomes in relation to the stressors [11, 18, 22, 23]. Stress is referred to as the overall transaction regarding these concepts.

Fig. 1. The research framework based on [22, 23].

The basic idea of the theory is that stress is created when the demands encountered by an individual exceed the individual's resources for dealing with them [22, 23]. Importantly, stress occurs because of the individual's own perception of the stressors [22, 33]. Thus, stress is subjective and two individuals can perceive a similar situation differently. In sum, we utilize the framework in our empirical study to identify different types of SNS strains as well as explain their underlying SNS-related stressors.

3   Method

To capture SNS users' strains and their underlying stressors, we chose a qualitative approach with real-life narrative interviews [34]. This approach was deemed suitable since it enabled us first to identify the strains that the SNS users suffer from and then to uncover the underlying reasons behind them. Such approaches have been found useful for uncovering users' perceptions and generating context-specific explanations about IT use [19, 20].

3.1   Data Collection

We chose to collect data with narrative interviews to tap into the users' actual experiences of technostress related to SNS use. Narratives are stories of how things have been: time-based descriptions of events comprising a beginning, middle, and end [35, 36]. Researchers have found narratives useful for explaining IT use and human behavior [35, 36]. By utilizing narrative approach, we could focus on the users' actual real-life experiences and avoid the risk of speculating about hypothetical use scenarios [37].

Altogether, we interviewed 32 SNS users who had experienced technostress. We utilized purposeful sampling [38]: We deliberately sought users who could provide first-hand experiences and relevant information regarding our research aims. Thus, we applied pre-screening to make sure that all interviews included actual experiences of technostress and SNS strains. For example, we used snowballing technique to reach potential interviewees. We first started with interviews of users of one popular SNS. As we wanted to broaden our focus so that our results would reflect also other types of

SNS, we continued by interviews with users of also other types of SNS. Half of the interviewees were women, and half were men. The interviewees were Finnish and their age ranged from 20 to 80 years. Altogether, they had varying occupational statuses, including employed, unemployed, student, and retired. To contextualize our data [19], we asked each interviewee to describe their background as well as what types of IT they generally use, for what purposes, and to what extent.

We structured the interviews to uncover real-life narratives. Regarding the aim of this study, we asked the users to identify their problems deriving from SNS use as well as to thoroughly describe how and why their problems and stressful situations with SNS had originated and affected them. With each interviewee, we asked several detailed questions about their real-life examples, practices, and perceptions. We followed the main guidelines of interviewing set by [39]. For example, we maintained flexibility and, when needed, added questions to our interview scheme.

We continued data collection until a sufficient level of saturation had been reached, no essentially new information appeared to emerge, and the benefit from conducting further interviews was estimated marginal. The interviews lasted approximately 47 min on average and contained altogether over 117,000 words. The interviews were recorded and transcribed for the relevant parts.

3.2   Data Analysis

In this study, the unit of analysis was the individual user's perception of technostress related to SNS use. We conducted the analysis by coding all interview text that reflected technostress according to the broad research framework [22, 23]. Such use of the framework assisted us to focus and make sense of the detailed data [40]. Thus, we placed relevant sets of words, sentences, or sets of sentences under SNS strains and SNS stressors accordingly and labeled them with names with the help of NVivo software. These detailed labels were then sorted and combined into higher-level categories based on their content. Although one author was primarily responsible for the initial coding, we utilized hand-written memos and discussed the possibility of multiple interpretations [19].

To ensure a detailed examination of the SNS strains, we utilized a reverse analysis approach: we started by identifying and paying attention to the users' SNS problems and strains and continued by tracing the strains back to what had caused them. This way, we were able to uncover the SNS stressors that contributed to the strains. Such reverse analysis was deemed suitable since it enabled us to find linkages behind the different types of SNS strains.

We found four different categories of strains that were sorted into two types of SNS strains (individual and social strains). Our analysis indicated that behind the individual strains there was a different set of SNS-related stressors than behind the social strains. As we followed the strains into their respective SNS stressors, we found out two essential stressors for the individual strains and three for the social strains. As a result, we had developed two different ways of how SNS strains are created with the help of the broad research framework and our detailed data. Regarding triangulation, we ensured that the main insights recurred in multiple interviews [19].

4   Results

On a general level, our data indicated that technostress caused reduction in the users' overall well-being via mental and physical fatigue. However, we deliberately wanted to pay close attention to the more specific strains of SNS use. Thus, our analysis highlighted four categories of strains that the SNS users suffered from: concentration problems, sleep problems, identity problems, and social relation problems. These four categories reflected two main types of strains: individual strains and social strains. According to our data, the two main types were caused by different sets of SNS stressors. We elaborate the two main types of strains one by one and present demonstrating quotations from the interviews.

4.1   Individual Strains: Concentration and Sleep Problems

One of the most recurrent strains was **concentration problems**: the negative effect of SNS use on users' ability to concentrate on a situation or a task at hand. These issues appeared because SNS use frequently distracted the users' attention and made it harder to concentrate on a specific issue at hand or even just to *"live in the moment"*. A recurrent situation was that the SNS draw the users' attention away from their formal or informal daily activities that they were supposed to focus on (e.g., studying or having a discussion with spouse). Many interviewees described how they felt their attention span had become weaker and shorter. Simultaneously, they portrayed how they had turned increasingly *"restless"*. For example, one of the interviewees narrated how his use of a particular SNS had drained his concentration abilities:

> "For instance with [a particular SNS] I realized that whether it's day or night, I use so awful lot of time with it. …I started to feel like I'm becoming a zombie. …I realized how much time and a certain type of thinking capacity, or whatever it is, it took from me. And so I couldn't properly concentrate on my studies and that kind of activities."

Another individual strain of SNS use was **sleep problems**: the disturbance of nightly SNS use on sleep. Almost all interviewees used SNS when in bed before sleeping and many of them as the last thing before falling asleep. Particularly, the interviewees perceived that their late-night SNS surfing concretely shortened sleep duration, harmed quality, and distracted timing. They perceived that their SNS use ate a portion of their potential sleep time per night and, at times, they were woken up by the sounds and lights triggered by SNS. Some of the interviewees used the terms *"sleep problems"*, *"sleep difficulties"*, and *"changes in sleep"* when talking about late-night SNS surfing:

> "…sleep problems, particularly at the time I used [SNS via smartphone] very much at night. … for several years, I kept the smartphone in my bed but then I decided that it is not wise anymore to mess around with it after 10 PM or especially when I try to sleep. I think [SNS and smartphone] comprised a quite clear contributor [to my sleep]."

4.1.1 Stressors Behind the Individual Strains: SNS Overdependence and Overload

In the interviewees' narratives, both of the individual strains can be traced back to two types of stressors: SNS overdependence and the constant feeling of SNS overload. By **SNS overdependence**, we refer to the users' high reliance on SNS in their behavior and daily activities[1]. The interviewees emphasized how their concentration and sleep were hindered particularly because SNS was present in nearly all areas of their lives, SNS dominated some of their daily activities (especially bedtime activities), and they were too accustomed to constantly use SNS. These aspects caused the users' tendency to frequently switch their attention to SNS as well as to stay awake past their bedtime. SNS and technology overdependence is illustrated by the following quotes:

> "Unfortunately, it really dominates, governs, and controls my day quite much. Like when I wake up to the beeping sounds of my smartphone in the morning. And when I'm going to sleep, I gaze at the screen as the last thing at night and see how many new followers I got on my [SNS] accounts."

By **overload**, we refer to the users confrontation with excessive amounts of information derived via SNS, various SNS channels, and the activities within SNS[2]. Most of the interviewees emphasized how they are continuously challenged by the on-going flow of information deriving from multiple sources and requiring for various types of actions. For example, overload derived via push notifications made the users constantly shift from one target of concentration to another. Such multifocus did not only hinder the interviewees much needed concentration abilities but also their sleep since it was perceived as an unfavorable state to fall asleep and decreased quality of sleep. The interviewees reported that overload reflected a feeling of having too much to process in their head. For example, one interviewee described his daily feelings of overload as follows:

> "I think, most of all, it's the about the information abundance where I live, so that the [information] comes from all places and to all channels. From all people. It's probably what I feel as the most negative issue. It's almost daily. …and then I can't reach the presence that I'd need for a particular situation at hand."

In sum, Fig. 2 maps the stressors behind the individual strains of SNS use.

4.2 Social Strains: Identity and Social Relation Problems

According to our data, SNS use can create strains tied closely to the users' social life. First of them is **identity problems**, by which we refer to the users' tensions related to their conceptions of themselves and communicating such conceptions to others. In practice, the interviewees highlighted how SNS use derived a pressure to constantly question and reassure one's own activities. This is due to the SNS' unprecedented possibility of seeing glossy peeks of others lives and posting updates about one's own life, which can cause negative self-image and disappointment to one's own identity:

---

[1] Dependence is different from addiction in that dependence is a broader term, it emphasizes users' reliance on SNS, and it does not necessary indicate compulsive behavior.

[2] In literature, different overloads such as information, technology, and social overload are used. In this study, we refer to a combination of them.

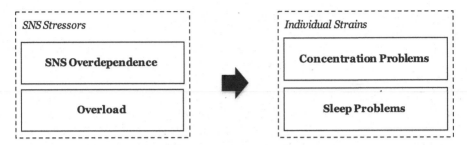

Fig. 2. Stressors behind the individual strains.

> "Somewhere down the line I noticed that [SNS use] influences me, so that the other users' status updates and posts have an effect on my self. So if everyone had many happy things posted [in their status updates] and if I wasn't doing that good in life, I noticed that [the updates] disturbed my self."

Identity problems also included the burden of forfeiting one's own identity and private information. According to the interviewees, SNS jeopardize identity-related information, since such information can be sold to a third party, stolen, or taken otherwise advantage of.

Another social strain was **social relation problems**, which refer to the harmful effects of SNS use on one's interactions with other people. A recurrent issue was negative changes in one's online relations. For instance, several interviewees mentioned how their perceptions had changed about some of their peers after their peers had posted provocative content. Further, discussions and debates over such content had a polarizing effect, since they tended to drive people to the opposite corners:

> "I've noticed that when I took a stand on an [SNS debate], and I received some initial attention from [the opposing side] or they assigned me with a certain profile, I began to attract even more attention than before. ...at first I didn't even realize [the harm], because it was fun, but if it went on for long, for like a year, I noticed how straining it was. It was so treacherous that you didn't see the mental energy that died out with it."

4.2.1   Stressors Behind the Social Strains: Life Comparison Discrepancy, Online Discussion Conflict, and Privacy and Security Uncontrollability

According to our data, the social strains can be traced back to three SNS stressors: life comparison discrepancy, conflicts in SNS discussions, and privacy and security uncontrollability. By **life comparison discrepancy**, we refer to the SNS users discomfort when comparing their own life to the lives of others via SNS. As one interviewee put it simply, it was about the negative and tiring aspect of "*stalking how others are doing*". The interviewees emphasized how easy it is to compare the constantly on-going SNS posts of others to their own life. Life comparison was perceived dangerous because it can form an infinite loop: one can always find an SNS post that showcases how someone is doing something better than its reader. The following excerpt illustrates the effects of such comparison to one's identity:

> "It's like when I hear my friends saying like, 'I've just browsed the profiles [in a particular SNS] for two hours'. Like I recently discussed [with my friends] that people go and peek at the lives of some friends of their friends or their ex [girlfriends and boyfriends], eh... It causes me

to start thinking too much about everything… It's probably like that I start to compare myself [and my life] to the others and that kind of stuff."

Online discussion conflict refers to the public or private disputes between two or more users of SNS. Several interviewees referred how they were displeased when they were driven into online arguments or witnessed other users' altercations. The subjects of the debates varied all the way from politics and religion to hobbies and leisure activities. Specifically, many interviewees emphasized how *"intense"*, *"nasty"*, and *"personal"* such conflicts got. For example, one interviewee described how a conflict within an SNS group of dog owners had evolved into a war that was reported even in a national newspaper:

"…I'm involved in a dog breed group [in a particular SNS]. And there's, I guess like every spring, some fight about whether that particular breed should be trimmed and cut the dog's fur to zero for summer [laughs]… So, an actual war breaks out. There was a really long discussion thread under one picture of a trimmed dog… People were like 'yuck how ugly it is' and 'the dog is ruined'. …so that, eventually, [a national newspaper] ended up writing a story about that particular [SNS] fight."

Privacy and security uncontrollability reflect the user's possibilities to control how their personal information is shared via SNS (both within the visible SNS or behind the scenes). Several interviewees perceived that sharing detailed private information could turn against them if their network members *"knew too much about"* them or their sensitive information ended up in wrong hands. The more severely perceived security risks included surveillance, theft of bank account information, and other profile hacking. These aspects contributed to identity pressures, since many interviewees thought they had to keep sharing personal information to maintain their identities via SNS despite the uncontrollability. For example, one of the interviewees described how he had been balancing between identity building and his concerns related to privacy and security:

"[Previously] all of my status updates were public. My pictures were public. …I just posted all kinds of personal stuff visible for everyone… All kinds of stuff that I still regret today. …[but nowadays] I tend to delete my [recent] updates after a while, basically after people have seen them."

In sum, Fig. 3 illustrates the stressors behind the social strains of SNS use.

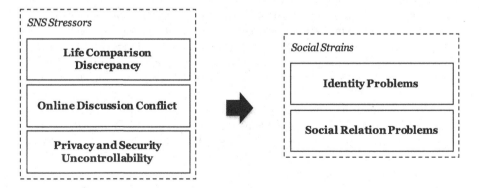

Fig. 3. Stressors behind the social strains.

5 Discussion

Despite the recent calls and a growing research interest on technostress (e.g., [2, 6, 8, 11, 16–18]), the extant studies have not explained what kinds of various strains SNS use can create and how can these strains be traced back to different stressors. To address the identified research gap, this study contributes by identifying four strains of SNS use and uncovering the SNS-related stressors underlying them (Table 1). Such knowledge is deemed important because understanding how actual problems are created can help individual users and their stakeholders to prevent the problems, attain stress-free SNS use, and improve their well-being [10, 13, 33].

Table 1. Summary of the findings

	SNS Stressors	*SNS Strains*
Way 1	• SNS overdependence • Overload	*Individual strains:* • Concentration problems • Sleep problems
Way 2	• Life comparison discrepancy • Online discussion conflict • Privacy and security uncontrollability	*Social strains:* • Identity problems • Social relation problems

5.1 Implications for Research and Practice

First, our data suggests that there are two different ways of how SNS strains are created: individual strains link with different underlying stressors than social strains. These new findings go beyond the prior studies on technostress in personal/leisure IT and SNS contexts, which have focused only on a few rather abstract and general strains (e.g., [2, 4, 6, 21]). By identifying different kinds of strains and their different determinants, it is now possible to help users and their stakeholders (e.g., families, friends, employers, medical professionals, and health organizations) to acknowledge their strains, understand how they are created, and increase their possibilities to avoid the strains in the future. This generates opportunities for researchers as they can use our findings to design and implement tailored interventions for technostress reduction that target certain types of strains. In sum, we suggest researchers to distinguish these different types of strains and their linkages with different stressors when studying technostress in the future.

Second, our study demonstrates how users can suffer from concrete problems deriving as side-effects from their SNS use. For example, we found out how users' concentration abilities had essentially decreased, how their sleep had been disturbed, and how they had faced identity problems due to SNS use. In contrast to the prior studies' focus on strains related to SNS use and SNS themselves (e.g., use discontinuance and SNS exhaustion) [2, 4, 6, 21], our findings extend the current understanding by recognizing the side-effects that "spill" further from the mere SNS use situations (e.g., to situations such as sleeping). Thus, this study aims to reveal a more precise picture about the SNS strains that seem to haunt the users in also outside of the actual SNS use situations. By highlighting such "spillover" effect of the SNS strains, our study aims to provide input for discussions about healthy ways to use IT in concord with other areas of human life.

Finally, our study reveals several more detailed new findings that, to our best knowledge, have not been discussed in the technostress literature. For example, we could not find any empirical studies on technostress that would account for concentration problems, sleep problems, social identity pressure, life comparison discrepancy, and online discussion conflict. There have been discussions of some alike aspects fragmented across different disciplines such as self-promotional and antisocial SNS behavior in psychology [41] and children's screen time and sleep in medicine [42]. However, most studies have applied rather general constructs and have not revealed a picture about the stressors underlying the strains. In this way, IS studies could potentially offer implications also for other disciplines than IS and enhance the much desired two-way interaction between IS and its so called reference disciplines [43]. For example, psychologists and medical researchers could potentially complement their studies with our findings regarding the different kinds of SNS-related stressors.

5.2   Limitations and Future Topics

There are certain limitations regarding this study. First, this study aimed to capture and distinguish the central stressors for both main types of strains (individual and social), although the stressors may not be completely exclusive and some interaction between them may occur. Second, since data collection with retrospective approaches may relate to recall and re-interpretation issues [44], we aimed to anchor questions, responses, and examples in real-life events and instructed the interviewees to think carefully about their past experiences. Third, we collected self-reported data about users' perceptions instead of physiological data [45]. However, such self-reported and perceptional data have been found reliable for studying technostress [8, 11]. Fourth, our study focused on the users' subjective experience of stress and it did not capture any potential effects of IT on a biological level (e.g., chemicals or radiofrequency radiation) [46]. Fifth, our interviewees were Finnish and, hence, some of the findings may relate to nationality and culture. Overall, we estimated that answering our research questions required data about users' actual experiences of technostress instead of hypothetical scenarios.

Based on the findings of this study, we suggest areas to be examined in the future. First, our study revealed various SNS strains but did not focus on investigating whether the problems are short-term or long-term. Thus, researchers could utilize longitudinal approaches to study how permanent and recurrent these problems are. Second, this study focused on SNS use in the personal/leisure context. Since SNS are nowadays becoming increasingly popular also with work IT, strains of work-related SNS could be studied in organizational contexts. Finally, we encourage researchers to study how the SNS strains could be reduced. The findings of this study could be utilized to examine at least two different ways to reduce the strains: one for individual strains and another for social strains.

References

1. Carter, M., Grover, V.: Me, myself, and I(T): conceptualizing information technology identity and its implications. MIS Q. **39**(4), 931–957 (2015)
2. Maier, C., Laumer, S., Weinert, C., Weitzel, T.: The effects of technostress and switching stress on discontinued use of social networking services: a study of Facebook use. Inf. Syst. J. **25**(3), 275–308 (2015)
3. Lin, K.Y., Lu, H.P.: Why people use social networking sites: an empirical study integrating network externalities and motivation theory. Comput. Hum. Behav. **27**(3), 1152–1161 (2011)
4. Luqman, A., Cao, X., Ali, A., Masood, A., Yu, L.: Do you get exhausted from too much socializing? Empirical investigation of Facebook discontinues usage intentions based on SOR paradigm. Comput. Hum. Behav. (2017)
5. Huffington Post: Why Do Social Networks Increase Stress? (2013). http://www.huffing tonpost.com/john-dick/social-networks-and-stress_b_3534170.html
6. Maier, C., Laumer, S., Eckhardt, A., Weitzel, T.: Giving too much social support: social overload on social networking sites. Eur. J. Inf. Syst. **24**(5), 447–464 (2015)
7. PBS Newshour: This is How Facebook Stresses You Out, According to Study (2015). http://www.pbs.org/newshour/rundown/social-media-stress-contagious/
8. Ayyagari, R., Grover, V., Purvis, R.: Technostress: technological antecedents and implications. MIS Q. **35**(4), 831–858 (2011)
9. Brod, C.: Managing technostress: optimizing the use of computer technology. Pers. J. **61**, 753–757 (1982)
10. Brod, C.: Technostress: The Human Cost of the Computer Revolution. Addison Wesley, Reading (1984)
11. Ragu-Nathan, T.S., Tarafdar, M., Ragu-Nathan, B.S., Tu, Q.: The consequences of technostress for end users in organizations: conceptual development and validation. Inf. Syst. Res. **19**(4), 417–433 (2008)
12. New York Post: Why Facebook Feeds Division and Stress (2017). http://nypost.com/2017/02/18/why-facebook-feeds-division-and-stress/
13. Krasnova, H., Widjaja, T., Buxmann, P., Wenninger, H., Benbasat, I.: Why following friends can hurt you: an exploratory investigation of the effects of envy on social networking sites among college-age users. Inf. Syst. Res. **26**(3), 585–605 (2015)
14. Pawlowski, S.D., Kaganer, E.A., Cater, J.J.: Focusing the research agenda on burnout in IT: social representations of burnout in the profession. Eur. J. Inf. Syst. **16**(5), 612–627 (2007)
15. Srivastava, S.C., Chandra, S., Shirish, A.: Technostress creators and job outcomes: theorising the moderating influence of personality traits. Inf. Syst. J. **25**(4), 355–401 (2015)
16. Tarafdar, M., Tu, Q., Ragu-Nathan, B.S., Ragu-Nathan, T.S.: The impact of technostress on role stress and productivity. J. Manag. Inf. Syst. **24**(1), 301–328 (2007)
17. Tarafdar, M., Tu, Q., Ragu-Nathan, T.S.: Impact of technostress on end-user satisfaction and performance. J. Manag. Inf. Syst. **27**(3), 303–334 (2011)
18. Tarafdar, M., Bolman, E., Pullins, E.B., Ragu-Nathan, T.S.: Technostress: negative effect on performance and possible mitigations. Inf. Syst. J. **25**(2), 103–132 (2015)
19. Klein, H.K., Myers, M.D.: A set of principles for conducting and evaluating interpretive field studies in information systems. MIS Q. **23**(1), 67–93 (1999)
20. Venkatesh, V., Brown, S.A., Bala, H.: Bridging the qualitative–quantitative divide: guidelines for conducting mixed methods research in information systems. MIS Q. **37**(1), 21–54 (2013)
21. Lee, Y.K., Chang, C.T., Lin, Y., Cheng, Z.H.: The dark side of smartphone usage: psychological traits, compulsive behavior and technostress. Comput. Hum. Behav. **31**, 373–383 (2014)

22. Lazarus, R.S.: Psychological Stress and the Coping Process. McGraw-Hill, New York (1966)
23. Lazarus, R.S., Folkman, S.: Stress, Appraisal, and Coping. Springer, New York (1984)
24. Salanova, M., Llorens, S., Cifre, E.: The dark side of technologies: technostress among users of information and communication technologies. Int. J. Psychol. **48**(3), 422–436 (2013)
25. Shu, Q., Tu, Q., Wang, K.: The impact of computer self-efficacy and technology dependence on computer-related technostress: a social cognitive theory perspective. Int. J. Hum. Comput. Interact. **27**(10), 923–939 (2011)
26. Wang, K., Shu, Q., Tu, Q.: Technostress under different organizational environments: an empirical investigation. Comput. Hum. Behav. **24**(6), 3002–3013 (2008)
27. Yan, Z., Guo, X., Lee, M.K.O., Vogel, D.R.: A conceptual model of technology features and technostress in telemedicine communication. Inf. Technol. People **26**(3), 283–297 (2013)
28. Tu, Q., Wang, K., Shu, Q.: Computer-related technostress in China. Commun. ACM **48**(4), 77–81 (2005)
29. Galluch, P., Grover, V., Thatcher, J.: Interrupting the workplace: examining stressors in an information technology context. J. Assoc. Inf. Syst. **16**(1), 1–47 (2015)
30. Kim, H.W., Chan, H.C., Chan, Y.P.: A balanced thinking–feelings model of information systems continuance. Int. J. Hum Comput Stud. **65**(6), 511–525 (2007)
31. Venkatesh, V., Thong, J.Y.L., Xu, X.: Consumer acceptance and use of information technology: extending the unified theory of acceptance and use of technology. MIS Q. **36**(1), 157–178 (2012)
32. Maier, C., Laumer, S., Eckhardt, A., Weitzel, T.: When social networking turns to social overload: explaining the stress, emotional exhaustion, and quitting behavior from social network sites' users. In: European Conference on Information Systems (ECIS) (2012)
33. Lazarus, R.S.: Coping theory and research: past, present, and future. Psychosom. Med. **55**(3), 234–247 (1993)
34. Myers, M.D.: Qualitative research in information systems. MIS Q. **21**(2), 241–242 (1997)
35. Pentland, B.T.: Building process theory with narrative: from description to explanation. Acad. Manag. Rev. **24**(4), 711–724 (1999)
36. Schwarz, A., Chin, W.W., Hirschheim, R., Schwarz, C.: Toward a process-based view of information technology acceptance. J. Inf. Technol. **29**(1), 73–96 (2014)
37. van der Heijden, H.: User Acceptance of Electronic Commerce: Contributions from the Bled eConference (2012)
38. Patton, M.Q.: Qualitative Evaluation and Research Methods. SAGE, Beverly Hills (1990)
39. Myers, M.D., Newman, M.: The qualitative interview in IS research: examining the craft. Inf. Organ. **17**(1), 2–26 (2007)
40. Reeves, S., Albert, M., Kuper, A., Hodges, B.D.: Why use theories in qualitative research? BMJ **337**, 631–634 (2008)
41. Carpenter, C.J.: Narcissism on Facebook: self-promotional and anti-social behavior. Personality Individ. Differ. **52**(4), 482–486 (2012)
42. Hale, L., Guan, S.: Screen time and sleep among school-aged children and adolescents: a systematic literature review. Sleep Med. Rev. **21**, 50–58 (2015)
43. Grover, V., Lyytinen, K.: New state of play in information systems research: the push to the edges. MIS Q. **39**(2), 271–296 (2015)
44. Folkman, S., Moskowitz, J.T.: Coping: pitfalls and promise. Annu. Rev. Psychol. **55**, 745–774 (2004)
45. Riedl, R.: On the biology of technostress: literature review and research agenda. ACM SIGMIS Database **44**(1), 18–55 (2012)
46. Yakymenko, I., Tsybulin, O., Sidorik, E., Henshel, D., Kyrylenko, O., Kyrylenko, S.: Oxidative mechanisms of biological activity of low-intensity radiofrequency radiation. Electromagn. Biol. Med. **35**(2), 186–202 (2016)

Like, Share and Follow: A Conceptualisation of Social Buttons on the Web

Jan Ljungberg[(✉)], Dick Stenmark, and Fahd Omair Zaffar

Department of Applied IT, University of Gothenburg, Gothenburg, Sweden
{jan.ljungberg,dick.stenmark,
fahd.omair.zaffar}@ait.gu.se

Abstract. In this theoretical and argumentative paper we analyse the implications of social buttons as used on social networking sites (SNSs). Although social buttons have been around for many years, there is still a scarcity of research on their effects despite their pivotal functions for the success of SNSs. We conceptualise these buttons as *Like buttons*, *Share buttons* and *Follow buttons* and analyse them and their associated actions through the lens of social capital theory. Our analysis shows how the clicker and the clickee are affected differently through these social buttons, and in the process, we also propose seven concepts to describe the social implications of these buttons. Having discussed these concepts, we conclude the paper by offering three contributions; (a) the distinguishing between the clicker and the clickee; (b) the subtle but yet distinct differences between buttons, and; (c) a set of ways through which social buttons become productive.

Keywords: Social buttons · Social capital theory · Social networking sites · Clicker · Clickee

1 The Social Turn of the Web

Social Media platforms and Social Networking Sites (SNSs) such as Facebook, Twitter, LinkedIn and Google Plus, have transformed the Web from 'the informational web' into 'the social web' [11, 12]. This transformation has been achieved by facilitating the creation of public or semi-public profiles, the exchange of user generated content, and the articulation of friend lists [6]. The social web can be understood as a digital environment that supports "collaborative development of content, cross-syndication and relations created between users and multiple web objects—pictures, status updates or pages" [12: 1351].

As a result of this transformation, the hits and links counters that were common in the informational web have largely been replaced by Like and Share dittos, whose numbers are generated through what might be referred to as 'buttonised' actions. These actions are made possible by the introduction of particular buttons, whose main objective is to allow interactivity between users and the content through a single mouse click. These features are referred to as 'social buttons' [11].

Social buttons allow individuals to share, endorse, or appreciate users or their content within and across various social media platforms. Unlike other SNS

© Springer International Publishing AG 2017
S. Stigberg et al. (Eds.): SCIS 2017, LNBIP 294, pp. 54–66, 2017.
DOI: 10.1007/978-3-319-64695-4_5

mechanisms such as updating a status, posting a blog entry or writing a tweet, social buttons support a set of pre-defined, single-click tasks. In addition, social buttons also provide means to visualise certain actions and turn them into tangible measurements that can be harvested, repurposed and sold. This can be illustrated by Facebook's *Like button* introduced in 2009, which has the capacity to instantly metrify and intensify users' affects, i.e. materialising emotions into numbers on the like counter [12].

Although social buttons have been around for ten or so years, there is scarcity of research that specifically study and analyse social buttons [3]. In addition, most research on clicking behaviour so far has focused on the person who clicks – the clicker – and tried to understand when and why people click on things. The clicker is obviously important since it is this actor who initiates the interaction by clicking the button. However, if the clicker would be the only actor involved it would make little sense talking about social buttons or social media. There is obviously also an actor behind the object being clicked; the person who posted the message, uploaded the photo, or shared the object. This actor – the clickee – is affected socially by being clicked, but this aspect of social button usage has thus far largely been overlooked.

In this theoretical and argumentative paper, we contribute to existing research on social media platforms as we conceptualise the social buttons and their capabilities through the lens of social capital theory. In addition, we pay attention to both involved main actors – the clicker *and* the clickee. Our main research question is: *What social implications do social buttons have for those who click them and for those who become clicked upon?*

2   Social Capital Theory

Social capital plays a central role in society through the various types of relations that bind together the members of social networks and communities [8, 18, 20]. Like financial capital, using social capital creates more of it, but what is used and created here is social relationships and the benefits that come with them [21]. Social capital was first defined by Bourdieu as: "the aggregate of the actual or potential resources which are linked to possession of a durable network of more or less institutionalised relationships of mutual acquaintance and recognition" [5: 248]. In line with this, Putnam defines social capital as social networks and their associated norms of reciprocity [18].

Thus, social capital is embedded into relationships among individuals and can be measured both at individual or group level [8]. It is embedded in the structure of social networks and location of individuals within such structures. Social capital has been considered as individual benefit, a network and its effects, as well as a process [21]. While we acknowledge Nahapiet and Ghoshal's [17] reminder that no single individual can monopolise social capital since it is always owned collectively, this paper focuses on the benefits individuals derive from interacting socially through these specific social media buttons.

For our analysis of the social buttons, we apply the three dimensions of social capital originally proposed by Nahapiet and Ghoshal [17] and later frequently used in research in a variety of fields, including IS (cf. [23]). The three dimensions are *structural social capital, cognitive social capital* and *relational social capital*, and although we shall below describe them separately and later use them separately to analyse social buttons, the boundaries between them are in reality blurred and interrelated.

Structural Capital refers to the connections between various actors in the network, be they individuals or organisations. Actors create and maintain relationships with or links between each other in their communities, and such ties are necessary for the development and utilisation of social capital [20] and provide the most fundamental form of social capital. Social networking sites offer a plenitude of opportunities for actors to create structural links by clicking and commenting on each other's posts and profiles. The more actors that are connected via these links, the higher density the network has, and the more likely it is that the actors act in compliance with the norms that are collectively established. In particular, centrally embedded actors, i.e. those with many ties to others, are expected to lead in such collective actions [23]. The frequency and the duration of the interactions between the actors reflect the level of structural capital build [24] and the number of ties can thus be used as a proxy for the structural capital an actor possesses [2]. Individual click actions are typically made visible on many social media platforms through the use of various counters.

Cognitive Capital means resources that enable shared interpretations and meanings among members of a network [17]. One important such resource is a common language since it provides a frame of reference for understanding the environment [23]. A shared language lessens the risk of misunderstandings [24] and facilitates knowledge sharing, behaviour regulation and conflict management among other things [20]. As an actor interacts with others, sharing the same practice and developing norms related to that practice, the actor learns the particular jargon, terms and words that are part of the discourse, and this develops the cognitive capital for that actor. The sharing of narratives or "war stories" are particularly useful in order to develop cognitive capital [17, 23]. On social networking sites, an actor may either be a resource by sharing of expertise and knowledge, or find resources by reading and interacting with others in the network. The more interaction, the better, since it has been argued that networks characterised by high density and frequent interactions are particularly likely to be beneficial to the development of cognitive capital (cf. [17]).

Relational capital relates more to the personal relationships amongst the individual actors, according to Nahapiet and Ghoshal [17]. In contrast to structural capital that primarily concerns the properties of the network as a whole, relational capital deals with the expectations and obligations felt by the actors in the network [20] and is developed when actors identify strongly with the collective and perceive an obligation to participate and contribute to the network [23]. Trust thus becomes an important element since it affects the level of social exchange that may occur between actors. The amount of personal information an actor discloses affects the amount of trust the actor receives from the community, but the willingness of an actor to share personal information also depends on the level of trust he or she has in the community. Reciprocity in terms of sharing information in order to receiving information is vital to the development and maintenance of relational capital [24]. Related to trust is the degree of social closure to the community [20]. A higher degree of closure enacts more observable norms and allows more efficient sanctions. When there is relational capital, actors perceive an obligation towards the collective, for example by helping other members, even if they are strangers.

3   Research Design

We departed with an understanding that *Like*, *Share* and *Follow buttons* may create social capital in different ways. Herein lies an implicit assumption that these buttons are used predominantly in a positive way. We acknowledge that you can *Like* a racist comment, *Share* false information and *Follow* someone in order to troll them, but we have chosen to reflect upon the constructive use of these buttons. We have hence also excluded buttons such as Sad, Angry, Dislike and Thumbs-down from our analysis. SNSs and the potential social capital that is more generally generated by people have been addressed by several scholars, often in a quantitative fashion (e.g. [9, 23]). We add to the understanding by providing a previously missing qualitative view on the conceptualisation of social buttons by applying social capital theory as an analytic instrument.

Gerlitz and Helmond define social buttons as features that allows individuals to "share, recommend, like or bookmark content, posts and pages across various social media platforms" [11: 1351]. Halupka [14] has a slightly narrow definition where he suggests that the main task of a social buttons is to allow interactivity between users and the content through a single mouse click. In this study, we join Halupka and focus only on such one-click buttons, thus eliminating status updates, tweets, commenting and other actions that require typing.

In order to identify various types of social buttons, we visited some of the biggest and most popular SNSs. There is no exact way to measure size or popularity of an SNS and there is an abundance of lists available on the Web ranking SNS according to various variables such as e.g. number of accounts, number of active users, or degree of activity. Although there are some differences between these lists, there is also much overlap, and we selected the eight SNS that consistently scored high on the four ranking lists that we examined. These sites include (in alphabetical order) Facebook, Google+, Instagram, LinkedIn, Pinterest, Tumblr, Twitter, and YouTube. Browsing each of these sites systematically, we identified and collected 73 different social buttons.

Next, we organised these buttons in groups based on similarities in function and purpose, thereby creating more general categories of social buttons. Many of the buttons were unique to a particular SNS but three distinct categories emerged as being common to all of these eight sites. Since these three types of buttons are the most common and cover the bulk of the activities supported by social buttons, we chose to focus solely on these three. The first category contained buttons that allowed the user to show appreciation of or express sympathies for an object. This included the 'Thumbs up' in Facebook, the 'Heart' in Twitter and the '+1' in Google+. The vocabulary differed between sites, but we chose to refer to this category as *the Like button*. The second category of buttons enabled users to redistribute content in a simple manner. In Twitter, this is known as 'retweet' whereas most other sites called it 'share' and hence we chose to refer to this as *the Share button*. Finally, our third category consisted of buttons that made it possible to monitor an account over time. YouTube call this feature 'subscribe' but we followed the majority of the sites and chose to label it *the Follow button*. The result of this process is shown in Table 1.

Table 1. List of (categorised) social buttons found on different SNSs.

SNSs	Social buttons		
	Like	Share	Follow
Facebook	Like Love Haha Wow	Share	Follow Add friend Poke
Google Plus	+1	Share	Follow
Instagram	Heart	Send	Follow
LinkedIn	Like Love Endorsement	Share	Follow Connect
Pinterest	Love Loved it Pin (save)	Share	Follow
Tumblr	Love	Share Reblog Send	Follow
Twitter	Love	Retweet	Follow
YouTube	Like	Share	Subscribe

4 Conceptualising Social Buttons

In the following section, we conceptualise the three main categories of social button identified above, and what these buttons imply for the clicker and the clickee, respectively.

4.1 The Like Button

The most obvious reason for a person to click on a *Like button* is that he or she actually likes the object in question; it could be a witty statement or an uploaded picture of a cute baby or someone having checked in at the theatre or at a restaurant. This would typically be the case when the object belongs to family members, friends or colleagues with whom the clicker has an established personal relationship. In these cases, liking would be a way of showing these individuals that the clicker has noticed and appreciates their posts. Clicking the *Like button* is thus a way to maintain an ongoing relationship. As these individuals, typically do not get thousands of likes, they would be able to see from the list of likers that the clicker has liked their posts. The clicker and the clickee would in this case be aware of one another.

However, the clicked object might also belong to an organisation issuing a call for action or promoting a new product or service. In this case, 'the organisation' is typically a nameless account who the clicker does not know personally. Even if the clicker probably do like the organisation or the object in question, clicking the *Like button* for that object would serve two other purposes; to actually support the organisation and to show the community that the clicker is a kind of person who *Likes* this sort of organisations. For example, liking the Red Cross is a way to support their cause but perhaps even more so a way to promote oneself as a responsible and caring person. As a clickee, an organisation or a celebrity would receive thousands of *Likes* and would probably not go through the list of likers, and even if they did, they would not recognise the clicker's name. The relationship, in this case, only goes one way. Nonetheless, the click would increment the clickee's *Like* counter.

Structural social capital amounts to having a large number of links within the community. Clicking frequently on *Like buttons*, the clicker would establish links to other users. When these users are known friends the links would be kind of bi-directional whereas when the clickee represents a more abstract entity (e.g. a celebrity or charity organisation), the link would tend to be uni-directional. In either case, the community would identify the clicker as liking very frequently and thereby creating many connections which would translate into structural social capital. On the receiving end, a clickee with a high *Like* counter would also be recognised as having structural social capital, regardless of who has generated the *Likes*.

Cognitive social capital means having many resources to tap into and to be such a resource to others, but it is also about having shared norms and a common understanding. Clicking the *Like button* is a way to endorse certain individuals or opinions, thereby fostering a network of people who reciprocally *Like* one another or one another's posts. In such communities, actors may develop shared habits or ideas that increase their cognitive capital but also risk making the community rather introvert. Within such networks, the clickee who receives many *Likes* earns cognitive social capital as being a resource of knowledge, but also the clicker benefits from having endorsed the clickee. Sometimes, liking can be a deliberate strategy for the clicker in order to build an identity and thus become a resource to the community.

Relational social capital is more personal in nature and does therefore primarily develop amongst actors who know and trust one another. The bi-directional nature of *Like* links between friends, and the fact that expectations, obligations and reciprocity are likely to exist, suggest that the clicker and the clickee both would increase their relational capital when the *Like button* is clicked. This situation may also apply to organisations if the clicker is personally involved, say as a paying member of a club or as an active volunteer for an organisation. The clicker would benefit from the future return *Likes* that can be expected due to the reciprocal nature of the relationship, whereas the clickee benefits from the increased *Like* counter.

4.2   The Share Button

To share experiences is a fundamental social aspect of human life which the *Share button* affords in an efficient way. One of the primary reasons to use the *Share button* is to forward content between sub-communities, when the clicker believes that the content is somehow meaningful for that other sub-community. A funny cat video or a useful piece of information posted by a friend or family member is typically *Liked* rather than *Shared*, since friends and family in the clicker's own community would most likely already have seen the original post. Sharing is thus not so much done amongst close friends, although friends and colleagues often belong to different sub-communities. Here, the clicker *Shares* an object just because of its content and do not care who the original contributor is; it may be a totally unknown actor but with a worthwhile post.

However, the opposite may also be true. The clicker may *Share* an object in order to endorse or acknowledge the authority of the object owner. The clicker *Shares* the "Save the Earth" call from Greenpeace in support of the organisation, wanting it to receive more attention from the community. Here, the identity of the clickee is important since what matters to the clicker is who the clickee *is* rather than what the message says. This sort of action also adds to the clicker's image.

The *Share button* builds structural capital primarily for the clickee, since a frequently shared object indicates some sort of popularity (either for the content *per se* or for its provider). However, it is not only the number of *Shares* that are displayed to the community; every time someone *Shares* something, a new entry is created, adding structural capital also to the clicker. Although these activities are spread out and not aggregated in a counter as for the object owner, they are still visible and implicitly adds up - especially if they are frequent.

By providing resources across communities, it is the clicker who adds to the cognitive capital of his or her sub-community despite not being the original source. The receiving community, who may not know the original source, relies on the judgement or expertise of the clicker who *Shared* the content. It is more important that the clicker is known and/or trusted, than is the clickee, and it is thus the clicker rather than the clickee who benefits from the *Share button* in terms of cognitive capital.

If the initiative to *Share* something with one's community is based on a perceived obligation to contribute to the network, relational capital is said to exist. The use of the *Share button* presupposes something worth of sharing and is thus not as casual as the *Like button*. Almost anything can be *Liked* whereas *Share* is done much more selectively. The *Share button* is therefore also not as bi-directional as the *Like button*; the clickee cannot immediately share back unless there is something to share. Whereas *Like* is directed towards the clickee, *Share* is directed towards the community, and thus builds very little relational capital for the clicker and the clickee.

4.3   The Follow Button

Unlike the *Like* and *Share buttons*, which are more instantaneous in their nature, the *Follow button* enables users to initiate more long-term relationships. Clicking the *Follow button* means that the clicker wants to receive continuous updates from the clickee, and this seems to be the case for friends and family as well as for organisations and other impersonal accounts. Being followed does typically not result in a follow back action and *Follow* is therefore in nature a uni-directional relationship, although there are exceptions as discussed below.

Following a friend or family member would strengthen the ties between the clicker and the clickee but does not add much to the greater community, since the clickee might be totally unknown. However, the clickee can also be a celebrity or an organisation in which case the act of following tells the community something about the clicker. In addition, the reasons for following a celebrity or an organisation could be either personal or professional. To illustrate, a supporter of President Trump can decide to *Follow* Trump for personal reasons, i.e. to support Trump and show this support to the community. Professionally, a journalist may choose to *Follow* the President in order to receive tweets to analyse without sympathising with or endorsing the President's views. Regardless of the reasons, though, each follower adds to the clickee's counter and thus to the clickee's popularity.

The *Follow button* creates more structural capital for the clickee, since it is obviously more important to have many followers than to follow many. The fact that a clicker frequently *Follows* others is less visible to the community and thus less likely to be recognised. In contrast, for a clickee who has millions of followers, the large number of connections is shown and thus helps build structural capital for the clickee.

Neither in terms of cognitive social capital does the clicker gain much from the *Follow button*. It is only the clicker, not the community, who receives notifications about the clickee's whereabouts, and the number of people the clicker is following is not clearly exposed. However, if many people in the community are following the same clickee(s) this may be seen as adding to the cognitive capital, since it helps communicate a common interest and may facilitate shared norms.

Following a public figure or an organisation with which the clicker has no existing relationship would not result in any relational capital gain, since relational capital is tightly linked to personal relationships. However, between family members and close friends the *Follow button* can be used to strengthen existing bonds. The clicker receives updates about the clickee's activities, thereby getting to know him or her better. The clickee, in turn, would be aware of being followed, and therefore feel obligated to somehow reciprocate or contribute to the shared agenda. Both can therefore be said to contribute relational capital from the *Follow button*.

5 The Social Implications of Like, Share and Follow

As described in the theory section, social capital is productive in the sense that it facilitates certain kind of actions [8]. In social capital theory, either organisations or persons can perform these actions, but in this paper, we stick mainly to how social capital can be resources for individuals. In the following, we will discuss how the *Like, Share* and *Follow buttons* draw on social capital, either by using it or contribute to creating it. When a button is clicked, an action is performed with implications for the clicker as well as for the clickee. To describe these actions and their implications we will introduce a set of concepts: building identity, bridging, bonding, popularising, acknowledging, creating awareness, and recognising.

5.1   Structural Social Capital

Structural social capital is constituted by the connections between individuals in a network [17, 23], in the form of strong or weak ties [13]. SNS are particularly well suited to the maintenance of weak ties, but also offers ways to manage different types of connections [22]. An SNS user would typically have a list of connections that includes both strong and weak ties, but also implicitly have access to a large number of latent ties (i.e. friends-of-friends). For an individual, the amount of structural capital is dependent on the position in the network in terms of the nature and number of connections. In an SNS, an individual can generate structural social capital relevant for a variety of contexts, ranging from strong ties among close friends, and in closed communities, over weak ties in different networks, to the huge number of latent ties constituted by the whole user base of an SNS. Similarly, an individual can draw on structural social capital as resource from these diverse contexts.

When the clicker hits the *Like*, *Share* and *Follow buttons*, it is a way to show appreciation, but also to show preferences and thus a way to build identity in relation to the wider network that constitute the base for the clicker's structural capital. We refer to this process as Profiling. In order to gain structural capital, the network need to be dense enough for the clicks to be observed by the others; otherwise no structural capital will be generated. For a person with a large amount of structural capital, this profiling will be efficient and wide spread, and further nurture the position in the network. For the clickee, it depends whether there already exists a strong or weak tie to the clicker, or no tie at all. The *Like button* favours instant, gut-fired, emotional, positive evaluations. This could be directed towards strong ties as friend and family, but also towards weak ties or total strangers. In the first case, it is the relations to family and close friends, i.e. strong ties that constitute the arena for structural capital. Being *Liked* implies an *acknowledgement*, it is something good, and it generates structural capital for the clickee.

In the case where the clickee is a weak tie or stranger, the network that constitute structural capital could be viewed as the whole SNS community, e.g. the community of all Facebook or YouTube users. Drawing on this very large base of potential clickers, gives a great potential to achieve large amounts structural capital for certain individuals. Thus, clicking the *Like* button may bring popularity to certain persons. Van Dijck [19] argues that the popularity principle is one of the core dimensions of SNS-platforms: Given the visibility featured by SNSs, and the algorithmic capability to further boost popular persons or topics, popularity generates even more popularity [12]. The very concept popular is not about being renowned or recognised, it is about fame [4]. In the context of SNS, it is all about numbers. Popularity is a quantifiable measure, which makes it manipulable since boosting popularity rankings is an important mechanism built into SNS [19]. Potential popularity for a clickee is generated by all the buttons - *Like*, *Share* and *Follow* - even if it might have strongest implications in the case of *Like*. The social buttons ability to accumulate mass attention, and making certain persons famous, draws on the large amount of structural capital that is generated. In some cases, this can translate into monetary capital, as for example in the case of YouTube star *PewDiePie*, who gains structural capital from all the YouTubers that

Like, *Share* and *Follow* him. This structural capital in turn can be converted to economic capital [1], i.e. in form of sponsor deals.

5.2 Cognitive Social Capital

Cognitive social capital refers to the common ground of a community, in the form of language, norms and culture [17, 23]. From an individual's perspective, cognitive capital is related to how well the individual masters these common resources. An individual that is at the core of a community (i.e. having plenty of structural capital) is likely to master the resources well, and therefore also have plenty of cognitive capital. What happens when the *Like* or *Share* button is clicked is that an act of bridging occurs. The concept of bridging was introduced by Putnam [18] to describe the impact of weak ties. The connections to a diverse set of people in different contexts, lead to exposure to a broad set of information and opportunities that strong ties would not provide. Hence, weak-tie networks are better suited for linking to external ideas and for dissemination of information and knowledge [21, 24].

When bridging, an item originating from outside the clicker's network is put forward to the network's attention. In the case of liking, this is an indirect effect, since the *Like* will be visible for the network, as part of the SNS's way to steer the flow of information. In the case of sharing, this a conscious act of bridging, were an item from outside is brought into the common resources of the network, adding to the cognitive capital. The more structural capital the clicker has, the more efficient the sharing will be, due to many connections. A clicker with plenty of cognitive capital would be able to assess if the item about to be *Shared* is relevant and compatible with the norms for the community, and hence, would be considered trustworthy.

A certain dilemma here is the diversity among connections. A friend list could connote a mixture of people that represents a range of different contexts: family, close friends, colleagues, communities and even total strangers. This mixture creates a great generative potential of latent ties that could generate structural capital. However, this could also cause problems in terms of items introduced that are incompatible with the common ground of the network. This 'context collapse' occurs when people from different social contexts come together in uncomfortable ways [15].

The *Follow button* creates mainly awareness for the clicker. For the clickee, all three buttons create recognition of the clickee as a provider of relevant content. This is different from popularity, because it draws on compatibility with the cognitive capital (especially in the case of sharing), rather than on structural capital. A person whose items often get *Shared* becomes recognised as a person whose contributions are worthy to pass on to others. Thus, a person with many followers receives recognition as a person worthy to *Follow*.

5.3 Relational Social Capital

Relational social capital is related to expectations and obligations as central to social capital in terms of trust, identity and system closure [8, 20]. This could concern the identification with the collective, the trust of others, and loyalty in terms of perceived obligation to participate [17]. Networks with plenty of relational capital tend to consist of dense, close and intimate connections, i.e. strong ties. Thus, it is not the accumulative number of (weak) connections in an SNS that provide relational capital (as in the case of structural capital), but the strong ties in terms of 'actual friends' [10].

When the clicker presses the *Like button* targeting a tightly coupled connection (e.g. friends and family members) an act of bonding occurs with the clickee. The concept of bonding was introduced by Putnam [18] to describe the impact of social capital for strong ties. The act of bonding relies on emotional support, access to scarce resources, and the ability to mobilise solidarity [18, 21]. In the context of an SNS, liking an object among close friends gives an impression of presence of strong ties between the actors. It is an act of the clicker expressing sympathy and emotional support for the clickee, but bonding brings relational social capital to both the clicker and the clickee.

As the bonding act is visible also to other strong ties, it may generate further emotional support for the clickee. One example of this is the way creators of memorial pages on Facebook perceive *Likes* as a direct and personal support [16]. The visibility of the bonding act among strong ties will also frame the clicker as an emotional and supportive person, generating relational social capital [7, 10]. Clicking the *Follow button* has similar implications for relational social capital as pushing the *Like* button. In contrast, the *Share button* does in essence not contribute any relational social capital; neither for the clicker, nor for the clickee.

5.4   Summarizing the Implications of Social Buttons

Social buttons and social networking sites (SNSs) have an increasing impact on our everyday practices. In this paper, we set out to identify what the social implications of such social buttons are for those who click them and for those who become clicked upon. Such findings contribute to our understanding of social networking sites and may also have implications for the design of such platforms. We conclude that social buttons facilitate relationship maintenance with low transaction costs, both in relation to strong and weak ties. We have in this paper conceptualised what social buttons are, and how users can generate and draw on social capital from different contexts ranging from strong ties, over weak ties to the whole range of latent ties constituted by an SNS-network as a whole. We have contributed to a deepened understanding of the role of social buttons in the transformation of the web. Firstly, we acknowledged the different nature of being a *clicker* and a *clickee*. Secondly, we identified three main categories of social buttons, and the subtle but yet distinct differences among them. Thirdly, we found a set of ways that the *Like*, *Share* and *Follow buttons* become productive in relation to social capital, with implications for the clicker and the clickee such as building identity, bridging, bonding, popularising, acknowledging, creating awareness, and recognising, as summarised in Table 2.

Table 2. Summary of the social implications of the *Like*, *Share* and *Follow buttons*.

Actors	Social buttons		
	Like	Share	Follow
Structural			
Clicker	Building identity	Building identity	Building identity
Clickee	Popularising Acknowledging	Popularising	Popularising Acknowledging
Cognitive			
Clicker	Bridging	Bridging	Creating awareness
Clickee	Recognising	Recognising	Recognising
Relational			
Clicker	Bonding (amongst friends)	n/a	Bonding (amongst friends)
Clickee	Bonding (amongst friends)	n/a	Bonding (amongst friends)

References

1. Adler, P.S., Kwon, S.W.: Social capital: prospects for a new concept. Acad. Manag. Rev. **27** (1), 17–40 (2002)
2. Ahuja, M.K., Galletta, D.F., Carley, K.M.: Individual centrality and performance in virtual R&D groups: an empirical study. Manag. Sci. **49**(1), 21–38 (2003)
3. Alonso, O., Kandylas, V.: A Study on Placement of Social Buttons in Web Pages (2014). arXiv preprint arXiv:1410.2828
4. Boltanski, L., Thévenot, L.: On Justification: Economic Ideas and Political Change in the Twentieth Century. Cambridge University Press, Cambridge (2006)
5. Bourdieu, P.: The social space and the genesis of groups. Theory Soc. **14**(6), 723–744 (1985)
6. Boyd, D., Ellison, N.B.: Social network sites: definition, history, and scholarship. J. Comput. Med. Commun. **13**(2), 210–230 (2007)
7. Burke, M., Kraut, R., Marlow, C.: Social capital on Facebook: differentiating uses and users. In: Proceedings of the SIGCHI Conference on Human Factors in Computing Systems, pp. 571–580. ACM Press (2011)
8. Coleman, J.S.: Social capital in the creation of human capital. Am. J. Sociol. **94**(6), S95–S120 (1988)
9. Ellison, N.B., Steinfield, C., Lampe, C.: The benefits of Facebook "friends:" social capital and college students' use of online social network sites. J. Comput. Med. Commun. **12**(4), 1143–1168 (2007)
10. Ellison, N.B., Steinfield, C., Lampe, C.: Connection strategies: social capital implications of Facebook-enabled communication practices. New Media Soc. **13**(6), 873–892 (2011)
11. Gerlitz, C., Helmond, A.: Hit, link, like and share. Organising the social and the fabric of the web. In: Proceedings of the Digital Methods Winter Conference, pp. 1–29 (2011)
12. Gerlitz, C., Helmond, A.: The like economy: social buttons and the data-intensive web. New Media Soc. **15**(8), 1348–1365 (2013)
13. Granovetter, M.S.: The strength of weak ties. Am. J. Sociol. **78**(6), 1360–1380 (1973)
14. Halupka, M.: Clicktivism: a systematic heuristic. Policy Internet **6**(2), 115–132 (2014)
15. Marwick, A., Boyd, D.: I tweet honestly, I tweet passionately: Twitter users, context collapse, and the imagined audience. New Media Soc. **13**, 114–133 (2011)

16. Marwick, A., Ellison, N.: "There isn't Wifi in heaven!" Negotiating visibility on Facebook memorial pages. J. Broadcast. Electron. Media **56**, 378–400 (2012)
17. Nahapiet, J., Ghoshal, S.: Social capital, intellectual capital, and the organizational advantage. Acad. Manag. Rev. **23**(2), 242–266 (1998)
18. Putnam, R.D.: Bowling Alone. Simon and Schuster, New York (2000)
19. Van Dijck, J.: The Culture of Connectivity: A Critical History of Social Media. Oxford University Press, Oxford (2013)
20. Widén-Wulff, G., Ginman, M.: 'Explaining knowledge sharing in organizations through the dimensions of social capital. J. Inf. Sci. **30**(5), 448–458 (2004)
21. Williams, D.: On and off the 'Net: scales for social capital in an online era. J. Comput. Med. Commun. **11**(2), 593–628 (2006)
22. Vitak, J., Ellison, N.B.: 'There's a network out there you might as well tap': exploring the benefits of and barriers to exchanging informational and support-based resources on Facebook. New Media Soc. **15**(2), 243–259 (2012)
23. Wasko, M.M., Faraj, S.: Why should I share? Examining social capital and knowledge contribution in electronic networks of practice. MIS Q. (2005)
24. Zhou, T.: Examining social capital on mobile SNS: the effect of social support. Program **50**(4), 367–379 (2016)

Principles for Enabling Deep Secondary Design

Jan Pries-Heje[(✉)] and Magnus Rotvit Perlt Hansen

Institute of People and Technology, Informatics,
Roskilde University, Roskilde, Denmark
{janph,magnuha}@ruc.dk

Abstract. User-based redesign after implementation has been studied in many contexts gone by many different names, such as appropriation of technology, malleable design and secondary design. The phenomenon of redesigning content has mainly revolved around technologies such as Facebook, Twitter, or Wikipedia or portal-based technology with configuration abilities, with very little focus on technologies where users can change both functionality, content and the level of technology complexity. We coin this type of secondary design *deep secondary design*. In this paper, we investigate how to enable deep secondary design by analyzing two cases where secondary designers fundamentally change functionality, content and technology complexity level. The first case redesigns a decision model for agile development in an insurance company; the second creates a contingency model for choosing project management tools and techniques in a hospital. Our analysis of the two cases leads to the identification of four principles of design implementation that primary designers can apply to enable secondary design and four corresponding design implementation principles that secondary designers themselves need to apply.

Keywords: Principles · Design theory · Secondary design · Case study

1 Introduction

Years ago, von Hippel [1] claimed that a type of users called *Lead Users* were using IT products in innovative ways, and next generations should be based on the practices of these users. As such, literature on user-changed reinvention has existed since the late 80s in the shape of e.g. participatory design [2] and emergent organizational workarounds [3]. Germonprez et al. [4] observed that IT systems can intentionally be constructed so that it is easy for the design "to be tinkered with and tailored for the creation of systems where people actively reflect on and engage with their local contexts, tasks, and technologies" [4, p. 665]. Today, many IT products are designed in a way that users can easily take the design into use and add their own content and use cases. The users redesign in a manner so they become designers of the original primary design; they become *secondary designers* of the product. This has been found to carry with it new functions for social interaction in non-organizational settings with the argument that secondary design of function in organizational settings can actually inhibit the tailorability and possibilities for users as secondary designers [4]. Furthermore, common design theory and principles, e.g. originating from Design Science Research, have primarily sought to provide prescriptions of how functionality of a

© Springer International Publishing AG 2017
S. Stigberg et al. (Eds.): SCIS 2017, LNBIP 294, pp. 67–82, 2017.
DOI: 10.1007/978-3-319-64695-4_6

design should be in order to attain a solution [5]. However, as secondary design has been defined as a process and not as an artifact only, we still seek to find a proper answer to how and when users take on the role of secondary designers who redesign the functionality, underlying logic and the level of technology complexity for a new target group or use situation. Prior research has focused on the users as *contributors*, while we still need knowledge of how to enable users to become *differentiators* of the content and function of the design [4]. We call this *deep secondary design* and distinguish it from tailoring content by preferences or new features of a product [6], and we seek to identify what enables these changes and how to enable it. Thus, the research question being answered in this paper is: *"How can secondary design be enabled?"*

We answer the research question by presenting two case studies of completed secondary (re-)designs, all concerned with relatively simple IT artifacts on different complexity levels (from manual paper-based scorings to spreadsheet macros and visualization). First, we review the existing literature on related research on secondary design and identify areas for potential research. Second, we explain our research method and methodology used on the two cases. Third, we analyze the cases to infer principles for enabling secondary design. Fourth, we discuss findings and contributions to the field, and finally we conclude the paper.

2   Previous Research

In this section, we show a gap in the field of research how to enable the phenomenon of secondary design. We argue that rather than providing principles of physical attributes of the design, we should focus more on the principles of process that can help primary designers successfully enable secondary design.

2.1   Intentionality and Problem-Solving

Design Science Research (DSR) aims to solve problems through designing solutions and contributing with prescriptive design theories to solve classes of problems [5, 7, 8]. Contributions to DSR require general and prescriptive theories to share and assist designers in solving specific design problems. As such, the DSR field is a strong contender for helping theorize of principles for secondary design. Design principles are a central part of design theories [9] and also a central part of "nascent design theory" (theories in progress) [10]. Gregor and Jones [11] specifically note that principles can be denoted as "form and function", explaining the physical attributes and constructs of the artifact, and "principles of implementation"; how to create the artifact. Recently, examples have been given of malleability to a design, divided into levels of customization (of certain preferences of the technology), integration (between other technologies), and extension (adding new capabilities of the artifact) [6]. The literature on DSR converges in agreement that design theories should focus on design and principles as inherent attributes of the artifact, or something the designers do to create the artifact with little regard to the outside context. Of special interest is the element of "principles of implementation", which indicates prescriptions for how to create the design artifact. We use this element to argue that in order to answer our research question, we need principles of design implementation for secondary design [11].

2.2 Tailorable Technology Design

In tailorable technology design, the designer intends the users to modify the design after use [12]. The process of tailorable technology occurs in two processes, a *default state* and an *ongoing act of tailoring* where the users gradually change the design as they see fit. Design principles for tailorable design include designers to provide flexibility of abstract tasks and using modifiable components to be reused and re-arranged without establishing best practices [12]. The concept of secondary design by Germonprez et al. [4] is conceptualized by defining a *functional* and a *content* layer. Secondary design of the functional layer is defined as users combine hardware and software solutions to solve problems. The content layer is defined as users being freely able to change the content to support various types of expressions, use ad interaction with other users. Common for the notion of tailorable technology design is that principles rely on the attributes, structures and technology choices of the artifact, similar to the notion of what DSR has noted. We see a gap between understanding how to distinguish artifact attributes and the processes that enable users to move beyond contribution of content to the artifact and into becoming a differentiator of function and content.

2.3 Relationship Between Designers and Users

In order to combine principles of the artifact and principles of design implementation of the process leading up to secondary design, it is imperative to position us in relation to other research areas revolving around design with stakeholders. Examples of research areas where designers engage with stakeholders to create new designs are for example the concept of co-realization [13], or the wide-spread participatory design [2, 14]. Co-realization is the notion of designing technologies-in-use over longitudinal periods based on an ethno-methodological approach so that the final design better corresponds to the reality it eventually is placed in. The principles of participatory design include that designers should have hands-on experience with the domain and that those who will use the design should also have decision power over what the final design should be. Common for these approaches is that users are seen as co-designers who learn design and that the designers are more facilitators than experts. Secondary design has been positioned as being different from this, as secondary designers are defined as autonomous once they begin their design journey [4] and only little or no interaction with the primary designers. We argue that this makes it crucial to focus on the very fleeting moments where a relationship can exist between primary designers and users in secondary design.

2.4   Organizational Appropriation of Technology

On an organizational level, unintended use of technology can be deemed as "appropriations of technology". These typically involve changes to processes post-implementation that are difficult to plan for or entirely unintended. Seminal research is that of Orlikowski and Hofman [3] who distinguished between emergent changes (new and difficult-to-observe changes to how technology is being used) and opportunity-based changes (changes captured and formally implemented by the organization). Davern and Wilkin [15] also created a matrix of types of changes that were either circumventions or innovations based on new, emergent practices. Richter and Riemer [16] defined malleable end-user software (MEUS) as software in the organizational space that changes how users act. With the previously defined layers of content and function, one can say that MEUS is designed specifically with the intention of content layer manipulation. Furthermore, this practice has been coined as *"as a social process of appropriation in which the software is interpreted and "placed" within the context of existing work practices"* [16, p. 196].

Common for the literature of appropriation of technology is that it focuses on what users do with and around the software, and how the organization can benefit from this. As such, it somewhat excludes the relationship between designers and users, as well as the opportunities for changes to the technology itself.

3   Method

We studied the above concept of secondary design in a multiple case study aiming at establishing a "replication logic" for contrasting results [17]. The two cases represent a diverse and different set of organizations and contingencies for secondary design. For each case, primary design and final secondary design were compared, and observations and interviews were made whenever possible. Furthermore, we observed the use of the secondary design in practice. Due to access limitations, case 1 only contained observations and artifact analysis. Table 1 provides details of the two organizations and settings represented in our cases.

For our analytical lens of the two cases, we were inspired by the concepts defined by Walls et al. [9] on how to understand IS design theories and combined it with the anatomy of a design theory by Gregor and Jones [11]. Walls et al. [9] define components of design theories to consist of meta-requirements that are answered by a meta-design. Both meta-requirements and meta-design are based on so-called *kernel theories,* referring to theories from the knowledge base of existing research. While the model was originally conceptualized as a prescriptive way to form design *theories,* we found that by abstracting an instantiated artifact into a similar version of their model, one can infer the overall components of from that specific artifact. We combine the concepts of meta-requirements and meta-design with "principles of implementation" by Gregor and Jones [11] who use that type of principle to derive at the specific product of the design. We combine these two design theory models to identify two sets of principles for secondary design: one describing the design and on describing how to use the design, the implementation guidelines (see Fig. 1). Hence, we use it to describe the

Table 1. Case details

Case	Name (pseudonym)	Secondary design characteristics	Data collection
1	Insurance Company	Fundamentally redesigning a decision model for choosing agile or plan-driven development in a specific project	Observation of knowledge transfer (of primary design) Participation in three design workshops Observing use Analysis of secondary design artifacts
2	Hospital	A contingency model for choosing project management tools and techniques based on contingencies	Observation of secondary design process over 9 months 6 status interviews held Analysis of secondary design artifact

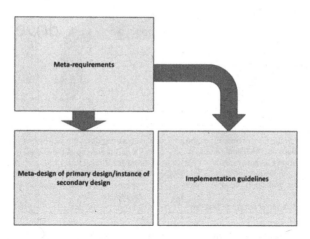

Fig. 1. Inferred components of an IS artifact design, combined from Walls et al. [9] and Gregor and Jones [11].

primary design and we use it show the secondary design giving us an overview of what secondary design involves. We specifically focus on meta-requirements, meta-design and implementation guidelines in this paper.

4   Analysis of the Two Cases

We first present the two cases' primary design and their secondary design counterparts, then we show the similarities by comparing them using the analytical lens and present the design implementation principles and their grounding.

4.1   The Insurance Company Case

The primary design in this case was a tool to assist an IT project manager in choosing between agile tools and techniques or a more classic plan-driven approach. The primary design was inspired by another designed artifact for the same purpose and used as a kernel theory [18]. The meta-requirements for the derived primary design came out of studies in many organizations considering agile but working in a classic plan-driven way. In these organizations, agile development was found to be suitable for only certain IT-projects, and there was a need for choosing between agile and plan-driven methods [19]. Another meta-requirement was that the choice of agile tools and techniques or plan-driven tools and techniques needed to be made early in an IT project again leading to the requirements that IT project managers need to be aware of core project characteristics early on. In Fig. 2 we have elicited the primary design from our analytical lens.

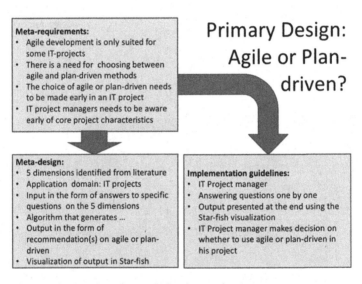

Fig. 2. The primary design in case insurance company

The primary meta-design (lower left box, Fig. 2) was based on a literature survey of what impacts the agile development: "requirements stability", "project size", "complexity", "project team", and "criticality". For example, "complexity" involved the ability to pre-define system requirements and scope as the central constraint [19]. An unclear scope makes requirements hard to define and an agile approach may be preferable because it will allow requirements to persist in near or full ambiguity (Fig. 3).

In the secondary design, the primary actor was a manager responsible for projects who needed to adapt the tool into the IT development department of the insurance company. The meta-requirements did not change as the organization still needed to be able to differentiate between choosing agile or plan-driven projects. The biggest

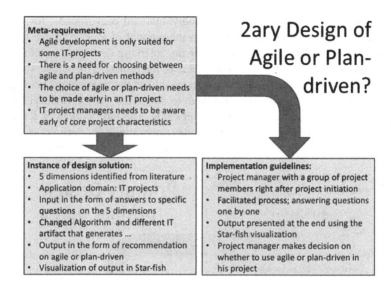

Fig. 3. Solution of the secondary design for case 1.

changes were the instantiation of the meta-design and its input in terms of the questions that were asked. For the secondary design to work and be comprehensible to the users, the questions needed to change, and included new questions on whether the project was staffed with full-time or part-time participants, and whether the result of the project was to be used by employees or customers. Furthermore, the algorithm for calculating a dimension was changed to assign different percentages to different dimensions and was built into an interactive spreadsheet.

The implementation guidelines were changed to be used in a workshop with the project manager and a chosen number of project participants. Furthermore, the workshop was facilitated using a projector so everyone could see and by one person from the "method and project office" who would fill out the interactive spreadsheet.

4.2 The Hospital Case

In Case 2, the primary design was called "the project radar" and was originally used as a tool to identify problematic issues of an existing project in the organization of Danske Bank [20]. The meta-requirements included the assumption that project management is a tool-heavy discipline and this can make it difficult for a project manager to use the right tool for the right problem in a project with varying variables such as size, aim, and number of stakeholders.

The artifact was an open technology incorporated into an interactive spreadsheet. A project manager would answer questions related to 8 dimensions including "task", "knowledge about", "individual and background", "environment", "team", "calendar time", "stakeholders", "quality/criticality" (identified from literature on project management). An algorithm for benchmarking would then generate recommendations for the project as a whole. The dimension of "individual and background", for example, could be identified by a high score based on the amount of time available to project participants. Solutions included proposals for documenting decisions, or aim at uninterrupted, successive work days for all members in the project. The output was a radar chart visualization where the project manager could see the problematic areas.

The implementation guidelines included to have the project manager answer questions and get an output visualization afterwards. The tool worked as a reflection tool providing the project manager with relevant suggestions and techniques (Fig. 4).

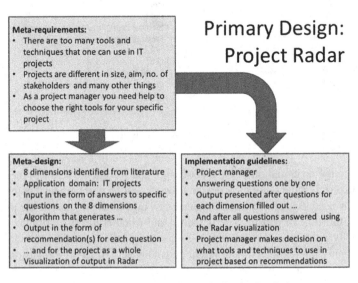

Fig. 4. Figure of the "project radar" primary design.

Two project managers that followed an Executive Master in Project Management were inspired by the primary design and felt that it was applicable in their own practical domain; a health care setting at a hospital. Both project managers had more than 20 years of working experience. The primary issue with how the hospital handled projects was that project teams were put together from random people from different departments. The requirements were more often than not based on their healthcare professional experience and competence and not on project management competences. As a result, they compared meta-requirements from the primary design with requirements from their own domain and found that only little knowledge existed on what project management tools were and how to select appropriately among them.

They tested out the primary design, the project radar, on 4 different projects. The two project managers would facilitate the test of the primary design by engaging in dialogue with the team members to help understand any project management specific jargon and also reshape the jargon used for the secondary design. The meta-design of the primary design was changed so first of all, a complex IT artifact was too technical for the target audience and instead, the project managers opted for evaluating by using pen and paper and operate an interactive spreadsheet for inputting values (without the project team members knowing). They removed the dimensions of "individual and background" and "environment", and replaced them with "implementation" and "communication", as well as rephrasing new questions for these dimensions. Rather than showing the proposals for improvement, they would manually write up a report of their results with proposals for how to solve the identified problems. The reason was that a certain level of formality was needed when the team members would spend time away from their daily work in order to help with the tests of the secondary design. Furthermore, a formal report would increase the likelihood of receiving management support for their project. The purpose of the tool was changed to inspire the project group rather than letting their project manager decide on a course of action, since many of the projects did not have a dedicated project manager (Fig. 5).

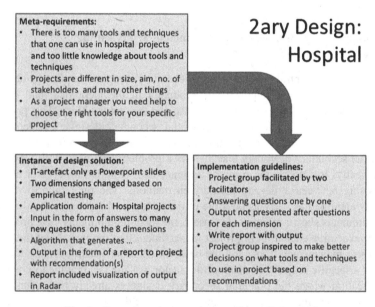

Fig. 5. Secondary design solution of case 2, hospital

5   Results – The Principles

From the two cases, we elicit two sets of four design implementation principles. The principles are dyadic in the sense that one set focuses on how primary designers can design the implementation of a primary design artifact to enable deep secondary design (changing both content and function). The other set is focused on how secondary designers should react so they can perform secondary design (shown in Table 2).

Table 2. Table of principles

Principle #	Design implementation principles for primary designer	Design implementation principles for secondary designer
1	Presenting meta-requirements	Understand meta-requirements and compare to own situation
2	Specifying relevance and advantage	Identify advantage and relevance to own domain
3	Unlocking meta-design and implementation guidelines	Understand all details of meta-design and guidelines and decide how supplementary needs can be met
4	Creating opportunities for trialability	Try out primary design and explicitly identify learning opportunities

5.1 Primary Design Implementation Principle 1: Presenting Meta-Requirements

This principle is the central enabler of deep secondary design. The primary designer is meant to present the meta-requirements grounded in the theoretical and empirical background, as well as show the domain-in-use and the compatibility. This principle is basically the design rationale that lets potential secondary designers understand the fundamentals for the design in the first place. It is up to the primary designer to convince the secondary designers that there is a problem or a need both theoretically and empirically. In Case 1, the primary designer had identified a need for assistance with choosing between agile and plan-driven methods. The right time to make this choice was identified as early as possible in the based on the dimensions identified in meta-requirements shown in Fig. 1. In Case 2, the meta-requirements were presented as part of the executive education in project management that problematized the standard use of project management tools and the need for deciding which of many tools were needed for a specific project. One supporting factor was the fact that the tool was a part of the education where the potential secondary designers already had a fundamental technical understanding of the project management field. The meta-requirements were thus presented as a review of existing knowledge in the project management field. The design rationale was presented through traditional class teaching, with the primary designers as facilitators responsible for creating an understanding of the artifact. Furthermore, the compatibility of the primary design was also grounded in empirical work, both grounded in prior sessions of the project management education as well as in peer-reviewed papers where the tool had been applied.

5.2 Secondary Design Implementation Principle 1: Understand Meta-Requirements and Compare to Own Situation

The logical extension for design implementation principle 1 for secondary designers is to make an effort into understanding the meta-requirements. This means thoroughly researching the theoretical and empirical backgrounds for the design rationale. While it is not given that secondary designers will always strive for this, it seems that the motivation for understanding the meta-requirements is correlated to how well the primary designers have fulfilled principle 1. In Case 1, the secondary designers decided to adapt a number of the questions of the five dimensions based on their own situation in the insurance company. Another example was to change the whole implementation process to be facilitated in a group instead of individual use by a project manager. This again was based on what had worked before in the insurance company and on who initiated the secondary design. In Case 2, the fact that standardized project management tools had been presented and used already was a central factor for how thorough the secondary designers understood the primary design: *"It could be really interesting if we had the possibility to change some of those questions [...] because we do not have projects with 300–400 employees, we have a completely different context."* – Secondary designer, Hospital case 2.

5.3 Primary Design Implementation Principle 2: Specifying Relevance and Advantage

The principle of specifying relevance and advantage includes that (a) the primary design must show its relevance by having a likeliness to the potential secondary designers' background, either through a common purpose within the same field of applicability or through linking a shared knowledge base (in this case: project management), and (b) the primary design must produce a solution that also solves a problem for the secondary designers. The principle was followed in Case 1 by being directly related to the secondary designers' current background; project management methodologies. The relevance aspect was solved by providing a simple decision: when to use agile or when to use plan-driven methodologies. As such the value in terms of relevance was simple in helping the users answer a problematic question. The principle was used in Case 2 through simplifying the variables of projects into simple answers that most project members could answer on a scale. The aspect of relevance was shown by having a list of relevant solutions of actions tailored to the specific projects that users needed: *"We need to be able to find a score and recommend x and y, because that is what helped us; how did it look in practice?"* – Secondary designer, Hospital case 2.

5.4 Secondary Design Implementation Principle 2: Identify Advantage and Relevance to Own Domain

While it is necessary for the primary designers to show relevance and advantages, it is impossible to specify completely due to the generic nature of primary design. The secondary principle following this is the principle of identifying relevance and advantages for the secondary designers' own domain. The secondary designers should compare the relevance and advantages to find areas where they could benefit from tweaking. In Case 1, the primary design had been presented to the insurance company with examples from the company – Danske Bank – where it was originally developed.

The insurance company recognized the need for a similar tool and some similarities between banking and insurance – administrative IT projects – that made it relevant to adapt to the insurance domain. In Case 2, an immediate need was identified and it was established that projects in the hospital were initiated based on healthcare related competences and not on the project competences. As a result, the primary design was seen as a better alternative to expensive, standardized project management education.

5.5   Primary Design Implementation Principle 3: Unlocking Meta-Design and Implementation Guidelines

The principle of unlocking meta-design and method indicates an open approach to technology. The principle covers four layers: (1) the content layer, (2) the algorithmic layer, (3) the complexity layer, and (4) the procedural layer. Unlocking the content layer makes it possible to change what is shown and what the purpose of the design is. Unlocking the algorithmic layer involves re-arranging the components and/or scoring of values between them. Unlocking the complexity layer means that the level of technology can be scaled all the way from paper-based, manual completion to high-tech, full-fledged IT application. Unlocking the procedural layer involves being able to change the use setting and the actors involved in this, e.g. from individual use to collective use, or to assessing a context area individually or collectively. In Case 1, we saw how the meta-design was flexible enough to include changes in questions and presentation, as well as how the practice of assessment was flexible enough to be used either as facilitative dialogue or personal reflection. In Case 2, the initial primary design was based on 8 dimensions but could easily be changed to more or fewer, with also the questions and benchmarking being open to change. Likewise, the different levels of complexity of the technology were already present in that several versions were created to show the various applications. One version was based on slideshows and manual, paper-based filling out questions, while a more embedded and structured version was also created to automatically visualize the results in a spreadsheet.

5.6   Secondary Design Implementation Principle 3: Understand All Details of Meta-Design and Guidelines and Decide How Supplementary Needs Can Be Met

For a secondary designer to take advantage of primary design implementation principle 3, it is necessary for the secondary designer to understand the underlying technology itself and decide how supplementary needs can be met in the mentioned layers. This can be done from experience or by being inspired by various versions of the primary design. In Case 1, supplementary needs were primarily met through changes in the specific questions, how the underlying algorithm was changed to take into account different benchmarking and the level of complexity of the IT artifact. Furthermore, they realized a need for a facilitated workshop process as opposed to an individual stand-alone process. In Case 2, two new dimensions replaced older ones to accommodate the specific domain, and new questions were included to reflect this. The secondary design tool was assessed with facilitators and rather than having immediate results with solutions, the designers decided to formalize a written report with specific suggestions.

5.7   Primary Design Implementation Principle 4: Creating Opportunities of Trialability

This principle means that the primary designer should actively design so that secondary designers get experience with the primary design from beginning to end. As artifact complexity increases, the designated workflow can also be difficult to overview without having tried it out. This entails that the primary design should be kept simple as high complexity can make it difficult for secondary users to get the required experience to comfortably change it. In Case 1, this was done by testing the artifact (spreadsheet) with the (updated and changed) questions and benchmarking three carefully selected projects. In these projects, the project manager had his assumptions challenged because the project management methodology has more or less been chosen in advance. In Case 2, the primary design was tested out in a class setting with a project that the students were already familiar with: *"My great "Heureka" moment was after using [the tool] [...] and we were visually able to see where our challenges were and confirm our suspicions we had when we were part of the project." – Secondary designer B, Hospital case 2.*

Since the primary design did not require real life subjects or real data, it could easily be tried out. Furthermore, the testing of the design also created opportunities for the secondary designers to identify relevance and advantages.

5.8   Secondary Design Implementation Principle 4: Try Out Primary Design and Explicitly Identify Learning Opportunities

The principle that follows here is that of actively trying out the primary design and explicitly identifying learning opportunities. The principle requires that the secondary designers gain hands-on experience with how the design is structured and used to properly estimate what needs to change. This principle further supports changing the design to accommodate a new domain-of-use.

In Case 1, the secondary designers learned that their three projects had a high interdependence and that if one project changed to agile, the other projects would also have to change to the same methodology. As a result, the level of interdependencies to other projects was built into the artifact as an addition to the secondary design during the final two workshops.

In Case 2, the two secondary designers saw that testing the primary design helped them gain the confidence they needed to assess required changes: *"If we are going to test it out for real and redesign it, adapt it to our world, we need to do [prototyping]. We cannot just change it. Now we have knowledge and experience which make it possible for us to start somewhere, and much more qualified." – Secondary designer, Hospital case 2.*

6 Discussion

We have now provided four dyadic "design implementation principles" that need to be applied in unison to enable *deep* secondary design. We contribute with the concept of deep secondary design by defining it as a redesign of a primary design that goes beyond original intentions in both domain-of-use, as well as include both changes to the function and content layer. We further contribute with findings of secondary design within an *organizational* domain, which hitherto has been described as being inhibitive for the secondary design process [4]. On the contrary, we found that by following the principles, secondary design in organizations certainly is viable.

However, the principles strongly relate to taking advantage of when to create a relationship between primary and secondary designers. Prior research on relationship between designers and users, (e.g. in co-realisation [13] or participatory design [14]) have noted the requirements of a flat and symmetrical relationship. While the primary designers were both consultants (in Case 1) and educators (in Case 2), the principles still created a short, facilitative role of the primary designers that enabled the secondary design. Especially the two principles of presenting the meta-requirements and testing out the primary design seemed to be important factors. One of the reasons for this was that rather than focusing on redesigning the product, the primary designers focused on assisting with the process of individual adoption and redesign, with no expectations of benefit realization of the product. The lack of expectations or straightforward cost-benefit measurement is also an important point made by Richter and Riemer [16] when supporting malleable end-user software. Our findings supported this and we also call for more research on applying secondary design principles as a diffusion process in organizational settings.

Our findings also extend the understanding of what "principles" are within DSR. Much literature within DSR has focused on principles of artifact design features, while the importance of having various editions of the artifact on different complexity levels (e.g. from paper to structured and embedded web-apps) have not been an important of the final design. This is seen in Gill et al. [6] who suggests that artifact designs make use of "openness" to enable malleability or in Germonprez et al. [12] who underscore the importance of componentization of the design. While this is important, it overlooks the importance of the use domain where secondary designers and their users might not have high technical design competences.

It is also possible that our findings only extend to the class of information system of our cases, a type of facilitative decision support system. As a result, we also call for more research on deep secondary design with other types of technologies to.

7 Conclusion

We have now defined deep secondary design as a phenomenon where secondary designers change function and content, as well as the complexity level of the tech-nology. We have described and analyzed two cases - all from the project management domain - where secondary designers fundamentally changed both meta-design and implementation guidelines as the result of how the primary designers implemented the primary designs. Our analysis of the two cases led to the identification of four principles of design implementation that primary designers can apply to enable secondary design and four corresponding principles that secondary designers themselves can apply. We contribute with these two-by-four principles that form a "nascent" theory on deep secondary design. Our practical contribution can help primary designers reflect on what they do with their design rather than how they designed its features. For users with the potential to become secondary designers, we practically propose actions that they need to perform to better grasp how to become better designers.

References

1. von Hippel, E.: Lead users: a source of novel product concepts. Manag. Sci. **32**, 791–805 (1986)
2. Kensing, F., Blomberg, J.: Participatory design: issues and concerns. Comput. Support. Coop. Work **7**, 167–185 (1998)
3. Orlikowski, W.J., Hofman, D.J.: An improvisational model for change management: the case of groupware technologies. In: Malone, T.W., Laubacher, R., Scott Morton, M.S. (eds.) Inventing the Organizations of the 21st Century, pp. 265–282. Sloan School Management, Cambridge (1997)
4. Germonprez, M., Hovorka, D., Gal, U.: Secondary design: a case of behavioral design. J. Assoc. Inf. Syst. **12**, 662–683 (2011)
5. Hevner, A.R., March, S.T., Park, J., Ram, S.: Design science in information systems research. MIS Q. **28**, 75–105 (2004)
6. Gill, T.G., Hevner, A.R.: A fitness-utility model for design science research. ACM Trans. Manag. Inf. Syst. (TMIS) **4**(2), 5 (2013)
7. Gregor, S.: The nature of theory in information systems of theory in information systems. MIS Q. **30**, 611–642 (2006)
8. Gregor, S., Hevner, A.R.: Positioning and presenting design science research for maximum impact. MIS Q. **37**, 337–355 (2013)
9. Walls, J.G., Widmeyer, G.R., El Sawy, O.A.: Building an information system design theory for vigilant EIS. Inf. Syst. Res. **3**, 36–59 (1992)
10. Heinrich, P., Schwabe, G.: Communicating nascent design theories on innovative information systems through multi-grounded design principles. In: Tremblay, M.C., VanderMeer, D., Rothenberger, M., Gupta, A., Yoon, V. (eds.) DESRIST 2014. LNCS, vol. 8463, pp. 148–163. Springer, Cham (2014). doi:10.1007/978-3-319-06701-8_10
11. Gregor, S., Jones, D.: The anatomy of a design theory. J. Assoc. Inf. Syst. **8**, 312–335 (2007)
12. Germonprez, M., Hovorka, D., Collopy, F.: A theory of tailorable technology design. J. Assoc. Inf. Syst. **8**, 351–367 (2007)
13. Hartswood, M., Procter, R., Slack, R., Voß, A., Büscher, M., Rouchy, P.: Co-realisation and participatory design. Scand. J. Inf. Syst. **14**, 9–30 (2002)
14. Simonsen, J., Robertson, T.: Routledge International Handbook of Participatory Design. Routledge, London (2013)
15. Davern, B.Y.M.J., Wilkin, C.L.: Evolving innovations through design and use. Commun. ACM **51**, 133–137 (2008)
16. Richter, A., Riemer, K.: Malleable end-user software. Bus. Inf. Syst. Eng. **5**, 195–197 (2013)
17. Yin, R.K.: Case Study Research: Design and Methods. Sage Publications, Thousand Oaks (2009)

18. Boehm, B.W., Turner, R.: Balancing Agility and Discipline: A Guide for the Perplexed. Addison-Wesley, Boston (2004)
19. Baskerville, R., Pries-Heje, J., Madsen, S.: Post-agility: what follows a decade of agility? Inf. Softw. Technol. **53**, 543–555 (2011)
20. Avison, D., Pries-Heje, J.: Flexible information systems development: designing an appropriate methodology for different situations. In: Proceedings of the International Conference on Enterprise Information Systems 2007, pp. 212–224 (2008)

Service Interaction Flow Analysis Technique for Service Personalization

Olli Korhonen[1]($\boxtimes$), Anna-Liisa Syrjänen[1], Marianne Kinnula[1],
Minna Isomursu[2], and Kari Kuutti[1]

[1] University of Oulu, Oulu, Finland
{olli.korhonen,anna-liisa.syrjanen,marianne.kinnula,
kari.kuutti}@oulu.fi
[2] IT University of Copenhagen, Copenhagen, Denmark
miis@itu.dk

Abstract. Service interaction flows are difficult to capture, analyze, outline, and represent for research and design purposes. We examine how variation of personalized service flows in technology-mediated service interaction can be modeled and analyzed to provide information on how service personalization could support interaction. We have analyzed service interaction cases in a context of technology-mediated car rental service. With the analysis technique we propose, inspired by Interaction Analysis method, we were able to capture and model the situational service interaction. Our contribution regarding technology-mediated service interaction design is twofold: First, with the increased understanding on the role of personalization in managing variation in technology-mediated service interaction, our study contributes to designing service management information systems and human-computer interfaces that support personalized service interaction flows. Second, we provide a new analysis technique for situated interaction analysis, particularly when the aim is to understand personalization in service interaction flows.

Keywords: Service personalization · Service interaction · Service management information system · Interaction flow · Interaction analysis

1 Introduction

Multilayered information and communication technology (ICT) affords delivering of services by sophisticated interfaces that are able to support complex service interaction. Complex service interaction is difficult to capture, analyze, outline, and represent for information systems research and design purposes. During the last decades the analytical interest has focused on perceived quality [47] and how it can be measured and attached to service providers and customers who, with their differing needs and goals, share service interaction and are seen as co-creating its value [8, 9, 11, 37]. Existing research on service management emphasizes that we should pay critical attention to the service quality formed across all moments of contact with organizations providing service [8, 13, 36]. We argue that there is still lack of understanding of how automated or technology supported service management could be implemented on the level of a

S. Stigberg et al. (Eds.): SCIS 2017, LNBIP 294, pp. 83–97, 2017.
DOI: 10.1007/978-3-319-64695-4_7

unique service process for achieving a personalized service flow which adapts to the needs of the actors taking part in the service delivery process.

Over decades, the idea of providing standardized services while treating each customer as a unique person has remained in the service marketing literature [44]. Service personalization means adaptation of service clerks' interpersonal behavior and interaction in a way it suits a particular customer's needs [15]. Today that interaction is often enhanced with technology, and the interaction is mediated through interfaces and devices [14]. In the human-computer interaction (HCI) and information systems (IS) fields, personalization interests join in the question of how to provide services online, in different contexts, and serving the needs of different kinds of users; the key interest to researchers being the delivery component, the interface [3] by which different interaction and service problems manifest themselves. [3] argues that there are still shortcomings around solid theoretical perspectives on which parts of service delivery should be computer-driven and which parts should involve humans, and also lack of research on evaluating different ways of how human service interaction could be delivered and which media would be appropriate in mediating it in different interaction situations. Accordingly, in information systems research and design there is an ongoing change from focusing solely on professional and managerial users to more heterogeneous audiences [3] including children [18], elderly, and persons with memory problems [26], together with many other user groups with special ICT needs.

Interaction and collaboration studies have shown that when compared to direct interaction between people *in situ*, use of technology in the interaction can make some issues even more visible [20, 27, 36]. One such instance is situatedness of action, seen as manifesting variation and thus necessitating understanding of different viewpoints of actors, in a situation where people interact without having a good model of each other's action, skills, resources, or location or other influential factors of that particular situation [40, 43]. While related studies have focused on how people refer to other people, objects of interest, and environment, and share information in documents or tangible things [12, 20], studies related to personalization of service interaction itself are scarce.

In this study, our aim is to understand and analyze variation of service interaction flow for personalization of service interaction, and to propose and demonstrate a new technique for doing that. Therefore, we ask as our research question: *How can we recognize and capture variation of personalized service flows in technology-mediated service interaction?* To answer this, we analyzed interaction in agreement-based car rental service where the service provider utilizes video-mediated communication (VMC) [12] in their service kiosk interfaces. Interaction Analysis method [19] was applied to investigate the human activities, and to identify and illustrate the variation in service interaction. The kiosks are highly interactive computer-based information systems that are located in public areas [17]. In our service case, these kiosks enable technology-mediated service encounters between service clerk and customer [14] and service provider's service management information system (SMIS) supports personalization of service interaction to meet the needs of both the service provider and each individual customer. Next, we discuss related research on personalization in service context, how it has been considered in service systems design, and how variation of service flows has been approached for service interaction analysis. After that, we describe our methodology, summarize and discuss with our results. We conclude by discussing the implications of our results to IS and HCI, limitations, and paths for future work.

2 Related Research

2.1 Personalization of Services

Service personalization is defined as *any behavior occurring in a service interaction intended to individuate the customer* [44]. In service literature, personalization is defined as adaptation of service clerk's interpersonal behavior and interaction in a way it suits a particular customer's preferences [10, 15]. In technology mediated services, this behavior and interaction is supported by an information system. Service personalization is often intertwined with another concept used to tune a service to individual customer preferences: service customization that focuses on configuration of the service content [10]. Both personalization and customization can be done in the interaction between service clerk and customer [15, 48].

Personalization has been conceptualized as option personalization, programmed personalization, and customized personalization. The first one focuses on the service outcome and latter two on service process [44]. *Option personalization* [44] means customization of service outcome, where customer configures the service, for example, by choosing a set of components from a pre-set menu to create a unique service [10, 48]. This can vary from use of fully customized unique service packages to services that include both customized and standardized components [21]. Service component here means a resource used in service delivery – be it human resource, ICT resource, or information. Use of SMIS allows real-time construction and support of a service flow to provide unique service packages with best available resources, as is done for digital services with web service composition [28].

Programmed personalization and *customized personalization* focus on personalizing the interactive process of the service and the way service is delivered for individual customer [10, 44]. Example of programmed personalization is the use of personalized small talk, where customer is called by name during the interaction. Customized personalization on the other hand focuses on interpersonal behavior adaptation, such as using similar dialects or vocabulary to personalize the service process [44].

In service systems design, personalization can be integrated in different *virtual systems* (e.g. online systems/websites), *physical systems* (e.g. human intervention, delivery, logistics) and *integration systems*, which should enable the seamless function of other systems [39]. As most of the systems utilize human-computer interaction, quality of services and potential for personalized service interaction is in effect dependent on it. In interactive services, service quality has been addressed to service providers' customer orientation, customers' service expectations for and experiences in services, and to the interaction by which quality service involves people, technologies, and organization and attaches economical costs and practical benefits to both sides [8].

Therefore, the sensitive point in service systems personalization is the customer – service provider relationship, depending on such factors as how well the needs of individuals and the suitable interaction styles for each of them are understood in service delivery.

In this paper, we propose that personalization is a technique for managing variation of service interaction flows when there is a need to adapt service interaction to the needs of actors participating in service delivery, such as the customer, front-stage clerk, and the organizations delivering the service. Advanced IS can support personalization better if the service interaction alternatives and logic are analyzed and understood by the designers.

2.2   Analyzing Service Interaction Flow

Traditionally, different aspects of variation in service interaction flows have been analysed in studies, which have aimed to challenge existing ways of thinking, analysing, and designing interactive technological systems [24, 27, 40, 43]. Regarding service-oriented thinking, [47] argue that standardization of the output of a service is much more difficult compared to standardization of goods. Contemporary services are more like "activities" or "processes", and rather than goods customers buy "offerings". In this line of thought, variation embodies harmony with "the individualized, dynamic demand of the customer" [47]. The authors argue that companies should construct also their goods to be more *service-like* by customizing the output according to the varying standards of consumers, and they show that companies that have realized this have gained competitive advantage [47].

Varying demands for use are well recognized in design activities where the need for supporting personalized service flows is seen as an existing and enduring challenge in everyday decision-making. Along with changing activities and conditions [5, 7, 31], variation usually entails continuous work with their reorganization, as well as distribution of collective capabilities [33]. Accordingly, analysis and design involve the capacity of capturing, analysing, outlining, and representing the essential situated aspects [42]. Design methods are situated by nature and can be supportive regarding different instances of situatedness, including situated knowledge, action and learning, and situating context [38].

According to [41] the basic idea in situated analysis is to challenge actors' assumptions on how activities are carried out by making visible something that is not apparent but essentially influences their working. Many invisible forms of work were recognized with a conclusion of "the better the work is done, the less visible it is to those who benefit from it" [41]. Hence, representations such as service interaction visualizations by texts, snapshots, state transition patterns, graphs of time-line, statistical mode, and state transition probability map [29], and results from ethnographic analysis and interaction analysis on using VMC in multidisciplinary medical team meetings [20] emphasise both the importance and the challenges of visualizing variation in multi-actor interaction.

[32] argue that service design is a growing practice and there is a continuous need for new tools, for making sense of the intangible and tangible qualities of services.

Patrício et al. [35] in turn maintain that service design is an emerging field where methods are not yet well established. Service process flows can be modelled with several methods and approaches. Basically all modelling techniques applicable to processes in general can be used to model service process flows in particular, such as IDEF diagrams or Petrinets [6], structured workflow modeling [22], and business process modeling in general [1]. More recently, service design methods addressing not only the service provider viewpoint, but also the viewpoint of customer and network of actors needed in the service process have emerged [46]. For example, customer journey method [50] can be used to describe the touchpoints between a company and its customers when experiencing a service. Service blueprinting [4] takes a customer perspective for visualizing the service processes. The technique can be also applied in a service situation with multiple actors with different motivations [49] and for designing adaptive services [25]. However, as service blueprinting visualizes all actions that are needed for a service to function [49] the support for capturing and modeling variation with that technology requires multiple blueprints to cover all the potential variations in the service interaction. Therefore, we propose an analysis technique to capture and model variation in service interaction.

3   Methodology

3.1   Context

Our study was conducted in 2012 with a service provider that offers agreement-based car rental services and had recently extended to a new kiosk-based service, configured as a special HCI setup for online face-to-face (F2F) service. The kiosk uses a secure data transmission connection over the internet between the provider's service management system and service clerks' and customers' locations. Interaction between a service clerk and a kiosk customer is mediated by VMC-based interfaces together with remote-controlled kiosk system's devices and peripherals especially designed for this type of service. These peripherals include functions for secure authentication, service agreement, payment, and releasing of car keys. The delivery model resembles video banking [34] and supports variation in communication by VMC.

3.2   Data

Our data consists of 16 video-recorded service processes of individuals (id1–id16; ages 22–63; seven women, nine men; Finnish and English languages, non-native) who used the service kiosk in a public space while the front-stage clerk worked over the internet following the service provider's standard rental procedure. All participants were new car renters for the provider and the analyzed interaction processes went through the standard phases of car renting process included in the service description. Eight phases for a typical car rental service process have been identified in [45]. However, as some of those phases consist of multiple acts (e.g. phase 6 includes personal details, signing the rental agreement, and paying), we decided to distinct the acts into separate phases of their own, resulting in 11 interaction phases in overall. The phases are: starting,

Table 1. Interaction phases and interface components.

Interaction phase	Interface components used
Start (greetings)	VMC by cameras
Needs	Microphones
Requirements	Video displays
Charge	
Add-ons	
Identity	VMC by cameras
Authentication	Document camera
Payment	VMC by cameras
	Credit card reader
Agreement	VMC by cameras
	Scanner
	Printer
Delivery	VMC by cameras
	Car key locker
Ending (parting)	VMC by cameras

identifying needs of the customer, discussing requirements, charging, discussing possible add-ons, identification of the customer, authentication, payment, making of a rental agreement, delivery of car keys, and ending the service process (Table 1).

The rental process lasted for 8–12 min and users were interviewed before (general background information) and after the rental process (evaluation of the experience related to service process). None of the participants had used this type of kiosk service interface before but all of them had used face-to-face services and self-services. Nine of them were first-time car renters and seven had prior experience of car rental process. We used parallel columnar transcript method [19] for transcribing verbal and nonverbal behavior of the use situations, making it possible to capture kiosk users' interaction at the kiosk interface, and the service clerk's interaction via VMC devices.

3.3   Analysis Procedure

Our analysis was inspired by work on situated interaction between the participants of a particular social situation [19]. However, instead of identifying regularities in participants' use of resources [19] in service delivery, our main goal in this paper is to identify and illustrate variation in service interaction. Therefore, our unit of analysis is a single **phrase** or an **act**. For instance:

- Service clerk (Sc) says: *"Welcome to Xxxxx car rental. How may I help you?"* <= this is a **phrase**.
- When a service clerk asks from the customer (C) personal details: *'participant showed personal details by setting her business card on a document camera area'* <= this is an **act**.

Based on the order of the phrases/acts and discussed issues, the phrases were compared with the service provider's standard procedure and divided into related phases and shown as flow points (•) in figures below. For instance (excerpt 1):

1. Sc: *"Welcome to Xxxxx car rental. How may I help you?"* <= this is related to the **start phase** (•).

When needed, phrases were further combined so that related answers/complementary questions were counted as a one-content unit. For instance (excerpt 2, excerpt 3):

2. C: *"I want... I want to rent a car."* Sc: *"OK."* <= this is **one unit**, related to the **needs phase** (•).
3. C: *"I have planned to visit ... to go to (Place), it is a family visit."* Sc: *"OK, to go to (Place), and would you need a car immediately today?"* C: *"No, I just need it on the weekend, next weekend."* Sc: *"OK... the forthcoming weekend, so that would be ...you need it on Friday?"* C: *"No, on Saturday...."* <= this is **one unit**, related to the **requirements phase** (•).

Correspondingly, multi-content phrases were divided into separate units based on the phases. For instance (excerpt 4):

4. Sc: *"It will be five euros additional │ but we will charge your credit card?"* <= here we have **two units**, the former is related to the **charge phase** (•), and the latter to the **payment phase** (•).

When the answer could not be interpreted to refer to a foresaid content item (e.g. credit card in this case), it was integrated with the latter one. For instance (excerpt 5):

5. Sc: *"It will be five euros additional │ but we will charge your credit card?"* C answering: *"Oh, very fine. Thank you so much!"* <= The customer's answer is related to the **payment phase** (•).

After this outlining, individual rental processes were represented as graphs using the flow points (•), which show how interaction flows between different service phases (e.g., **requirements** were discussed in several occasions), the lines connecting the flow points showing advancement in time. Finally, the processes were compared by layering flow graphs of four corresponding customer service situations on top of each other (four is the maximum number of cases for the figures still to be readable in this paper). See Figs. 3 and 4 as examples.

We consider this degree of precision in representation as appropriate in illustrating relevant aspects of variation in a manner we see useful for systems study and design in practice.

4 Analysis Results

Using the standard car rental service process as a frame for describing individual service interactions, we were able to identify and capture variation caused by personalization in service interaction. Service interaction was personalized by actors participating in service delivery, such as verbal variation in flow of service interaction as well as sequential variation, for instance, the temporal re-orderings within service phases.

In our analysis, we first represent an example by phrase units, which is one of the common ways of visualizing variation in spoken interaction [19]. Second, by using the flow points defined earlier for the graphs, we exemplify variation in temporal interaction changes by following the content shifts in the service process.

4.1   Verbal Variation in the Flow of Service Interaction

Verbal variation in service interaction was recognised as different vocabulary was used in the service process. That is exemplified in the excerpt 3 where the requirements for the starting time of rental were specified by using five different time measurements: *"on the weekend"*, *"next weekend"*, *"forthcoming weekend"*, *"Friday"*, and *"Saturday"*. However, neither the customer nor the service clerk serving her used the exact date recorded into the provider's SMIS or the terms used in the rental agreement. We consider this as epitomizing customer-oriented communication [8] regarding the interaction needs and modes of individual customers; in other words, tuning the communication and interaction style to the specific needs of the customer [44].

The examples manifest different kinds of variation, such as different vocabulary and conventions, used in personalized interaction, showing conceptual variation [40] in interaction modes, and situational variation in action [43]. Despite the variation, the standard service process was loosely followed.

4.2   Sequential Variation in Flow of Service Interaction

Sequential variation in individual service process realizations is demonstrated in service interaction flows (Figs. 1 and 2) of two participants (id16 and id8).

The linear standard service interaction flow (the blue dotted line in Figs. 1 and 2) is most closely followed during the few first steps and at the end of the interaction. After the first steps, the anomaly increases by discussion deviations going to *delivery* issues, from these to *add-ons* and *charge* negotiations, and then back to *delivery* again, and so on. Steps between *add-ons*, *charge*, *authentication*, and *payment* show supportive connections and temporal re-organization of the phases in course of the interaction. In Fig. 1, shaping of the service outcome for *delivery* has been an important topic throughout the interaction (six separate steps). In addition, the flow captures variation in total of 24 steps and shows the interaction as progressive: all needed phases were completed and the service could be delivered.

The same is also visible in the flow of id8, though the interaction itself was differently organized (Fig. 2). The interaction flow of id8 has a linear flow of five steps from *start* to *add-ons*. After that it proceeded variably going from discussing of *charge/add-ons* to *identity/requirements* and *authentication/charge*. The outcome of the service has been nearly finished in the middle, except the additional service spurt at the end.

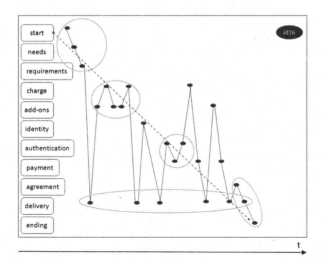

Fig. 1. Service interaction flow of id16 (*dark blue steps*). (Color figure online)

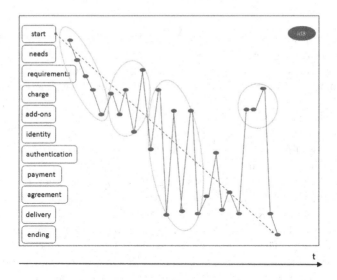

Fig. 2. Service interaction flow of id8 (*pink steps*). (Color figure online)

Individual interaction flows can also be compared with the flows of other customers by layering graphs on top of each other. The flow comparisons enable capturing of the relationship between the varying interaction changes [40] on the one hand, and, on the other hand, the factors affecting each other by the sifting focus of interests of actors [30] in their interaction situation. For instance, from the flow comparison of four individual users (group A in Fig. 3) we can see that *requirements/charge/add-ons* steps have close-knit internal connections but *identity, payment,* and *delivery* discussions disperse unevenly.

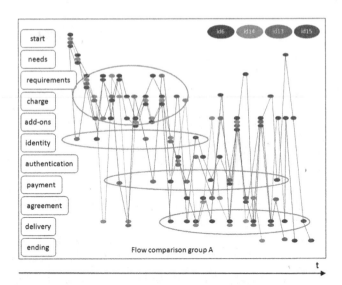

Fig. 3. Comparisons of service interaction flows by a group of four individual users (*group A*).

From the flow comparison of group B (Fig. 4), we can identify the linear starting steps, the repeated, close temporary *add-ons/charge* connection, and see that throughout the interaction *add-ons* have been an important factor in shaping of the total service outcome for *delivery*. These are just few examples of what can be analyzed by the flows.

We consider that the comparisons have potential for making generalizations and new observations related to service interactions, for instance when asking what kinds of strategies to adopt for service interaction or process design and how these match with the customers' interaction modes.

Furthermore, when creating understanding on a certain interaction process, we can look at what changes and what does not change in the process. For example, there is only one flow (Fig. 3, group A, id13, red) which did not follow the common *start-needs-requirements* line in the beginning, and one flow (Fig. 4, group B, id2, green) with two ending steps. Therefore, we can ask whether variation is more characteristic to certain types of interaction processes, certain service phases, or interaction modes, and what makes the other processes, phases, or modes to be more integrated?

Comparisons also show that in spite of this dynamicity and variation in service interaction, all service situations were performed successfully and produced a personalized service interaction flow and service outcome for each participant. In fact, we were not able to identify any interaction flow that would have followed the standard service process *per se* or even similarly-ordered interaction flows. However, most participants' interaction flows followed a common line from *start* to *needs* to *requirements* and all the service interactions ended with parting rituals.

As a result, we argue that with the analysis technique presented in this section we have been able to capture and show variation derived from the original situational service activities. In other words, our measures are not separated from the sources;

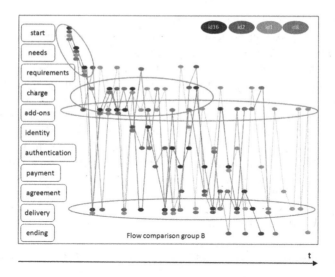

Fig. 4. Comparisons of service interaction flows by a group of four individual users (*group B*).

rather they combine essential interaction contents into new forms as situations emerged [23]. We also claim that with this technique we were able to capture personalization of service interaction in the car rental context, and to find shaping points for service outcomes according to the varying requirements of customers, as is suggested by [47].

5   Concluding Discussion

This paper inquired *how can we recognize and capture variation of personalized service flows in technology-mediated service interaction.* This was studied in the context of agreement-based car rental service that uses a special HCI setup for service delivery.

5.1   Summary of the Results

Our aim for this study was to understand what implications variation of service interaction flows has for personalization of service interaction. By analysing and modelling interaction between customers and a service clerk, we focused on capturing evidence on how variations of service flows can be made visible in technology-mediated service environment. We present an improved analysis technique that models the service interaction flow step by step, adding a visual dimension to the interaction analysis [19] and going in the micro-level in interaction compared to customer journey analysis [50]. With this technique we were able to capture and model variation in personalized service flows, derived from the original situational service activity. Variation can be seen as incorporated on certain levels of situated service interaction, phrases, service phases, and interaction flows. These have been outlined as (1) verbal variation in flow of service interaction, and (2) sequential variation in flow of service interaction.

We argue that this technique has the capacity of showing essential elements of service interaction personalization and revealing variation in the personalized service flows, and propose that understanding gained from that can be used for designing service management systems and interfaces that support construction and delivery of personalized service interaction flows. As we have shown with our data, personalization of service interaction flows contributed to shaping of the service process and outcomes, according to the actors' varying needs. In our context, service interaction personalization can be seen as framed by the provider's standard service procedure which, however, became re-constructed by the service clerk who applied it in the actual service interaction, adapting to each unique service situation. Service interaction personalization took therefore place (1) within individual service processes, (2) in individual service phases, (3) in temporal reorganization of phases by close-knit internal content connections, and (4) in unique content combinations via several phases.

5.2   Implications for Research and Practice

Our findings show that even in a relatively simple service, as illustrated in our case study, a lot of variety between individual service interaction flows took place during service encounters. We claim that this has two implications for practice and research. First, when an information system is used as a resource in a service process, it needs to adapt to the varying nature of actual service interaction flows. In our data, SMIS used by the service clerk allowed entering data in the natural order of the service interaction flow, and it provided consistency checks necessary to make sure that the process was completed successfully. Second, if some parts of the service interaction flow were automated or supported by a service management system, service interaction flow models could be used for implementing automated and real-time service composition and consistency check features similar to methods developed for web service composition [28] aiming at service orchestration done through coordination models [2]. SMIS could compose a service in real-time, adapting to the needs of the actors and context where the service is delivered, thus managing a variety of different contextual parameters [16] relevant from the service personalization point of view.

Our analysis technique can also help researchers and designers to understand interaction flows of services that have not been formalized into a defined model, but have been formulated through experience over time. It can also help both researchers and practitioners to identify different phases in service interaction flows as well as variety in the unique interaction flows of individual customers. Another possibility would be to design which parts of the service are fully standardized and which parts allow more customization [21].

5.3   Limitations and Future Research

The results have some limitations to be noted. We studied service interaction in a relatively simple service setup of car rental service. The analysed service interaction flow was completed during a relatively short time, and the service was entirely delivered in interaction between one service clerk and a customer. It may be that new insights could be revealed from a more complicated service setup [14], where several service providers work together to compose a holistic personalized service experience. However, we argue that the analysis technique utilized in our study is very versatile and has potential also in the contexts of more complex service research and design areas. For instance, in usability, user experience, and interaction design studies, and when complementing situated design methods for collaborative processes [38]. It would be interesting to see future studies utilizing the technique for deeper understanding of what happens in a service delivery situation where the service delivery spans over a longer period of time and requires collaboration of several actors and service providers.

References

1. Aguilar-Saven, R.S.: Business process modelling: review and framework. Int. J. Prod. Econ. **90**(2), 129–149 (2004)
2. Barbosa, M.A., Barbosa, L.S.: A perspective on service orchestration. Sci. Comput. Program. **74**(9), 671–687 (2009)
3. Benbasat, I.: HCI research: future challenges and directions. AIS Trans. Hum. Comput. Interact. **2**(2), 16–21 (2010)
4. Bitner, M.J., Ostrom, A.L., Morgan, F.N.: Service blueprinting: a practical technique for service innovation. Calif. Manag. Rev. **50**(3), 66–94 (2008)
5. Bødker, S., Christiansen, E.: Designing for ephemerality and prototypicality. In: Proceedings of the 5th Conference on Designing Interactive Systems: Processes, Practices, Methods, and Techniques, pp. 255–260 (2004)
6. Bosilj-Vuksic, V., Giaglis, G.M., Hlupic, V.: IDEF diagrams and petri nets for business process modeling: suitability, efficacy, and complementary use. In: Sharp, B., Filipe, J., Cordeiro, J. (eds.) Enterprise Information Systems II, pp. 143–148. Springer, Dordrecht (2001)
7. Büscher, M., Gill, S., Mogensen, P., Shapiro, D.: Landscapes of practice: bricolage as a method for situated design. Comput. Support. Coop. Work. **10**(1), 1–28 (2001)
8. Campbell, C.S., Maglio, P.P., Davis, M.M.: From self-service to super-service: a resource mapping framework for co-creating value by shifting the boundary between provider and customer. Inf. Syst. E-bus. Manag. **9**(2), 173–191 (2011)
9. Concilio, G., Deserti, A., Rizzo, F.: Exploring the interplay between urban governance and smart services codesign. Interact. Des. Archit. **20**, 33–47 (2014)
10. De Blok, C., Meijboom, B., Luijkx, K., Schols, J.: The human dimension of modular care provision: opportunities for personalization and customization. Int. J. Prod. Econ. **142**(1), 16–26 (2013)
11. Ekelin, A., Eriksén, S.: Citizen-driven design: leveraging participatory design of e-government 2.0 through local and global collaborations. In: Boughzala, I., Janssen, M., Assar, S. (eds.) Case Studies in e-Government 2.0, pp. 67–85. Springer, Cham (2015). doi:10.1007/978-3-319-08081-9_5
12. Finn, K.E., Sellen, A.J., Wilbur, S.B.: Video-mediated communication. Lawrence Erlbaum Associates, Hillsdale NJ (1997)
13. Gabbott, M., Tsarenko, Y., Mok, W.H.: Emotional intelligence as a moderator of coping strategies and service outcomes in circumstances of service failure. J. Serv. Res. **14**(2), 234–248 (2011)

14. Glushko, R.J.: Seven contexts for service system design. In: Maglio, P.P., Kieliszewski, C. A., Spohrer, J.C. (eds.) Handbook of Service Science, pp. 219–249. Springer, New York (2010)
15. Gwinner, K.P., Bitner, M.J., Brown, S.W., Kumar, A.: Service customization through employee adaptiveness. J. Serv. Res. **8**(2), 131–148 (2005)
16. Ho, S.Y., Bodoff, D., Tam, K.Y.: Timing of adaptive web personalization and its effects on online consumer behavior. Inf. Syst. Res. **22**(3), 660–679 (2011)
17. Holfelder, W., Hebmann, D.A.: Networked multimedia retrieval management system for distributed kiosk applications. In: ICMCS, pp. 343–351 (1994)
18. Iivari, N., Kinnula, M., Kuure, L.: With best intentions–a Foucauldian examination on children's genuine participation in ICT design. Inf. Technol. People **28**(2), 246–280 (2015)
19. Jordan, B., Henderson, A.: Interaction analysis: foundations and practice. J. Learn. Sci. **4**(1), 39–103 (1995)
20. Kane, B., Luz, S.: Multidisciplinary medical team meetings: an analysis of collaborative working with special attention to timing and teleconferencing. Comput. Support. Coop. Work **15**(5–6), 501–535 (2006)
21. Kellogg, D.L., Nie, W.: A framework for strategic service management. J. Oper. Manag. **13** (4), 323–337 (1995)
22. Kiepuszewski, B., Hofstede, A.H.M., Bussler, Christoph J.: On structured workflow modelling. In: Wangler, B., Bergman, L. (eds.) CAiSE 2000. LNCS, vol. 1789, pp. 431–445. Springer, Heidelberg (2000). doi:10.1007/3-540-45140-4_29
23. Klein, H.K., Myers, M.D.: A set of principles for conducting and evaluating interpretive field studies in information systems. MIS Q. **23**(1), 67–93 (1999)
24. Kuutti, K., Bannon, L.J.; The turn to practice in HCI: towards a research agenda. In: Proceedings of the 32nd Annual ACM Conference on Human Factors in Computing Systems, pp. 3543–3552 (2014)
25. Lee, M.K., Forlizzi, J.: Designing adaptive robotic services. In: Proceedings of IASDR'09 (2009)
26. Leinonen, E., Syrjänen, A., Isomursu, M.: Designing assistive and cooperative HCI for older adults' movement. In: Proceedings of the 8th Nordic Conference on Human-Computer Interaction: Fun, Fast, Foundational, pp. 877–882 (2014)
27. Löwgren, J., Reimer, B.: The computer is a medium, not a tool: collaborative media challenging interaction design. Challenges **4**(1), 86–102 (2013)
28. Milanovic, N., Malek, M.: Current solutions for web service composition. IEEE Internet Comput. **8**(6), 51–59 (2004)
29. Miwa, H., Fukuhara, T., Nishimura, T.: Service process visualization in nursing-care service using state transition model. In: Advances in the Human Side of Service Engineering, p. 312 (2012)
30. Nardi, B.A., Engeström, Y.: A web on the wind: the structure of invisible work. Comput. Support. Coop. Work **8**(1), 1–8 (1999)
31. Newman, M.W., Sedivy, J.Z., Neuwirth, C.M., Edwards, W.K., Hong, J.I., Izadi, S., Marcelo, K., Smith, T.F.: Designing for serendipity: supporting end-user configuration of ubiquitous computing environments. In: 4th ACM Conference on Designing Interactive Systems: Processes, Practices, Methods, and Techniques, pp. 147–156 (2002)
32. Nieminen, J., Mattelmäki, T.: Navigating in the World of Services-Visualizing a system of systems. Nordes, 4 (2011)
33. Orlikowski, W.J.: Knowing in practice: enacting a collective capability in distributed organizing. Organ. Sci. **13**(3), 249–273 (2002)
34. Paradi, J., Ghazarian-Rock, A.: A framework to evaluate video banking kiosks. Omega **26** (4), 523–539 (1998)

35. Patrício, L., Fisk, R.P., Constantine, L.: Multilevel service design: from customer value constellation to service experience blueprinting. J. Serv. Res. **14**(2), 180–200 (2011)
36. Reinders, M.J., Dabholkar, P.A., Frambach, R.T.: Consequences of forcing consumers to use technology-based self-service. J. Serv. Res. **11**(2), 107–123 (2008)
37. Scott, M., DeLone, W.H., Golden, W.: IT quality and egovernment net benefits: a citizen perspective. In: ECIS 2011 Proceedings (2011)
38. Simonsen, J., Svabo, C., Strandvad, S.M., Hansen, O.E., Samson, K., Hertzum, M.: Situated Design Methods. MIT Press, Cambridge (2014)
39. Sousa, R., Voss, C.A.: Service quality in multichannel services employing virtual channels. J. Serv. Res. **8**(4), 356–371 (2006)
40. Star, S.L.: The structure of ill structured solutions: boundary objects and heterogeneous distributed problem solving. Distrib. Artif. Int. **2**, 37–54 (1989)
41. Suchman, L.: Making work visible. Commun. ACM **38**(9), 56–64 (1995)
42. Suchman, L.: Practice-based design of information systems: notes from the hyperdeveloped world. Inf. Soc. **18**(2), 139–144 (2002)
43. Suchman, L.: Human-Machine Reconfigurations: Plans and Situated Actions. Cambridge University Press, Cambridge (2007)
44. Surprenant, C.F., Solomon, M.R.: Predictability and personalization in the service encounter. J. Mark. **51**, 86–96 (1987)
45. Syrjänen, A., Kinnula, M., Kuutti, K., Sihvola, V.: A facilitated VMC-based remote service kiosk interface for information systems. In: Proceedings of IADIS Interfaces and Human Computer Interaction Conference, pp. 157–164 (2013)
46. Tax, S.S., McCutcheon, D., Wilkinson, I.F.: The service delivery network (SDN) a customer-centric perspective of the customer journey. J. Serv. Res. **16**(4), 454–470 (2013)
47. Vargo, S.L., Lusch, R.F.: The four service marketing myths remnants of a goods-based, manufacturing model. J. Serv. Res. **6**(4), 324–335 (2004)
48. Voss, C.A., Hsuan, J.: Service architecture and modularity. Decis. Sci. **40**(3), 541–569 (2009)
49. Wreiner, T., Mårtensson, I., Arnell, O., Gonzalez, N., Holmlid, S., Segelström, F.: Exploring service blueprints for multiple actors: a case study of car parking services. In: 1st Nordic Conference on Service Design and Service Innovation. Oslo, Norway (2009)
50. Zomerdijk, L.G., Voss, C.A.: Service design for experience-centric services. J. Serv. Res. **13**(1), 67–82 (2010)

Accelerated Tuning of Platform Boundary Resources

Amir Mohagheghzadeh[1](✉) and Daniel Rudmark[2]

[1] University of Gothenburg, Forskningsgången 6, 41756 Gothenburg, Sweden
`amir.mohagheghzadeh@ait.gu.se`
[2] RISE Viktoria, Lindholmspiren 3A, 41756 Gothenburg, Sweden
`daniel.rudmark@ri.se`

Abstract. Platform owners develop boundary resources to transfer design capabilities to third-party developers and boost innovation within platform ecosystems. The literature on boundary resources suggests the concept of tuning to depict the process where such resources are shaped through an interactive process involving platform owners, third-party developers and other actors within the platform ecology. While the literature on the tuning of boundary resources is promising and emerging, there is to our knowledge no current studies on platform owners' measures to speed up this often prolonged process. In this research, we studied how a platform owner sought to accelerate the tuning process of its boundary resource through a case study at Volvo Group Truck Technology. In doing so, Volvo used an innovation contest where third-party developers used several boundary resources and engaged in an accelerated tuning process with Volvo Group Technology.

Keywords: Digital platform · Boundary resources · Tuning · Innovation contest

1 Introduction

Traditionally, firms have relied on internal resources to improve and innovate their service and products. However, through an increasing degree of digitalization, many firms have also started to draw heavily on external ecosystems to propel product and service innovation [1]. By investing in digital platforms and applying platform thinking, organizations increasingly seek to incorporate innovative ideas or even complementary services and products by reaping innovators from new domains.

For organizations to draw on external software innovators, they need to transfer sufficient design capabilities to third parties through artifacts such as APIs, SDKs, intellectual property, and documentation. These *boundary resources* provide the means for platform owners to govern external arms-length contributions [1]. A major inducement to engage in such third-party development is to attract actors from insofar untapped innovation habitats. Hence, as platform owners and external innovators inevitably belong to different social worlds [2–4], boundary resources must be "plastic enough to adapt to local needs and constraints of the parties employing them, yet robust enough to maintain a common identity across sites" [5]. The conundrum of the

© Springer International Publishing AG 2017
S. Stigberg et al. (Eds.): SCIS 2017, LNBIP 294, pp. 98–110, 2017.
DOI: 10.1007/978-3-319-64695-4_8

platform owner is thus to grasp and understand the demands and practices of external innovators to transfer the necessary design capabilities to external developers efficiently. As third-party developers' interpretation and usage of the resources typically differ from the platform owners' intentions, the shaping of boundary resource design is often contested. This interactive, multi-stakeholder process has been denoted *tuning* [6].

The tuning of boundary resources is typically a lengthy process that requires designing boundary resources, exposing them for third-party development, engage external innovators to work with the boundary resources, gathering feedback and assessing the need to take necessary actions to evolve the boundary resources. Also, not only is the tuning of resources a time-consuming process but a risky one: once boundary resources are deployed, and a wide range of third-party developers contribute to the platform ecosystem, any significant change to the exposed boundary resources may result in breaking compatibility with existing third-party applications. In such cases, the platform owner must spend substantial resources to communicate breaking changes and urge third-party developers to invest additional work in their applications to stay compatible.

Hence, there is an inherent need for platform owners to find alternative ways of tuning its boundary resources that are less protracted and risk-prone. However, while the literature on the tuning of boundary resources is promising and emerging [6, p. 393] there is to our knowledge no current studies on platform owners' measures to speed up this process. Consequently, we in this research explore the research question: *how do platform owners accelerate the process of boundary resource shaping?*

To answer this question, the paper proceeds as follows. First, we discuss relevant background literature on platforms, boundary resources and more specifically how such resources are tuned through an interplay between resistance and accommodation. Next, we give a brief account of innovation contests followed by the research setting of this paper. We conducted a case study at Volvo Group Truck Technology that was able to significantly tune its boundary resources over a period of mere ten weeks. We continue with a discussion of our findings in relation to the extant literature.

2   Shaping Platform Boundary Resources

Digital platforms lie at the very heart of distributed digital innovation and are defined as "the extensible codebase of a software-based system that provides core functionality shared by the modules that interoperate with it and the interfaces through which they interoperate" [1]. Complementary add-on modules can be added on top of these modular software-based systems to extend its functionality [1]. These modules, often in the form of applications can be designed and developed by third-party developers. As third-party applications are vital complementary assets to the platform, third-party developers often add significant value to the platform ecosystem.

Given the importance of third-party developers, there is a growing body of literature examining different aspects of these actors. This include developer motivations [7, p. 676], work practices [7], developer relationships [8], onboarding strategies [9], business relationships [10], generativity [11] and longitudinal value of third-party development [12]. Platform owners typically work under the assumption that they will benefit by engaging more independent third-party developers which in turns results in application variety and ultimately the value of the platform ecosystem. Given that, platform owners must work intensely to extend the installed base through enlarging the community of third-party developers by bringing a wider range of developers on board [13]. This action can boost innovation in the platform ecosystem by providing various types of third-party applications [14]. Considering the importance of third-party applications as complementary assets to the platform, one of the essential goals in designing digital platform is thus to facilitate the third-party development process [14].

To understand the relationship between platform owners and third-party developers, existing research have suggested the concept of *boundary resources* [11, 12]. Platform boundary resources are defined by Ghazawneh [15] as the "software tools and regulations that serve as the interface for the arm's-length relationship between the platform owner and the application developer". Boundary resources can take many forms such as software-based artifacts like application programming interfaces (API) and software development kits (SDK) but also include guidelines, agreements, documentation and licensing of intellectual property [5]. From a platform owner perspective, boundary resources enable the platform owner to transfer selected design capabilities to third-party developers [5, p. 174]. From the viewpoint of third-party developers, they are dependent on that boundary resources are malleable for their purposes enabling them to contribute to the platform ecosystem by developing software applications and serve end-users [16, 17].

Engaging in shaping boundary resources, platform owners can face a conflict between innovation regimes [5, p. 175]. This conflict can be seen either in market dynamics, competing logics in the firm or architectural design [7, 17–19]. The concept of tuning, defined by Pickering (1993) provided a theoretical lens for the contradictions which may appear as humans interact with the material agency. According to Pickering (1993) [20], tuning is a generative process that deals with the tension between resistance and accommodation. Pickering describes *resistance* as human failure in practice to achieve predesignated objectives. For human agents to overcome this material resistance, *accommodation* is necessary [21]. Accommodation can take several forms; "revision to goals, modifications to the material form of the technology, shifts in human frames and activities, and adjustments in the social or political relations associated with the innovation" [22]. More recently, Barrett et al. (2012) [22], brought the tuning perspective into the context of digital innovation. Barret et al. (2012) [18] highlighted the clash between many actors' values, norms and practices in the context of digital innovation. They argued that during the tuning process, *materialities* can both be changed and expanded and *knowledge* may be generated, become obsolete or be reframed. Finally, existing *plans* may need revision to institutionalize new practices. [18]. Recently, Eaton et al. (2015) applied the concept of tuning to illustrate how platform boundary resources shape and evolve in a digital ecosystem. They suggest that shaping platform boundary resources is a continuous dialectic process engaging multiple actors rather than a mere design matter for the platform owner. In other words, shaping boundary resources require continuous interaction and negotiation between third-party developers and platform owners. [1]

3   Innovation Contests as a Setting for Tuning

While third-party development may offer significant value to a platform owner, its arm-length organization can be challenging: as third-party developers are not paid upfront for their work there is little agency that can be exercised by the platform owner onto third-party developers. To this end, the platform owner may engage in other types of endeavours where the result can indeed be influenced. One such action is organizing innovation contests.

Terwiesch and Xu (2008) describe innovation contests as an approach where "a firm (the seeker) facing an innovation-related problem (e.g., a technical R&D problem) posts this problem to a population of independent agents (the solvers) and then provides an award to the agent that generated the best solution" [23]. By arranging the contest including submission categories and evaluation criteria the organizer may hence influence the development into a direction that is aligned with its business objectives. Hence it is perhaps not surprising that innovation contests are becoming a widespread practice which may span different stages of the development process, from ideas to prototypes to market-ready solutions.

Traditionally the generation of novel ideas and products has been the sole purpose of organizing innovation contests. However, these arrangements seem to offer organizers spill-over opportunities to tackle third-party development issues. For instance, Haller et al. (2011) argued that innovation contests can be used to target potential recruitment candidates [24]. Moreover, in a recent study, Smith et al. (2016) found that innovation contests may serve as a useful vehicle for knowledge transfer between the platform owner and third-party developers [25]. One of the key arguments to organize an innovation contest is to accelerate the development of ideas and solutions for a specific purpose. Consequently, given that tuning of boundary resources seem to be inevitable yet both risky and lengthy, the semi-controlled setting of an innovation contest could be used as an arena for accelerated tuning of boundary resources. In what follows, we describe the tuning that took place within Volvo Group Truck Technology during an innovation contest.

4   Research Setting

To study a firm's practices to improve the process of boundary resource shaping, we conducted a qualitative study at Volvo AB. Volvo AB is a well-known bus, truck, and construction equipment manufacturer and has conducted a wide range of research projects to improve its business through digitalization. This study is focused on one such project where Volvo sought to engage in the digital ecosystem around Google's Android platform, by transferring design capability to third-party developers through boundary resources. Senior engineers from Volvo Car Cooperation and a Swedish IT consultant firm with relevant experience within infotainment system development were also part of this project team to boost creativity in the project. Volvo Group Truck Technology, however, played the leading role in the project. To avoid confusion, wherever "Volvo" is used in this paper, we are referring to Volvo Group Truck Technology.

In this paper, we conducted a single case study [18] to explore Volvo's decisions and actions to speed up shaping boundary resource process. There are three main motivations behind choosing a qualitative approach in a case study method: (1) Since we in this research are studying a complex and contemporary socio-technological phenomenon, the research setting lends itself well to a qualitative approach [23, p. 152]. (2) As argued by Yin (2009), the type of *how*-question explored in this research through a multitude of data sources is well suited for the case study method. (3) Finally, the first author had unique access to this research project with the opportunity to observe and analyse the actions, reactions, and interactions in the project closely. We consider this research as a revelatory case study [26], as the subject of accelerating tuning to our knowledge has yet to be studied.

4.1   Data Collection and Analysis

We have used several data sources to understand Volvo's actions in shaping boundary resources in an accelerated manner. First, we examined 34 biweekly project reports containing the notes on actions and opinions of Volvo experts and senior engineers as they were trying to solve arising problems and tensions. Second, we accessed an online project database where the Volvo project team's actions and decisions were archived and assigned to a different group of experts within Volvo for follow-up and action. For this project, the database in all contained 150 decisions and 55 actions. This data source was used by the project to record important suggestions and comments by the project members. The biweekly project reports were built upon this database and highlighted rationales for important decisions and actions. Third, we acted as observers in 5 problem-solving workshops where the project team tried to share the latest tensions and challenges in fulfilling the project objectives. A crucial workshop agenda item was major decisions and actions that had been taken since the previous workshop, and the workshop provided a forum to discuss and describe these. All conversations that took place in these 5 workshops were audio recorded.

Regarding third-party developers' feedback, there were three main resources that have been used for the analysis. First, we used the questions asked by third-party developers' in the project's online forum. The purpose of the forum was to have third-party developers ask any type of question regarding the boundary resources or to report related technical problems (such as a bug). A group of experts in the Volvo project team was assigned to review the questions, filter out redundant topics and answer to new issues. Altogether 21 unique questions and 45 responses (by the project team or by other third-party developers) were posted. Second, we used an online survey filled out by third-party development teams. Each team answered 3 questions about the boundary resources they had used. The questions were asked to highlight whether third-party development teams found the resources useful or not, how often they used the resources and an open question asking for any other feedback that they like to give to Volvo. The development teams also gave their views about the boundary resources and their rationale for usage or non-usage. In the online survey, third-party developers were also able to reflect their general opinions and suggestions on how to improve the boundary resources. 27 out of 30 third-party development teams replied to the online survey. The remaining 3 teams withdrew from the contest. Finally, we undertook interviews with development teams during the 10-week contest. Selected portions of these interviews were presented and reported back during the biweekly meetings with the project team.

Moreover, to understand Volvo's opinion on the development team's feedback, complementary interviews were conducted with Volvo's experts that were engaged in the project. Altogether 25 interviews were carried out with development teams and the project teams. 8 interviews were with Volvo staff where 4 of these were transcribed. Table 1 presents the data sources used in this research together with a brief description.

Table 1. Data sources

Data Source	Description	Quantity
Interview	With Volvo staff	8
	With testing teams	17
Biweekly reports	Project team reports	34
Action/decision list	Actions	55
	Decisions	150
Workshop	Problem solving internal workshops	5
Online forum	Questions of internal and external developers	21
	Project team's replies	45
Online survey	Number of questions for each team	3
	Number of responsive testing teams	27

We used qualitative analysis software, Atlas.ti, to analyse the collected data. In our analysis, we have conducted interactive approaches in our analysis based on Miles and Huberman (1994). This approach is based on iterative data reduction, data display and conclusion. Data collection and data analysis should be conducted in parallel. We could identify the gaps in data while analysing them with this approach.

We started by reviewing Volvo's actions and underlying intentions to develop the boundary resources under study. Initially, the 10 boundary resources that Volvo developed as the output of this project were selected as an output for the etic coding. These 10 boundary resources were categorized as 3 APIs, 3 Documentation and guidelines and 4 SDKs. For data reduction, we used the biweekly project reports to focus our analysis on the boundary resources that had been reshaped during the contest. For data display, we explored the actions and decisions for shaping the boundary resources as the analysis of the biweekly project reports highlighted the project team's rationale for the shaping of these resources. We also analysed the feedback given by external developers'. At this stage of our analysis, we also used the questions posed in the online forum and categorized them, based on their relationships to each boundary resource. To increase our understanding of the third-party developer feedback, we triangulated their feedback with the interviews with the testing teams and online surveys.

For the conclusion part of the analysis, we analysed the interviews with Volvo staff, together with the project final report to explore the tensions in design and development of the boundary resources together with how Volvo's dealt with the tension. The results of our analysis are presented below.

5 Results

5.1 Background

The SICS[1] project's objectives were to design, develop and evaluate an open platform concept to be used in a built-in infotainment system with applications that also met state-of-the-art safety recommendations. The research project started in early 2013 and ended in January 2015 where boundary resources were being designed, developed and evaluated during these 2 years. The resources were intended to facilitate the development of third-party applications for the automotive industry, regardless of the developer's prior industry background. In order to evaluate the boundary resources, in September 2014, 172 bachelor students in software engineering were asked to use 8 boundary resources to develop their application within 10 working weeks. The students were divided into 30 groups of 5 to 6 persons to develop novel and innovative applications in the contest. Three main pre-defined evaluation criteria were given to the groups to guide their ideas: (1) Safety, (2) Innovation and Creativity and (3) Business potential. These criteria were explained through a lecture to the groups. A jury of seven experts in different fields such as innovation contest, software development, and business analysis were assigned to evaluate the applications using software for pairwise comparisons.

5.2 Tuning of Self-assessment Tool

Assuring safety in in-car infotainment apps is paramount for the automotive industry. To ensure a valid safety assessment of the applications the project team thus reviewed two different standards dealing with these matters: NHTSA[2,3] and ISO[4]. The goal with this work was introducing safe visual interaction with the infotainment system while driving to third-party developers. In addition to these design recommendation, the standards came with two different test methods for assessing the degree of visual distraction within the applications. By applying one of these test methods before submitting their contest submissions, developers could assess the degree of safe visual interaction of their application while driving. The NHTSA method was based on a driving simulation environment along with the use of eye tracking technology to measure driver distraction. Albeit a powerful evaluation method, the NHSTA standard required both complex and expensive infrastructure and the method was thus considered as unrealistic by Volvo in the context of third-party developers.

---

[1] Safe Interaction Communication & States.

[2] Visual manual NHTSA (National Highway Traffic Safety Administration) driver distraction guideline for in-vehicle electronic devices.

[3] Since this standard was originally developed for cars and not for trucks, it was matter of debate at Volvo Group. Although not formally adopted by Volvo Group, the project team found it interesting as it was simple to apply. Evaluating this test method in an experimental project would make a valuable contribution.

[4] ISO (International Standard Organization) 16673 Occlusion method to assess visual demand.

ISO, on the other hand, was instead based on a method employing a so-called occlusion test. The ISO test method originally relied on occlusion goggles to block user interaction and thereby enforce a certain use pattern. While this method was widely used within Volvo, the reliance on occlusion goggles made it difficult for third-party developers as they had to obtain such a device. After careful consideration, Volvo kept working with the occlusion method as the most reliable way of assessing visual distraction.

In fall of 2013, a Swedish consultant firm (a project team member) was assigned to develop an application called the Occlusion App 1.0. This application did not require occlusion goggles for testing but was instead running in parallel with the test object, so that the Occlusion App simply blocked the device screen, in accordance with the performance acceptance criteria. This behavior afforded developers to assess their applications using any standard Android device without having to obtain the occlusion goggles. When the screen was operating in normal mode, the user could only interact with the screen for no more than 1.5 s and when the screen was blocked by the Occlusion App they could not. If the total interaction time for completing a particular task exceeded 12 s, the application did not meet the acceptance criteria. While the Occlusion App was deliberately designed only to be used for self-assessment *at the end* of the development process, it turned out that developers instead used the app frequently throughout their development process. This way, they continuously assessed the safety performance of their application.

This unanticipated usage stirred a debate within the Volvo project team regarding the function of this resource. The resource was explicitly designed with the purpose to be used for final self-assessment by third-party developers, yet the students also tested and redesigned their application using the Occlusion App. As a result, the final evaluation of the developed application was performed with the same tool as was used throughout the development process. However, according to existing guidelines, occlusion test method was not the only suggested test method, the project team decided to reconsider eye-tracking technology in addition to occlusion technology to afford developers testing their application both during the process (rapid testing) and at the end (final test) with two different self-assessment tools.

The eye-tracking technology was a verified test method, where the firm relied on a considerable amount of internal studies and experiences. In comparison with real-world driving research, using a driving simulator was a less expensive way of investigating driver behaviour. However, access to driving simulation stations was not an option for participating third-party developers. To tackle this barrier, Volvo decided to adopt an open source driving simulator software called TORCS[5]. This software could simulate driving situation to be used while testing third-party applications. Equipping the teams with an eye tracker for this test method was however still a problem.

To resolve this issue, Volvo investigated whether Smartphone cameras could be used, as this equipment was widely available within the contestant teams. More specifically, Volvo developed supplementary eye-tracking software by using an open

---

[5] The Open Racing Car Simulator.

source framework called Open CV[6] Eye tracker. This framework was then integrated the TORCS software and given to the third-party developers.

While these test methods would enable developers to assess their application performance, real-world tests were still important to Volvo's. For several years, a number of best practices regarding setting up reliable and valid tests with end-users had been developed and documented by the organization. This document (that insofar had been an internal resource) included recommendations regarding sample size, age and gender balance of testers, and the number of tests to be executed. To consider third-party developers' test results as a valid and reliable self-assessment, Volvo had to educate developers bout these test practices. While the knowledge about the best practice document was transferred within a lecture session to the third-party developers, there were still uncertainties among third-party developers about the test method and its execution.

The best practice document was transformed into a test assistant tool called the Test Leader App, as an effort to reduce the barriers for conducting self-assessment. The Test Leader App would afford developers to monitor, record and moderate several test results more easily.

With these actions, third-party developers could use the Occlusion App 1.0 to test their application during design and development. In addition, they were given three other resources for final evaluation of the application; The Open CV Eye Tracker, the simulator TORCS and the Test Leader App. The resources enabled developers to test their application both throughout the development process as well as for final testing, according to the platform owner's safety expectations. These three resources could also be used within Volvo as they did not require any specific device or station.

5.3   Tuning of Business Portfolios Analysis

Another resource that potentially could facilitate third-party development was Volvo's data and information about its customers. This resource was called Business portfolios analysis. The underlying data had been collected for several years, and the portfolio contained several personas including sex, age, market profile, and their daily demands. This resource could help third-party developers exploring customers' demands which in turn could facilitate the identification of critical areas of improvements. According to an expert at Volvo, this resource could afford developers to "put themselves into the shoes of end-users to understand what their needs are." The analyses could thus be a useful asset for developing more useful and value-adding applications, especially since one of the key criteria of the innovation contest was business potential. In other words, more valuable applications for the end user could yield a better result in the contest.

However, as the business portfolios analyses were a source Volvo's competitive advantage, they had been strictly confidential, and the initial decision by the Volvo project team was hence not to release the analyses.

---

[6] Open Source Computer Visioning.

As soon as third-party developers got engaged in the innovation contest, they used alternative ways of understanding truck drivers' demands and develop an application based on their requirements and daily tasks. To ensure that applications were aligned with users' preferences, some third-party developers conducted interviews with truck and bus drivers at different carriers to map their preferences and application features to be used while driving. When the Volvo project team reviewed the application proposals, it became evident that Volvo needed to facilitate the third-party developers' understanding of user needs by publishing their insofar-confidential resources. The project team thus extracted specific parts from the Business Portfolio Analyses to mitigate the potential revelation of business secrets. They eventually arrived at creating just one persona, that gave developers a limited range of users' basic information such as age, sex, type of truck, logistics company profile, daily tasks, and driver desirable service as an application. The project team realized that more personas would likely help developers more, but given the firm's resistance to reveal its Business Portfolio Analyses Volvo preferred to limit its portfolio to this resource, before introducing additional ones. According to third-party developers, even this limited version of business portfolio, helped them to "get to know" the end-users' (truck drivers in this case) demands better. The assessment by third-party developers was that the business portfolio significantly aided in their design and development efforts, to create more useful applications.

6 Discussion

In this research, we have explored how a large automotive manufacturer sought to accelerate its boundary resource shaping. By arranging an innovation contest Volvo could shape its boundary resources in interaction with third-party developers and their innovation practices in a more accelerated manner than what is currently found in the literature. Within a limited timeframe of 10 weeks, several boundary resources were introduced to third-party developers who started to use them. As soon as third-party developers engaged in developing applications using the given boundary resources, the platform owner could receive feedbacks from developers.

We observed how Volvo within 10 weeks of the innovation contest, undertook far-reaching changes to the resources connected to self-assessment and business portfolios. While the Occlusion App resource indeed were accommodated in the self-assessment of third-party applications, developers resisted the initial purpose of usage (final testing) and thereby challenged the validity and reliability of the final testing. As a response, Volvo explored eye-tracking technology (that traditionally only were used within a driving simulator) and developed TORCS and Open CV eye tracker. In addition, Volvo developed the Test leader app to accommodate the monitoring and recording of eye-tracking test results. This response by the platform owner, triggered by the encountered resistance can be perceived as a *revision to the goal* [27]. While Volvo initially intended to provide an application for final assessment, the response from developers' convinced Volvo to revise the initial goal of the resource and instead offer developers two different resources for self-assessment; one for the development process and one for final testing.

To handle developers' resistance towards using the eye tracking test method within driving simulation station, Volvo sought to resolve this tension by *modifying the form of the technology* [26]. This test method had been used extensively within Volvo to evaluate visual distractions while driving. However, to facilitate usage of this test method for developers without access to eye-tracking devices, Volvo changed the material form of technology by providing the open eye tracking software that enables developers to merely download, install and use it for eye tracking (without specialized hardware).

In addition to revision to goals and changes to the material form of technology, we noted additional forms of accommodation; *social and political relations associated with innovation* [18]. Educating third-party developers about the end-users of the new digital platform required shaping a new boundary resource by drawing on Volvo's business portfolios analyses. The challenge in this phase the potential would revelation of sensitive market intelligence, carefully gathered by the organization. By scaling down and re-packaging the analyses according to developers' requirements, Volvo could contain sensitive market information within the organization while simultaneously facilitate third-party development.

Regarding accelerating the tuning process of boundary resources, our case shows that innovation contest is indeed a suitable context as developers' behavior, norms and practices were comparatively easy to observe and monitor. As tuning of boundary resources is a dialectic process [18], access to developers feedback, monitoring their practices, behavior, norms and their perceptions on functions of the boundary resources is crucial. Innovation contests enables the platform owner to observe third-party developers' interaction with the boundary resources within in a shorter distance and relatively short time. In addition, because of the context and the developers' motivation to win, many actively contributed in the dialogue with platform owner representatives through informal interviews and forum discussions.

The innovation contest reported on in this research is longer than the typical 24–48-h setup of a hackathon. The purpose of this prolonged contest was that a shorter innovation contest would not allow the platform owner to study third-party developers' behavior sufficiently. As much of the feedback and basis for tuning did appear later in the contest we hypothesize that it is necessary third-party developers must be given sufficient time to grasp the underlying rationale for the boundary resources, understand their more precise affordances and start to interact with them. Besides, through the innovation contest, platform owner had enough time to analyze third-party developers' reported tensions and conflicts and took proper action to them.

7 Conclusion

In this research, we studied how a platform owner accelerated the process of boundary resource shaping. We found that while innovation contests typically are used for boosting innovation within an organization, it may also be used for the tuning of boundary resources. Platform owners can conduct the innovation contest within a relatively condensed timeframe, and receive a wide array of feedback from third-party developers. This way, Volvo were able to tune their boundary resources in a significantly shorter time than reported in the current literature.

In this research, we would highlight limitations that should be considered. First, the testing group consisted of university students. While such participants typically lack substantial software development experience for the automotive industry, this sample may be representative of an untapped innovation habitat (due to their lack of domain knowledge). However, given their limited prior knowledge of application development and lack of vested business interests, a group of professional developers may have led to tensions not exhibited in our case study. Second, we have conducted a single case study. Innovation contest as a suggested method to accelerate the tuning of boundary resources can be explored in different cases with different settings. Third, in our empirical material the platform owner did not introduce any modifications that broke applications' compatibility with the platform. Consequently, we have not identified any resistance of this type. We however expect that a different setting could have exhibited such resistance. Finally, we studied an innovation contest, which can be seen as one of many possible approaches that can be utilized to shape boundary resources in a more rapid manner. We hope that future studies can help identify additional settings that can be used to conduct accelerated tuning.

References

1. Eaton, B., et al.: Distributed tuning of boundary resources: the case of Apple's iOS service system. MIS Q. **39**(1), 217–243 (2015)
2. Dougherty, D., Dunne, D.D.: Organizing ecologies of complex innovation. Organ. Sci. **22**(5), 1214–1223 (2011)
3. El Sawy, O.A., et al.: Research commentary-seeking the configurations of digital ecodynamics: it takes three to tango. Inf. Syst. Res. **21**(4), 835–848 (2010)
4. Nambisan, S., Sawhney, M.: Orchestration processes in network-centric innovation: evidence from the field. Acad. Manag. Perspect. **25**(3), 40–57 (2011)
5. Ghazawneh, A., Henfridsson, O.: Balancing platform control and external contribution in third-party development: the boundary resources model. Inf. Syst. J. **23**(2), 173–192 (2013)
6. Star, S.L., Griesemer, J.R.: Institutional ecology, translations' and boundary objects: amateurs and professionals in Berkeley's Museum of Vertebrate Zoology, 1907–39. Soc. Stud. Sci. **19**(3), 387–420 (1989)
7. Tiwana, A., Konsynski, B., Bush, A.A.: Research commentary-platform evolution: coevolution of platform architecture, governance, and environmental dynamics. Inf. Syst. Res. **21**(4), 675–687 (2010)
8. Bergvall-Kåreborn, B., Howcroft, D., Chincholle, D.: Outsourcing creative work: a study of mobile application development. In: ICIS. Citeseer (2010)
9. Qiu, Y., Gopal, A., Hann, I.: Synthesizing professional and market logics: a study of independent iOS app entrepreneurs. In: ICIS (2011)
10. Bosch, J.: From software product lines to software ecosystems. In: Proceedings of the 13th International Software Product Line Conference. Carnegie Mellon University (2009)
11. Evans, D.S., Hagiu, A., Schmalensee, R.: Invisible Engines: How Software Platforms Drive Innovation and Transform Industries. MIT Press, Cambridge (2008)

12. Messerschmitt, D.G., Szyperski, C.: Software Ecosystem: Understanding an Indispensable Technology and Industry. MIT Press Books, Cambridge (2005)
13. Remneland-Wikhamn, B., et al.: Open innovation, generativity and the supplier as peer: the case of iPhone and Android. Int. J. Innov. Manag. **15**(01), 205–230 (2011)
14. Boudreau, K.J.: Let a thousand flowers bloom? An early look at large numbers of software app developers and patterns of innovation. Organ. Sci. **23**(5), 1409–1427 (2012)
15. Ghazawneh, A.: Towards a boundary resources theory of software platforms (2012)
16. Bergman, M., Lyytinen, K., Mark, G.: Boundary objects in design: an ecological view of design artifacts. J. Assoc. Inf. Syst. **8**(11), 546 (2007)
17. Yoo, Y., Henfridsson, O., Lyytinen, K.: Research commentary-the new organizing logic of digital innovation: an agenda for information systems research. Inf. Syst. Res. **21**(4), 724–735 (2010)
18. Barrett, M., et al.: Reconfiguring boundary relations: robotic innovations in pharmacy work. Organ. Sci. **23**(5), 1448–1466 (2012)
19. Gawer, A., Cusumano, M.A.: How companies become platform leaders. MIT Sloan Manag. Rev. **49**(2), 28 (2012)
20. Godoe, H.: Innovation regimes, R&D and radical innovations in telecommunications. Res. Policy **29**(9), 1033–1046 (2000)
21. Svahn, F., Henfridsson, O.: The dual regimes of digital innovation management. In: 2012 45th Hawaii International Conference on System Science (HICSS). IEEE (2012)
22. Pickering, A.: The mangle of practice: agency and emergence in the sociology of science. Am. J. Sociol. **99**, 559–589 (1993)
23. Terwiesch, C., Xu, Y.: Innovation contests, open innovation, and multiagent problem solving. Manag. Sci. **54**(9), 1529–1543 (2008)
24. Haller, J., Bullinger, A., Möslein, K.: Innovation contests: an IT-based tool for innovation management. Bus. Inf. Syst. Eng. **3**(2), 103–106 (2011)
25. Smith, G., Hjalmarsson, A., Burden, H.: Catalyzing knowledge transfer in innovation ecosystems through contests. In: AMCIS (2016)
26. Yin, R.K.: Case Study Research: Design and Methods. 4. udgave. Sage Publications, London (2009)
27. Kaplan, B., Maxwell, J.A.: Qualitative research methods for evaluating computer information systems. In: Anderson, J.G., Aydin, C.E. (eds.) Evaluating the Organizational Impact of Healthcare Information Systems, Health Informatics, pp. 30–55. Springer, New York (2005)

"Maybe Some Learn It the Hard Way": A Nexus Analysis of Teachers Mediating Children's Online Safety

Heidi Hartikainen[✉], Netta Iivari, and Marianne Kinnula

INTERACT Research Unit, Faculty of Information Technology and Electrical Engineering, University of Oulu, P.O. BOX 3000, 90014 Oulu, Finland
{heidi.hartikainen,netta.iivari,
marianne.kinnula}@oulu.fi

Abstract. Worries over children's online safety increase as ever younger children have their personal digital life. As digital technology use also increases in schools, teachers have natural opportunities to mediate children's online safety. However, a better understanding of how it can be integrated with schoolwork is needed. We study how teachers mediate children's online safety in primary schools. Through nexus analysis, we examine discourses of trust, control, and involvement that the teacher's engage in. We also uncover many actors and history and experience related issues that shape the mediation of children's online safety. This study results in a variety of ideas as regards how IS research can support teachers and schools in mediating children's online safety.

Keywords: Online safety · Safety mediation · Children · Teachers · Schools

1 Introduction

Mobile and online technologies open great possibilities for learning, identity creation, and participation [1] and ever younger children have a digital life [2]. Their digital literacy and safety skills increase with use, and European teens and preteens are generally not unskilled [3]. Younger children however tend to lack skills and confidence [3]. Worries over children's online safety increase [2], e.g., as Internet use is becoming more private [4], and as youthful tendencies for heightened risk-taking and independence can sometimes be magnified by the opportunities of online interactions [5]. Threats associated with Internet use include 'content threats', i.e., inappropriate (e.g. adult/abusive) content [6], 'contact threats', i.e., grooming, bullying, privacy loss [6], 'conduct threats' where a person participates in activities such as illegal file sharing or bullying [7], or 'computer threats', e.g., malware, phishing, data theft/loss, password stealing/cracking, Internet addiction [6]. These threaten information security (i.e., protecting private information and systems from unauthorized access, use, disclosure, disruption, modification, or destruction [8]), and personal safety (i.e., ability to go about their everyday life without threats or fear of psychological, emotional or physical harm [9]). Online safety can thus be defined as protecting persons' physical and

© Springer International Publishing AG 2017
S. Stigberg et al. (Eds.): SCIS 2017, LNBIP 294, pp. 111–124, 2017.
DOI: 10.1007/978-3-319-64695-4_9

psychological safety as well as their reputation, identity, and property online [10], property including hardware, software, information, and intellectual property.

Parents and peers are usually identified as significant actors in children's online safety [11]. However, teachers are also central actors [11]; they together with parents are 'significant adults' in children's lives, whom children are dependent on in many respects [12]. As use of digital technologies increases in schools [13], education leaders, policymakers, and teachers face the question of how to promote technology use while safeguarding children [14]. Teachers are in a central position, as they have good opportunities to inform children about online safety [11] and to shape children's attitudes and behaviour [11, 15]. Yet, they are currently under-researched actors [16]. Even though information security is an established field within information systems (IS) research, research concerning children and their online activities is still lacking [17]. We believe IS research could contribute to this fascinating field, especially in the school context.

To this end, we ask in this study: How do teachers mediate children's online safety and how IS research could help teachers in this significant task? We answer these questions though a nexus analytic [18] enquiry into how Finnish primary school teachers use digital technologies in their classroom and what they do to mediate children's online safety. We focus on primary school teachers as there is a lack of research particularly on younger children [16]. This inquiry offers a nuanced and rich account as well as opens a variety of possibilities by which IS research can support teachers in this important endeavour. Moreover, IS researchers interested in school context in general can get valuable insights into teachers' multifaceted work and how technology shows in it.

This paper is structured as follows: The next section contains related research on mediation of children's online safety and teachers' role in. This is followed by introducing the research design and the theoretical lens used to make sense of the data. Then our results are outlined, and finally the implications of them are discussed together with limitations and paths for future work.

2   Related Research

Online safety of children is mediated using different mechanisms developed by industry, policy makers, and governments [17]. People close to children also seek to help children to make the most of online opportunities while minimizing possibility of harm [11]. Parents and peers are important actors here, but teachers are also central [11]. People close to children use different strategies to mediate children's online safety, including, e.g., active mediation by talking and offering help or restricting and monitoring Internet use [11]. It is argued that restrictions reduce online risks but they reduce also online opportunities and skills [19]. Although monitoring is recommended, there are considerations whether it is ethically acceptable [6]. Usually, active mediation is encouraged as it is linked to lower risk and harm and to children having more online activities and skills [19].

Teachers and schools mostly practice technical mediation [20] or restrictive mediation by setting rules for Internet use [11]. Teachers' active mediation mostly focuses on instructive remarks [15]. Teachers who incorporate digital technologies in their every-day life are more effective in promoting online safety also in the class compared to those less enthusiastic about digital technologies [21]. However, despite growing interest in digital literacy within educational policies, guidance of how it should be included in teaching is lacking [22] and teachers sometimes find themselves responsible for delivering the online safety message with little support [23].

Educating children about online safety can be problematic, e.g., if children feel that they are better users of digital technologies than their teachers [24]. Researchers report, e.g., on teachers' lack of knowledge about online safety [13], cloud-based applications [25], and activities that pupils engage in [25]. Some report complexities when teachers connect with children online [26]. However, if a knowledge gap exists, it can be closed by gaining skills and interacting with digital technologies [27]. As some teachers might lack skills for exploring the Internet with children and giving guidance, a more systematic approach to online safety in schools is advocated [21]. If rules and procedures are not defined, in many cases restrictive mediation is employed [28]. Information campaigns targeted at teachers are recommended [11] as well as training to increase teachers' knowledge of threats, policies, and programs, thus increasing their capability to provide help [29]. To this end, there are many materials already produced, including, e.g., educational games [24] and guidebooks for teachers [30]. There, however, is a lack of research on what works and what does not [16].

Schools are also advised to engage with parents and peers in online safety education as they can help shape children's behaviour [31]. While it can be difficult to effectively involve parents [32], schools can assist them in becoming Internet savvy and help them in monitoring home usage, thus strengthening home-school relationship [33]. Positive experiences also indicate that online safety message can be better received from peers than from awareness-raising exercises [34].

Discourses on control, trust and involvement have been identified to characterize public debate on online safety of children and argued to have an effect on the practice as well [35]. *Control* aims at predictable behaviour [36], e.g., by setting rules, goals and rewards [35]. Sometimes adults, however, have to rely on children behaving responsibly even when they don't know where children are or what they do [37]. They have to trust children, such *trust* being based on the knowledge of children's past and present behaviour [37]. This knowledge can be obtained by children voluntarily sharing information, adults actively asking for the information from children, or adults setting rules and restrictions [38]. *Involvement*, then again, is seen to include communication, supervision, adults' aspirations for children, and active adult participation [39] and it can, hence, be seen as interlinked both with control and trust. Thus, it is important to notice that these concepts are not mutually exclusive but intertwined [35] and a close and caring relationship between children and adults combined with a suitable amount of control is considered to reduce children's undesirable conduct [40].

3 Methodology

3.1 Theoretical Lens

As our theoretical lens, we use nexus analysis (NA) [18]. In NA, the unit of analysis is social action that happens in a specific moment in place and time but is viewed as a cross-section of three different aspects: historical bodies [41] of participants, interaction order [42] between them, and discourses in place [18]. In this study, the social action under scrutiny is mediation of children's online safety, as carried out by teachers. *Historical body* of a person refers to histories of actors that affect the situation. For example, teachers' personal histories as pupils, teachers, and digital technology users may shape the social action under scrutiny. *Interaction order* can be used to explain why and how people interact in certain ways in different groupings and how this affects the social action in question. For example, teachers' interaction with pupils or parents can shape how they mediate children's online safety. Finally, *discourses in place* means that all social action and discourses circulating around happen in real time and place, the participating actors using different resources available to make the action meaningful. NA is interested both in discourses in specific place and time as well as in the broad discourses of our social life and how they are engaged in our everyday life [18].

3.2 Data Gathering

Data for this study consists of theme interviews (duration 20–63 min) of nine teachers from our three partner schools. Selection of the teachers was purposive, which is usual in qualitative research [43]: they were chosen due to their familiarity of the subject, i.e., use of digital technologies in classroom and efforts to educate children on online safety. Teachers of 9–12-year-olds were approached as there is a lack of research on younger children on this topic [16] and some data collection tools we use require participating children to be able to read and analyse their own behaviour at a certain level. We asked all teachers of grades 3–6 to participate in our research and also sent out reminders. Out of the 43 teachers contacted, nine volunteered.

The interviews were carried out at schools. Interview themes were based on the literature review and included teachers' digital technology and Internet use; teachers' assumptions on children's digital technology and Internet use; online safety mediation at school; and, guidelines and training related to mediating online safety. This was an exploratory study; we wanted to keep an open mind and gather as diverse data as possible. The interviewees were allowed to concentrate on the issues they felt important. We let the conversation flow freely, trying to stay neutral in our language and reactions. Interviews were transcribed and, to ensure authenticity, the transcripts were sent to the interviewees for credibility check.

3.3 Data Analysis

The interview texts were first coded into different categories emerging from the data, going through the interviews several times until no new categories could be identified.

Then, the authors discussed the results examining first discourses of teachers, using the existing literature on discourses of trust, control and involvement as a sensitizing device [35]. Afterwards, the NA lens guided us to identify how the teachers' historical bodies and their interaction with other actors were shaping the social action of mediating children's online safety.

4 Results

4.1 Discourses in Place

Regarding discourses in place, we examined the interview talk to see how the teachers positioned themselves and children when talking about online safety: how they discursively constructed children's online safety and their own role. There was variety in the teachers' talk and several discourses could be identified. Then again, one teacher could be engaged in different discourses during their interview. We noticed that particularly the discourses on control, involvement, and trust that have been seen to permeate debates on children's online safety in our society [35] stood out also in these interviews: the discourse on **trust**, characterized by the teachers' trust in children's skills and capabilities in technology use; the discourse on **control**, characterized by the teachers arguing for more control over what children do, and the discourse on **involvement**, characterized by the teachers asking for more involvement from different actors – parents, children, themselves, school administration, and possible external parties. Example quotations from our data are seen in Fig. 1.

In the discourse on **trust**, the teachers constructed children as skilled digital technology users who might learn a bit of a hard way, but the more they grow and interact with technology, the more skilled technology users they become (DP1 by teacher 6 in Fig. 1). They viewed children as sometimes even capable of instructing their teachers on digital technology use and positioned themselves as enthusiastic and open-minded in experimenting and teaching with digital technologies (DP2, DP3). Children were viewed as capable of handling problematic online safety issues, e.g. scary material, by themselves (DP4) and capable of determining what they can or cannot do online and instructing also others, e.g. not to spam on WhatsApp (DP5).

In the discourse on **control**, the teachers criticized children's digital technology use as light-hearted or entertainment oriented. Children were seen as handy with social media, gaming, and smart phones, but their basic computer skills (e.g. in productivity software use) were seen to be limited (DP7). As for online safety, the emphasis was on control. Even though children might be viewed as handy with many things, they were also seen as unthinking and easily excited and their skills and knowledge as lacking (DP8). Teachers and parents were to monitor, instruct, and limit children's technology use (DP9). Addiction was a concern and it was seen as legitimate to restrict technology use at school (e.g. banning smart phone use during recess) and the teachers hoped parents would do the same at home (DP10). The teachers positioned themselves as overseers of children and they were to inform also parents about possible problems (DP16). The teachers also advocated parental control while acknowledging that it is challenging nowadays because of mobile devices and data (DP11).

Trust	Control	Involvement
• They experiment with things, use of WhatsApp and such increases. Knowledge increases. Maybe some learn the hard way, what they should and shouldn't do (DP1:T6).	• If one says they are digital natives. That they use a computer with ease. It's a bubble. They use social media and games. They are handy. But it is amazing how unaware they are about many things (DP7:T3).	• 9 out of 10 students already have a smartphone. Implement "bring your own device". They carry them around anyway, we should think how to take them part of learning (DP12:T3).
• I am open minded, I like to test things and see what I can make use of and do with the students (DP2:T1).	• They live with eyepatches on. In the moment. They don't think a week forward, let alone 20 years, or 10. [...] There are always those that don't understand, no matter how hard you try (DP8:T5).	• Discussing it when they understand: "we're talking about my actions, this is targeted at me, I'll benefit from listening" (DP13:T3).
• Some are so advanced they teach me. [...] We constructed a Greek city state in Minecraft. I asked pupils if we could do it. I had no idea if it's possible. They immediately got excited (DP3:T9).	• We keep the phones in the backpacks, not out in the open. They are not used without permission (DP9:T8).	• The best way to get them excited is when they can experiment with a game or something (DP14:T6).
• They search for pictures, say "well, that was an ugly", and disregard it. They don't dwell on them, at least not here. On things they find using Google (DP4:T1).	• Good night, phone off. 10-15 minutes later the kid thinks the situation is over and starts playing or something. Then they are wiped out tired (DP10:T4).	• We went through these things in class with fifth graders. Then they prepared a lesson for smaller kids (DP15:T9).
• When they start saying inappropriate things, or spamming, very quickly they're told to "Stop spamming" (DP5:T3).	• It used to be easy with desktop PCs. Took out some cords and that was it. And the computer was in a common room. It could be monitored. Now everyone has Wi-Fi, and mobile devices. I don't envy parents at all (DP11:T3).	• We have talked about WhatsApp with parents, I have messaged them that they should keep an eye on what is happening there when there have been some disturbances, swearing or other stuff (DP16:T2).
• They are quite good nowadays, they don't give their passwords to friends anymore. They know it is not something you should do (DP6:T1).		• I pity parents if they let their child disappear into gaming without being involved. If they don't show interest they won't know what goes on. And they should know (DP17:T3).

Fig. 1. Example quotations regarding discourses in place.

Finally, the discourse on **involvement** can be characterized as emphasizing cooperation among adults and with children. The teachers within this discourse tried to bring digital technology important to children (e.g. smart phones) into classroom in a meaningful way (DP12). When it comes to online safety, teachers maintained that lecturing is not the answer, but issues were to be addressed on the spot, when they naturally emerge (DP13). Concrete examples, learning by doing and reflection were encouraged, as was inviting children to teach each other (DP14, DP15). The teachers were collaborating with children in digital technology use and supported and helped each other in integrating technology and online safety into the classroom. Parents were to be involved, too: teachers were to inform parents and vice versa, e.g. if they had noticed problems or new developments (DP16). Parental responsibility was also called for and it was pointed out that it is a pity some are not involved in their children's life online, citing reasons such as unfamiliarity with the technologies that children use (DP17).

4.2 Historical Body

When looking at our data, interesting issues related to historical bodies of the teachers as well as of the pupils could also be identified – shaping teachers' mediation of children's online safety. Example quotations from our data are seen in Fig. 2.

Teachers' historical bodies	Children's historical bodies
• I use a smartphone, social media: Instagram, Facebook. Read email, online magazines (HB1:T8).	• No matter the device, they learn quickly to use it. It's easy to see they were born into a world of devices and have used them since they were little (HB12:T1).
• I have Facebook, WhatsApp, Instagram, Twitter. Many accounts, but I'm not that active [...] Technology needs to be restricted, you get carried away. It's something that I've thought concerning my children, it's addictive (HB2:T2).	• For girls it is about photos, of yourself and with friends. For boys, it is more about games and videos. Boys have made gaming videos and have their own YouTube accounts where they upload them (HB13:T1).
• I'm not on Facebook – I wanted to see how it plays out. I don't need to be the first to try new things (HB3:T9).	• They use a lot of things I've never heard of and can't list. I know they use Instagram, Twitter and Facebook (HB14:T8).
• I'm trying to hang on, to be able to use new things. Me and technology is usually wondering why something isn't working, why it's broken, or what it is in the first place [...] I use digital technology, there are things it's necessary for. But I know what it's like to sit in front of it all night. So I keep my distance (HB4:T4).	• WhatsApp and others. Playing games, fiddling with their phone [...] it's like cotton candy. Entertaining fluff. I'd say that basic digital technology skills have... It would be wrong to say plummeted. Or lowered. But developed into a more frivolous direction, towards entertainment (HB15:T4).
• I'm especially active at school, as I'm one of those responsible for digital technology. I also use it actively with the kids, and on my free time (HB5:T7).	• We have a lot of students who use a computer a lot, but for gaming and such. At school, they use Wikipedia, and search engines. But for example word processing skills are lacking. [...] We have talked about this, that we need to focus on these skills, they are needed in the future (HB16:T5)
• We make videos, animations, documents, use the Internet [...] Office programs, writing, attaching and modifying photos in Word. PowerPoint. We have a blog, teachers and students post about school activities. More photos than text. Parents can read it, keep up to date (HB6:T1).	• There are also children that don't use computers at home at all. Even now, on fourth grade. Not interested, or allowed to, or don't have Internet and such (HB17:T5).
• We listen to music every once in a while. For example during art classes. When it is a little bit more free you are allowed to do it (HB7:T9).	• They're attached to their phones. Or other device, all the time. Their thoughts revolve around them. There's also those that game too much. Sit on the computer all day (HB18:T1)
• I understand that [Social media] is a part of children's life, their world. Because of this we're trying to figure out how to bring it to classes. It would relate to their life (HB8:T9).	• They've had messages circulating on WhatsApp saying if you don't forward it to ten people in 30 minutes, awful things will happen (HB19:T1).
• It depends on the teacher's own activity how much digital technology is used (HB9:T2).	• They've started WhatsApp groups and there has been some name calling. And messaging in the middle of the night. [HB20:T8]
• We use it when we can. If we don't have obstacles like now, our bad wifi (HB10:T2).	• Boys had name calling that got out of hand (HB21:T4)
• We have too few computers, they are a bit outdated and slow (HB11:T4).	

Fig. 2. Example quotations regarding historical body.

The teachers' own historical bodies in the sense of their digital technology use skills and experiences influenced in the background. All interviewed teachers told they have their own smartphones as well as PCs, laptops or tablet computers. Some were, however, hesitant towards using digital technologies on their free-time, e.g. as it takes too much time. Most interviewees described their technology skills as average. One even jokingly confessed of being a bit of a bungler when it comes to technology use (HB4). Only two of the teachers identified themselves skilled with computers. One had previous education and experience in digital technologies and the other one was responsible for technology support at school. Both were avid technology users and experimenters.

The teachers explained that it depends on them how much digital technologies are used in the classroom (HB9). All reported using digital technologies in their teaching at least weekly. They believed that basic computer skills will be important in the future, and the children practiced, e.g., searching for information online and using productivity software like word processing and presentation programs (HB6, HB16). Transitioning to cloud computing was seen as a learning situation for children and a big change for the teachers.

Regardless of their own skillset, some teachers had a more enthusiastic approach to introducing new digital technologies into children's education. Smart phones were utilized, e.g., to search for information or to listen to music during art classes (HB7).

One teacher noted that utilizing smart phones is a nudge towards trying to connect to the children's world, as children carry them around anyway (DP12). Children also learned content production at school, in the form of, e.g., photography, animation, and videos. Some of the work had also been uploaded to social media (HB6). Class-related WhatsApp groups were also common. The teachers who were more reserved in using new digital technologies in class cited reasons such as excessive free-time technology use, need for the children to learn the basic functions of a computer first, or techno-logical issues like lack of computers or bad wireless connections at school (HB10-HB11).

Issues related to children's historical body became also foregrounded during the interviews. The teachers described their understanding of their pupils' historical bodies regarding technology use and expressed their beliefs that most of the children spend a lot of their free-time using a computer or a smartphone (HB16, HB18). However, the teachers also acknowledged that there are children who cannot use digital technologies on their free-time, or even wish to do so (HB17). The teachers reported on gender differences in the pupils' use of digital technologies. For girls, photos were seen as important and one of their social media favourites was Instagram. On the other hand, the teachers believed that boys were more active in gaming and in making videos that some uploaded also to YouTube (HB13). According to the teachers, the most popular use of Internet among pupils was WhatsApp; they however also noted that they might not even know all of children's favourites (HB14). Online safety issues had also manifested in school or some children had taken them up – such issues therefore already being part of children's historical body. These issues included content threats like scary material, contact threats like cyberbullying, and computer threats like data theft, and privacy loss (HB19-HB21).

In general, the teachers believed children to be quick to learn and quite handy with technology, while individual differences could be big. The teachers more enthusiastic about technology also saw children's historical bodies with technology in a more positive light, positioning children as skilled and capable, while others were concerned of children's skills or the lack thereof.

4.3   Interaction Order

In our data, it was also evident that various kinds of interactions with a multitude of different stakeholders were involved in teachers' mediation of children's online safety: the participants, naturally, included children themselves and their parents, but also educational administration and different kinds of external actors. Example quotations from our data are seen in Fig. 3.

Some educators from outside institutions, such as a school police and an infor-mation security specialist from Microsoft, had visited the schools holding seminars and classes to children on online safety. Their visits were usually mass events meant for the whole school, and the teachers believed the impact might be limited (IO14 in Fig. 3). Parents were positioned as important actors in ensuring children's online safety. Par-ents and teachers also cooperated when troubles had emerged e.g. concerning smart phone use (IO5). However, sometimes the division of responsibilities between parents

Children	Parents	Colleagues/Schools	Other actors
• We discussed online etiquette. It was the kind of issue that in principle should be handled home. As it manifested in school work and I knew there was an argument, I handled it at school. They understood and there hasn't been issues since. (IO1:T9)	• I noticed a pupil was tired and kept my eye on him. When we had a meeting I brought it up. It was the smartphone (IO5:T4).	• We have a group that has produced content for classes where children work together. Age limits and such (IO9:T8).	• The police talked about the world of social media with all kind of side effects. Cyberbullying, and other things (IO13:T9).
• Repetition, repetition, repetition. Little by little they're starting to understand what I'm talking about (IO2:T3).	• Parents sometimes messaged about scary messages. The kids were stressed wondering what they are, where they come from (IO6:T1).	• There' s a plan on digital technology skills, how to proceed. Very little about social media. [...] Guess it's up to everyone to decide as there's no common guidelines, besides age limits (IO10: T6).	• It would have been good If he could have visited classes, but this is too big school, he would've had to pick classes (IO14:T3).
• I said he can't sleep if he has WhatsApp on. Then someone explained they've agreed to send messages until 10pm, after that it's not allowed (IO3:T5).	• They think using the smartphone is a school thing. Why isn't the school monitoring it? You're the one paying the bill, not the school (IO7:T5).	• This is not easy for any teacher to tackle on their own. Everyone knows this, something has to be done (IO11:T6).	• Video said a password is like your underpants; you shouldn't lend it to friends or go without. They laughed at it and remember it well (IO15:T1).
• Waving your finger, saying "now we'll discuss information security", some automatically shut their ears (IO4:T3).	• School doesn't say how [phones] should be used. We make recommendations. They create limits (IO8:T1).	• I like to test new things and also share my recommendations with others (IO12:T7) .	• We've had parent conferences for example from Mannerheim League of Child Welfare (IO16:T8).

Fig. 3. Example quotations regarding interaction order.

and teachers was seen a bit confusing. The teachers maintained that they do educate children, but parents should take more responsibility and become involved in their children's life online (IO7-IO8). To this end, some education and guidance was already provided by the school for parents, e.g. during parent nights (IO16).

When it came to interacting with children and teaching them online safety, the teachers were sceptical if traditional lecturing makes a difference (IO4). They felt that online safety related issues were not a major concern among pupils. Children had managed smaller problems in their groups, and if there had been problems that manifested in class (e.g. cyberbullying or addiction), the teachers had handled them when they occurred (IO1). Indeed, the teachers felt that when the message was tied to the children's own experiences, it was more readily received than through lecturing (DP13, DP14). The teachers also emphasized the power of repetition to get their message through (IO2).

The teachers were also collaborating with children in online safety education as well as in digital technology use, for example inviting older children to teach the younger ones (DP15). However, there was a variety in how the teachers saw their and children's relationship in online safety mediation, as mentioned: some saw themselves as controllers and instructors, others saw children even as teaching their teachers, while many saw active collaboration with children as the way to go.

There were common guidelines given to schools about educational use of digital technology, and what skillsets children should acquire during each school year (IO10). To some extent teachers had also supported and helped each other in integrating technology and online safety into children's education, e.g., by gathering material to be used in classes (IO9). However, there is so much material available that the teachers had difficulties in managing this information and selecting the best pieces. Some extra education was offered, but taking part was voluntary, and the teachers attended only if they felt it added some important knowledge.

The teachers felt they were left mostly on their own to decide how much digital technologies are used in their lessons, and if online safety issues are taught during them (HB9, IO10, IO11). As this might produce big differences in the skillsets of the pupils, the teachers were hoping that the schools would make more effort to help them. The teachers' concern for help from the school also reflects more broadly the background and history of Finnish school system, in which the pedagogical independence of teachers is emphasized. This leaves teachers quite alone regarding digital technology use and children's online safety education, balancing between wanting to provide them with new, exciting opportunities, and wanting to keep them out of harm's way.

5   Concluding Discussion

This study enquired *how teachers mediate children's online safety and how IS research could help teachers in this significant task.* We examined three discourses (trust, control, and involvement) on children's online safety in primary school teachers' talk and on how they taught it in school, and explored how the concepts of historical body and interaction order shaped the situation. Our analysis showed the complexity of teachers' work, trying to connect digital technology use and online safety to everyday schoolwork in a meaningful way, at the same time needing to collaborate with multiple stakeholders. Next, we present the three main issues that emerged from our study and where we think IS research could make a difference.

5.1   Developing Teaching Practices that Fit Children's World

In line with previous research, the importance of integration of digital technologies and web 2.0 to school life [13, 14] was visible in our data. The discourse on involvement was connected with this: even though not all teachers were enthusiastic about new technologies in their personal life, they were trying to incorporate those tools into their teaching when possible, in a safe environment (cf. discourse on control). They tried to prepare children for the future and to close the gap between school and children's free-time by utilizing tools that children are familiar with. This is an important step from the point of view of children's rights, too, as digital technologies continue to be an important part of their lives from an early age. Instead of focusing on controlling and restricting, one should concentrate on improving the supply of information and offering opportunities for self-expression and participation together with adult support and awareness [16].

With regards to online safety, the teachers believed that traditional lecturing of online safety is not very effective, but instead tying the teaching into children's experiences as issues arise (cf. [15]). The teachers believed educational materials from different organisations can be useful in teaching children online safety. Most effective seemed to be, e.g., videos with a message, games, and exercises where children reflect on their actions together in a group. However, there is a lack of research concerning which of these materials actually work and which do not [16].

5.2   Developing a Systematic Approach to Online Safety

In today's rapidly changing world teachers sometimes struggle to deliver online safety education to children. The reasons mentioned by the teachers echo those identified in the previous research: lack of common policies and educational resources [22, 23] and lack of knowledge in activities that children engage in [25]. Previous research has suggested that if there are no common policies in place on how to manage online safety, a common response will be restricting access [28]. Indeed, relying on the discourse on control, some teachers noted that restrictive mediation of online safety is warranted, e.g., when it comes to children's smart phone use. Monitoring was practiced, e.g., in WhatsApp. Then again, relying on the discourse on trust, most teachers favoured active mediation, as also is recommended in the previous research [19]. They approached online safety matters as they emerged in school. At the same time, however, they acknowledged that children might not be telling them everything that is going on.

We concur with the previous research [21, 28] that a more systematic approach is needed for teaching online safety in schools. Some schools had already tried to compile their own educational packages based on different materials, but the efforts were not consistent. In addition to tackling issues that emerge in school life, we need to find interesting ways to educate children also on the matters that do not emerge naturally there: even if children have not experienced certain threats in their digital life, it doesn't mean they shouldn't learn what to do if they ever encounter those. A systematic approach to online safety should include an investment in teacher training to increase their online safety knowledge and capability to provide help in difficult situations [11, 29]. Some education had been arranged for teachers, but not much and only on voluntary basis. The interviewees wished for more guidance. They had tried to get familiar with the educational materials produced by different actors, but there was simply too much available and it was sometimes considered extra work. Common policies and training would reduce the pressure of an individual teacher.

5.3   Linking School and Other Actors Together

The discourse on involvement as well as the nexus analytic concept of interaction order made visible how schools are an important nexus of activities that contribute to children's online safety. This nexus connects peers, parents, teachers, and other actors in a shared dialogue. As previous research [11] suggests, teachers position parents as important mediators of children's online safety. Previous research stresses the need to educate also parents [33], and the teachers reported efforts of this, e.g., in the form of arranging lectures for parents. The teachers also gave parents advice on online safety and hoped for a more active role for parents in online safety mediation (cf. discourses on control, involvement). Previous research also suggests involvement of peers [34] in children's education. This is also connected with our findings: the teachers reported positive experiences of using children to teach online safety to each other, e.g., older children teaching younger ones or children setting rules for digital technology use by themselves, maybe even teaching their teacher. However, the teachers found their responsibilities and roles sometimes conflicting or blurry. Engaging in a dialogue for making responsibilities between different actors clearer would help keep children safer in the online world.

5.4   IS Research Could Make an Important Contribution Here

IS research has remained negligent of this important topic, while our study enables IS research to start taking action. IS expertise, e.g., in information security policy building and organizational education and awareness should be applicable in the school context. We should combine that with teachers' expertise on meaningful teaching practices and with children's knowledge of their lifeworld, issues, and interests, and through this contribute to the development of novel education practices that engage children and fit their lifeworld. Especially Scandinavian participatory design community could make a valuable contribution here – by arranging and facilitating collaboration among these various actors involved in ensuring children's online safety. Online safety education as well as associated tool support should be collaboratively developed. It would be game changing to focus our efforts to schools as the next "organisation of interest": helping schools to educate children to become responsible, knowledgeable, cyber savvy citizens. As professionals in the field, we should take responsibility – we have technical knowledge and methods for helping to find solutions for this problem area. No child should learn about online safety the hard way.

Regarding limitations for the study, as typical for qualitative research, this study has a relatively low number of participants and rather than statistical logic, we hoped to build a convincing narrative based on richness and detail. In addition, this research has been carried out in one urban area in Finland. We maintain, however, that the discourses we examined can be used as a lens for studying mediation of children's online safety also in other contexts and countries, even when school system characteristics and actors differ, taking into account that emphasis between them may vary in different cultures. Then again, only teachers' viewpoint was asked in this exploratory study, as we were interested in seeing how teachers, in the position of great influence on children's education and behaviour, see the situation. However, as evident both in the previous literature and our data, children's online safety is an issue that requires teamwork from many parties. While we feel that this was a good way to explore this area, also other methods are needed for capturing the interplay between different actors. We plan to continue such research, within which we will include children and parents as informants, and study how they approach and appreciate online safety, and how they think related technical and educational solutions should be developed.

References

1. Livingstone, S., Smith, P.K.: Annual research review: harms experienced by child users of online and mobile technologies. J. Child Psychol. Psychiatry **55**, 635–654 (2014)
2. Holloway, D., Green, L., Livingstone, S.: Zero to Eight. Young Children and Their Internet Use, p. 36. EU Kids Online, LSE London (2013)
3. Livingstone, S., Haddon, L., Görzig, A., Ólafsson, K.: Risks and safety on the internet: the perspective of European children. 1–170 (2011)
4. Livingstone, S.: Children and the Internet. Polity, Cambridge (2009)
5. Wisniewski, P., Xu, H., Rosson, M.B., Carrol, J.M.: Adolescent online safety: the "moral" of the story. In: Proceedings of the CSCW2014, pp. 1258–1271 (2014)
6. Magkos, E., Kleisiari, E., Chanias, P., Giannakouris-Salalidis, V.: Parental control and children's internet safety: the good, the bad and the ugly. In: Proceedings of the ICIL, p. 18 (2014)
7. Boyd, D., Hargittai, E.: Connected and concerned: variation in parents' online safety concerns. Policy Internet **5**, 245–269 (2013)
8. Harris, S.: Cissp Certification Exam Guide. Osborne/McGraw-Hill, Berkeley (2002)
9. Waters, J., Neale, R., Hutson, S., Mears, K.: Personal safety on university campuses. In: Proceedings of the ARCOM2004, vol. 1, pp. 411–418 (2004)
10. Nigam, H., Collier, A.: Youth safety on a living internet. OSTWG (2010)
11. Hasebrink, U., Görzig, A., Haddon, L., Kalmus, V., Livingstone, S.: Patterns of Risk and Safety Online. EU Kids Online, London (2011)
12. Read, J.C., Bekker M.M.: The nature of child-computer interaction. In: Proceedings of the BCS-HCI 2011, pp. 163–170 (2011)
13. Nguyên, T.T.T., Mark, L.K.: Cyberbullying, sexting, and online sharing: a comparison of parent and school faculty perspectives. Int. J. Cyber Behav. Psychol. Learn. **4**, 76–86 (2014)
14. Ahn, J., Bivona, L.K., DiScala, J.: Social media access in K-12 schools: intractable policy controversies in an evolving world. Proc. Am. Soc. Inf. Sci. Tech. **48**, 1–10 (2011)
15. Shin, W., Lwin, M.O.: How does "talking about the internet with others" affect teenagers' experience of online risks? New Media Soc (2016)
16. Ólafsson, K., Livingstone, S., Haddon, L.: Children's Use of Online Technologies in Europe: A Review of the European Evidence Base. EU Kids Online, London (2013)
17. Hartikainen, H., Iivari, N., Kinnula, M.: Children and web 2.0: what they do, what we fear, and what is done to make them safe. In: Proceedings of the SCIS2015, pp. 30–43 (2015)
18. Scollon, R., Scollon, S.W.: Nexus Analysis: Discourse and the Emerging Internet. Routledge, New York (2004)
19. Dürager, A., Livingstone, S.: How Can Parents Support Children's Internet Safety? EU Kids Online, London (2012)
20. Lorenz, B., Kikkas, K., Laanpere, M.: Comparing children's E-safety strategies with guidelines offered by adults. EJEL **10**, 326–338 (2012)
21. Anastasiades, P.S., Vitalaki, E.: Promoting internet safety in Greek primary schools: the teacher's role. J. Educ. Technol. Soc. **14**, 71–80 (2011)
22. Hall, R., Atkins, L., Fraser, J.: Defining a self-evaluation digital literacy framework for secondary educators. Res. Learn. Tech. **22**, 17 (2014)
23. Sharples, M., Graber, R., Harrison, C., Logan, K.: E-safety and web 2.0 for children aged 11–16. J. Comput. Assist. Learn. **25**, 70–84 (2009)
24. Reid, R., Van Niekerk, J.: Snakes and ladders for digital natives: information security education for the youth. Inf. Manag. Comput. Sec. **22**, 179–190 (2014)

25. Lorenz, B., Kalde, K., Kikkas, K.: Trust and security issues in cloud-based learning and management. In: Proceedings of the ICWL2012, pp. 99–108 (2012)
26. de Zwart, M., Henderson, M., Phillips, M., Lindsay, D.: 'I like, stalk them on Facebook': teachers' 'privacy' and the risks of social networking sites. In: Proceedings of the ISTAS2010, pp. 319–326 (2010)
27. Helsper, E.J., Eynon, R.: Digital natives: where is the evidence? Br. Educ. Res. J. **36**, 503–520 (2010)
28. Lorenz, B., Kikkas, K., Laanpere, M.: Bottom-up development of e-safety policy for Estonian schools. In: Proceedings of the ICEGOV2011, pp. 309–312 (2011)
29. Baker, K.M.: Teacher perceptions concerning internet dangers for students. Doctoral dissertation (2010)
30. Hinduja, S., Patchin, J.W.: Bullying Beyond the Schoolyard: Preventing and Responding to Cyberbullying. Corwin Press, Thousand Oaks (2008)
31. Valcke, M., Schellens, T., Van Keer, H., Gerarts, M.: Primary school children's safe and unsafe use of the internet at home and at school. Comput. Hum. Behav. **23**, 2838–2850 (2007)
32. Ozcinar, Z., Ekizoglu, N.: Evaluation of a blog based parent involvement approach by parents. Comput. Educ. **66**, 1–10 (2013)
33. Hernandez, S., Leung, B.P.: Using the internet to boost parent teacher relationships. Kappa Delta Pi Record **40**, 136–138 (2004)
34. Atkinson, S., Furnell, S., Phippen, A.: Securing the next generation: enhancing e-safety awareness among young people. Comput. Fraud. Sec. **2009**, 13–19 (2009)
35. Hartikainen, H., Iivari, N., Kinnula, M.: Should we design for control, trust or involvement? A discourses survey about children's online safety. In: Proceedings of the IDC2016, pp. 367–378 (2016)
36. Kirsch, L.S.: Portfolios of control modes and IS project management. Inf. Syst. Res. **8**, 215–239 (1997)
37. Kerr, M., Stattin, H., Trost, K.: To know you is to trust you: Parents' trust is rooted in child disclosure of information. J. Adolesc. **22**, 737–752 (1999)
38. Stattin, H., Kerr, M.: Parental monitoring: a reinterpretation. Child Dev. **71**, 1072–1085 (2000)
39. Fan, X., Chen, M.: Parental involvement and students' academic achievement: a meta-analysis. Educ. Psychol. Rev. **13**, 1–22 (2001)
40. Fletcher, A.C., Steinberg, L., Williams-Wheeler, M.: Parental influences on adolescent problem behavior: revisiting stattin and kerr. Child Dev. **75**, 781–796 (2004)
41. Nishida, K.: Intelligibility and the Philosophy of Nothingness. Maruzen, Tokyo (1958)
42. Goffman, E.: Forms of Talk. University of Pennsylvania Press, Philadelphia (1981)
43. Miles, M.B., Huberman, A.M.: Qualitative Data Analysis: An Expanded Sourcebook. Sage, Thousand Oaks (1994)

Wickedness in Design of e-Health Systems for People Diagnosed with Schizophrenia

Susanne Lindberg[(✉)]

Högskolan i Halmstad, Box 823, 301 18 Halmstad, Sweden
susanne.lindberg@hh.se

Abstract. With the digitisation of society, e-health systems support new contexts that are different from traditional Information Systems contexts, and therefore need to be better understood. In design for complex, new and sensitive contexts, it is not possible to apply known methods and solutions without deeper contextual understanding. The paper intends to answer how the wickedness of the design context when designing digital services for people diagnosed with schizophrenia can be understood – a context that is contradictory and complex, that is, a wicked design context. The paper presents a grounded theory analysis of stakeholder interviews and focus group interviews with people diagnosed with schizophrenia. Four wicked problems are identified: struggle of dependence, contradiction of social interaction, contradiction of trust and counteracting improvement behaviour. The paper also shows the viability of the use of grounded theory for uncovering and describing contextual wickedness.

Keywords: e-Health · Wicked problems · Wickedness · Schizophrenia · Grounded theory · Design

1   Introduction

During the last decades, technical advances have created a digitalised society. This has in turn expanded the use of digital technology to new contexts and user groups; groups that are heterogeneous, and that use the digital technology in a multitude of contexts [1]. E-health systems are no exception. With the digitalisation of society, e-health systems have to be designed to support user groups who have previously not been supported. Examples include Tokar and Batoroev [2] who explore mobile health care for people with depression, Aardoom, Dingemans and Van Furth [3] who study e-health systems for people with eating disorders and Kowatsch, Maass, Pletikosa Cvijikj, Büchter, Brogle, Dintheer, Wiegand, Durrer-Schutz, Xu and Schutz [4] who study the design of a health information system for reducing childhood obesity. Advances such as these have paved the way for innovative ways to support patients at different stages of their lives.

In order to design digital services, it is necessary to understand the context in which they are to be designed and used [5]. It is not possible for one person to have all the necessary knowledge of the complexities of a design context; it therefore becomes imperative to involve stakeholders and support their communication and collaboration [6]. When the design context has been frequently designed for in the past, or is easily

© Springer International Publishing AG 2017
S. Stigberg et al. (Eds.): SCIS 2017, LNBIP 294, pp. 125–139, 2017.
DOI: 10.1007/978-3-319-64695-4_10

relatable, there is little effort in creating an understanding [7]. However, in design for new, complex and sensitive contexts such as health related contexts with vulnerable users, it becomes more difficult to both study and understand the context.

This paper focuses specifically on understanding the context of design of e-health services for people diagnosed with schizophrenia. Approximately 1% of the world's population is diagnosed with schizophrenia [8] and have symptoms such as hallucinations, psychoses, apathy, and cognitive impairment [9]. Symptoms and treatment for schizophrenia can affect the ability for creative thinking [10], clear expression of ideas [11], and social interaction [12]. The treatment for schizophrenia is typically antipsychotic medication, but this has only a limited effect [9].

Designing an e-health system for people diagnosed with schizophrenia means encountering contradictory and sensitive problems that affect the design situation, such as paranoia and delusions [8], and social stigmatisation [13, 14]. These types of problems that are contradictory, incomplete or have constantly changing requirements, have previously been referred to as "wicked problems" [cf. 15]. Design, which is aimed at solving problems, is particularly suitable for handling wicked problems [5, 16]. Understanding a wicked problem is also part in understanding its possible solution, since they are only possible to be understood once they have been solved [15]. This makes understanding the wickedness of a design context critical to the entire design process.

Understanding the wickedness of the context when designing for people diagnosed with schizophrenia is therefore essential but challenging. However, not attempting to gain a complete understanding of the complexities of the design context when it is possible to do so can not only have negative consequences for the quality of the designed system, but can also be considered unethical. Therefore, this paper intends to answer the question: *How can the wickedness of the design context when designing digital services for people diagnosed with schizophrenia be understood?*

Due to the explorative and open nature of the aim, this paper proposes a grounded theory analysis to uncover the wickedness of the context. The purpose is to both describe the wickedness of the context, as well as to discuss the applicability of the grounded theory approach to uncover wickedness in design contexts.

2   Background

2.1   Schizophrenia

Symptoms of schizophrenia can be positive (constituting an addition of abnormal symptoms and behaviours), negative (constituting a lack of normal symptoms and behaviours), or cognitive [8, 9]. These symptoms can be manifested to a different degree among individuals [9]. Positive symptoms can include delusions and hallucinations [9]; in essence a loss of contact with reality [8]. Negative symptoms include flat affect, social withdrawal and reduced speech [8, 9]. These symptoms are less fluctuating than the positive symptoms and also have a greater effect on the person's social life [8]. Many also have cognitive impairments, such as problems with attention, learning and memory, illogical thinking, confusion, delusion and strange linking of thoughts [8, 11, 17].

There is no cure for schizophrenia, only ways to cope with the illness. Most recover after the first onset, but about 10% never do [9]. The outcome seems more promising in developing countries than in developed countries [9]. The primary treatment in developed countries is antipsychotic medication that primarily treats positive symptoms [9]. Antipsychotic medication does not appear to improve cognitive function, and even though other symptoms improve, these cognitive symptoms tend to remain [17]. Psychosocial treatment such as supported employment and social skills training has been found to improve the outcome of schizophrenia [8].

The social and emotional limitations that people diagnosed with psychotic disorders, such as schizophrenia, experience can often lead to isolation [18]. Social support has been found to have several benefits for people diagnosed with schizophrenia and similar severe mental illnesses [19–22]. However, due to both social stigma and symptoms such as reduced vocal ability, lack of motivation, and difficulties with memory and concentration, it is difficult for people diagnosed with schizophrenia to organise social support themselves [18]. Increasingly, people diagnosed with schizophrenia are turning to social media not specifically designed for their needs for support, risking low quality support and being identified as an individual with such an illness and its associated stigmatisation [23]. People diagnosed with mental health conditions in younger generations are also more likely to use social media to build friendships [24].

2.2   Wicked Problems

The concept of wicked problems was initially described by Rittel and Webber [15]. The difference between typical, simple problems with established procedures and wicked problems, is that wicked problems do not have clear solutions, it is not always possible to know when or if they have been solved, and they are not possible to delineate and clearly define [15]. Social problems [15] and the problems approached using non-linear design processes are usually of a wicked nature [25]. In fact, all problems except those taken on by routine design are wicked problems [5]. There is no single right or wrong solution [26]; the solution of a wicked problems lies in the world view of the solver [15], in this case the designer [27].

In the attempt to solve wicked problems, all actions taken will affect the surrounding context and there is thus no way to undo mistakes [15]. Therefore, it becomes important to reduce the possibility for mistakes. Yet there are no categories of wicked problems, nor are there any predefined ways of solving them; all wicked problems are unique [15]. Wicked problems must be handled in a manner appropriate to their complexity, ambiguity and uniqueness, with a focus on achieving a desirable outcome instead of a clear problem solution [26]. The common collaboration between different people in design is suitable for tackling wicked problems [28].

The aim for this paper is to begin the process of understanding, and thus enable handling of, some of the wicked problems that exist in the design context when designing digital services for people diagnosed with schizophrenia. Dealing with complex problems requires that the designer considers the whole as well as the parts; that is, to not only focus on the specificities of the identified problem but also on the context in which the problem resides [26]. Instead of oversimplifying, it is important to consider the problem on different levels, systemically [26]. Familiarizing oneself with the context is also an important step in better utilizing the empirical material to create theories [29], and there are calls for more systemic ways of expressing and using context in theory development [30]. This paper is a step towards creating a deeper contextual understanding of the wickedness of design of e-health systems for people diagnosed with schizophrenia.

3 Method

This paper employs a grounded theory analysis to answer how the wicked problems in the design of e-health systems for people diagnosed with schizophrenia can be understood. The approach was considered appropriate because it is a way to make sense of stories told by interviewees, a way to stay close to the empirical material, and to learn about the contexts and settings under study [31]. Grounded theory was first introduced by Glaser and Strauss [32] and has since developed in different directions. This paper relies on the work of Charmaz [31] as a foundation for the methodology employed. Charmaz [31] emphasises that theories are not found, but constructed by the researcher in an interpretive process of analysis. Grounded theory can be successfully combined with design research, and one use of performing a grounded theory analysis can be in the early stages of a design process, in order to gain a systematic and deep understanding of the context and problem area [33].

It is becoming increasingly popular to use grounded theory in the Information Systems (IS) field, as it is considered useful for describing processes and phenomena [34]. However, the existence of some myths about the nature of grounded theory has been considered the cause of misuse or lack of use of grounded theory in the field [35]. These myths include for example the misconception that literature cannot be studied before performing a grounded theory analysis [35, 36]. Instead, literature should be studied beforehand, but not in order to integrate into the yet unidentified theory [35]; it should be used strategically [31]. In this paper, the intent was not at the onset of the analysis to identify wicked problems. However, the results that emerged from the application of grounded theory showed many complex and contradictory situations within the studied context, and these were identified to be wicked problems. The literature on wicked problems was then incorporated.

3.1 Study Design

The empirical material included in this study consisted of: semi-structured stakeholder interviews, four with relatives of people diagnosed with schizophrenia and three with medical professionals; and two focus group interviews, each with two people diagnosed with schizophrenia. The focus group interviews were part of the first of three design workshops with the aim to design an e-health system. The empirical material consisted of a total of 540 recorded minutes.

The individual and focus group interviews were all transcribed and coded line-by-line using open coding. The open codes were then grouped into categories using focused coding. The core to grounded theory is considered to be constant comparison between data, codes and categories [31]. The open and focused coding was therefore done iteratively, and each new code was compared with the existing codes and categories. Category identification was done by using the most significant or the most frequent codes as a starting point. Examples of categories identified at this stage include *depending on others*, *having illness awareness*, and *using strategies*.

The relationships between the identified categories were then axially coded. This was done using software visual mapping functionality. For example, the category *depending on others* related to the category *fearing* since fear affects the ability to depend on other people. It was at this stage that the wicked problems were identified in the conflicting nature of the categories. Theoretical coding was then done, but those results will not be possible to include in this paper. Memos were also written throughout the analysis process, as recommended by Charmaz [31]. These were important for recording insights and interpretations throughout the analysis.

The results presented in this paper are only part of the results from the grounded theory analysis. As the result was rich and diverse, it became more suitable to present it over the course of more than one paper for the sake of clarity. The results from the grounded theory analysis thus related to more than the wicked problems described in this paper.

3.2   Research Context

The research in this paper was performed within a research project aimed to design an e-health system for people diagnosed with schizophrenia. E-health systems have been designed for similar contexts. For example, Melling and Houguet-Pincham [37] study an e-health system for people who are experiencing depression, Webb, Burns and Collin [38] develop en e-health system for adolescents who are experiencing mental health difficulties, and Lederman, Wadley, Gleeson and Alvarez-Jimenez [39] design online social therapy meant to detect warning signs among young people with psychoses. Each of these cases illustrates the complexity of the context, and the necessity to understand the context as part of the design process, in order to adapt both the design process and the final e-health system. The data collected here is part of an early part of the project. The following part of the project included design workshops together with people diagnosed with schizophrenia with the aim to collaborate in design.

3.3   Participants

The participating stakeholders were four parents of people diagnosed with schizophrenia, one activity coordinator, one psychiatric nurse, and one assistant nurse working with housing support. The participating target users all had a diagnosis of schizophrenia, were between 45–51 years old, and had been treated for more than 10 years. They all relied on support from medical treatment and were on a disability pension. In total, four people diagnosed with schizophrenia participated in pairs in the focus group interviews. All participants' and their relations' names have been changed. There was no relationship between the participants. Table 1 below gives an overview of the participants and their roles.

Table 1. Overview of participants.

Participant role	Participants
Parent	The mother of Jack The father of Brock The mother of Carl The mother of Dani
Medical professional	Alfred, activity coordinator Benjamin, psychiatric nurse Chris, assistant nurse
Target user	Frank Scott David Angela

3.4   Ethics

The regional ethical review board approved the project (Dnr 2011/267) from which the collected empirical material in this paper comes. When the context is sensitive, as in this paper, there is a risk to the participants' welfare. The participants' wellbeing may be affected, and if the information on their participation would be made public, they can suffer social consequences due to the stigmatization of mental health illnesses such as schizophrenia [14]. During the interviews, the relatives of people with schizophrenia expressed concern that if their participation became known, it would negatively affect their children. As a result, all participants' names have been altered, and any information that might lead to their identification has been excluded.

Furthermore, one of the researchers who participated in the focus group interviews had a background in nursing, and many years of experience working with people diagnosed with schizophrenia. As the focus group interviews were only the first in a set of three workshops, she maintained contact with the participants between and after the time of the workshops, in order to ensure their wellbeing.

4   Findings

This section presents the results from the analysis of how the wicked problems in the design of e-health systems for people diagnosed with schizophrenia can be understood. Table 2 below summarizes the uncovered wicked problems that are described in detail in this section.

4.1   The Struggle of Dependence

The analysis indicates a struggle between being dependent and wanting to lead an independent life. The illness usually manifests itself in your twenties, when quite abruptly something starts to feel wrong, and normality is lost. Medical professional Alfred describes it like:

Table 2. Summary of the identified wicked problems.

Contextual wickedness	Description
Struggle of dependence	Living with schizophrenia causes dependence on others. The treatment system does not support independence, and some struggle with the collective treatment. People diagnosed with schizophrenia also tend to use little digital technology, leaving them outside of the increasingly digitized society, deepening their dependence
Contradiction of social interaction	People diagnosed with schizophrenia lose most social connections yet acquire many medical contacts. This, along with stigmatization, makes interaction impersonal and people are often lonely. Medical contacts enhance social behavior that serves to alienate others
Contradiction of trust	Due to being dependent, people diagnosed with schizophrenia have to trust others. However, the rationale behind trust is sometimes contradictory. People in trustworthy positions, such as medical personnel, may be mistrusted, while strangers are trusted. Trust also affects digital acceptance. Fear of technology and consequences of previous naïve use can reduce trust of technology
Counteracting improvement behavior	Some behavior directly counteracts possibilities for improvement. People diagnosed with schizophrenia tend to use avoiding coping strategies and isolating behaviors, increasing their loneliness. Balance tends to disappear

The withdrawal [from society] starts because something happens in your body or your head that you can't really... that doesn't feel right.

And Frank says that when he fell ill:

It didn't add up for me at all, my damn voices.

However, the memory of a normal life still exists and is something that the users in this study expressly want. Angela describes how she attempts behaviours and activities that the group home personnel do, because it seems healthy:

The staff at the group home work out a lot and that and... /.../ they feel well so I thought that I will do the same.

Similarly, Brock's father describes how it gives his son, who has recovered enough to maintain a regular job, pleasure in life to be able to buy things like everyone else. Nevertheless, Alfred explains that the treatment system does not have as a goal to create a normal life for people diagnosed with schizophrenia. Instead, the system treats the care recipients collectively, removing independence. David describes how he is no longer allowed to work by the Social Insurance Agency, despite previously being able to maintain a part-time job. Jack's mother describes her son's group home as "storage", and psychiatric nurse Benjamin describes his patients as being "preserved":

The illness becomes a kind of formalin. You get stuck where you become ill sometimes, and there is little new added.

Frank says that in some ways he felt better when he lived on the streets, because he was able to make his own decisions.

People diagnosed with schizophrenia are described by the participants as having no or few hobbies, and even fewer that they can afford. As a result, they are dependent on others to be activated. Dani's and Jack's mothers, psychiatric nurse Benjamin, and David all describe a need for other people to help with activation. However, the care system does not currently provide adequate support for this.

Furthermore, people diagnosed with schizophrenia use little digital technology. This is due to a combination of factors. For one, the user group is to a large extent on disability pension and therefore cannot afford digital technology. Frank and Scott both own smartphones, but explain that most in their situation do not, and that they have only been able to buy them since mobile subscriptions became more affordable. Medical professional Alfred tries to help:

We try to offer different kinds of study groups, and it's often computers that is being requested. So it's not about not being interested, but about not having the opportunity to.

Additionally, psychiatric nurse Benjamin describes issues with cognitive ability to learn how to use digital technology:

Patients that are chronically ill with a psychotic illness and have recurring periods of symptoms get a kind of cognitive impairment as well. /.../ They may have a more difficult time to take it in.

There is a need to increase digital technology use among this user group. Jack's mother describes it as this group being left out, and therefore also ending up outside of society. As a result, they become even more dependent. Nevertheless, this is a generational issue. Several stakeholders agree that with the coming generations, some of the issues described will no longer be valid. However, it will still be many years when these issues stay relevant.

4.2   The Contradiction of Social Interaction

The analysis further shows a contradiction in the social interaction of people diagnosed with schizophrenia. People diagnosed with schizophrenia are described as exceedingly lonely. For example, assistant nurse Christ says that social life becomes minimal after becoming ill, Carl's mother says that her son has lost all former friends and made no new ones, and Jack's mother says that her son's friendships have been forced on him, as they are all people who live in the same group home. Medical professional Alfred summarises:

When the person in question falls ill most contacts disappear. You have your parents left, and maybe some childhood friend who gets in touch once in a while, mostly because they feel guilty.

Nevertheless, despite the lack of close relationships, people diagnosed with schizophrenia meet a great number of people in their everyday lives. The majority of people they meet are medical professionals. Many have weekly visits from nurses, housing support help with everyday tasks, and most have to meet an assistant nurse daily to take their medication, as they are not allowed to handle it themselves. Yet, this is only superficial social interaction. Frank describes the isolation as the worst part of the illness:

> The hardest part of the illness was the isolation, the loneliness in the beginning, at first when you were lying at home.

Scott says that there cannot be too much social interaction. Yet both Frank and Scott agree that it is easier to interact with others who have a similar understanding of the illness. Scott wants more information from self-experienced online, and Frank chooses friends that have similar experiences.

Another issue that is raised is the stigmatisation of the illness. Psychiatric nurse Benjamin explains that the diagnosis itself can act as a deterrent, something that Frank experienced when he tried telling people around him about his experiences. Both Brock's father and Carl's mother express concern about revealing their names, as they fear that their sons will be negatively affected if the interviews can be traced back to them.

Further, people diagnosed with schizophrenia can sometimes engage in alienating behaviours that may strengthen that stigmatisation. For example, assistant nurse Chris describes how some of his patients have lost any chance to befriend their neighbours because they have tried to borrow money from them in the past. Further, Frank explains how he has had to learn that the kind of behaviour his nurse and care staff want is not acceptable elsewhere:

> It's mostly medical personnel and those who have experience... that get to hear some things. /.../ The friends... they just think that you're insane and that it can't be right, you know.

Since the people he mostly meets, medical professionals, enforce a behaviour that alienates his other relationships, he has had to adapt his behaviour in order to maintain the friendships that he values.

4.3   The Contradiction of Trust

From the analysis emerged a contradiction in how people diagnosed with schizophrenia trust others. Due to their dependence on others, people diagnosed with schizophrenia have to place a great deal of trust in the people they are dependent on. However, people diagnosed with schizophrenia often have misplaced suspicions, and can sometimes be paranoid. Jack's mother describes how he does not trust the staff at his group home:

> He experienced chest pains he told me one morning last week or a fortnight ago... And he hadn't said anything to the staff. He doesn't have that much confidence in them.

At the same time, she describes her son as being too trusting of strangers:

> He thinks good of people and... he gets robbed. That's why he doesn't have an ATM card anymore. /.../ They emptied it for him. So he is a bit unsuspecting- has become after the illness.

The other stakeholders describe similar behaviours in their children or patients. Dani's mother says that her daughter always wants to be able to keep an eye on any visitors, even when it is her mother. Brock's father describes his son as being kind to the verge of wanting to buy friends with gifts. Angela tells us of how she has repeatedly been robbed of large sums of money.

People diagnosed with schizophrenia are a group of people vulnerable to fraud and theft, yet one symptom of schizophrenia is paranoia, as Jack's mother describes:

He called my house... and accused me of having started the second world war /.../ and he couldn't eat because the food was poisoned...

Trust and distrust appears to be misplaced and irrational. Yet people diagnosed with schizophrenia have to rely on and trust other people to help them to manage their everyday lives. Dani's mother describes it as:

They should actually have a real personal assistant all the time, really.

Irrational fear also affects digital technology acceptance and use. Jack's mother describes how she has to take care of his finances because he refuses to own as much as an ATM card. He flushed his mobile phone down the toilet due to his fear of technology. Similarly, Scott says that he has never dared use Facebook because he is afraid that everyone in the world will see his information.

Furthermore, there are also risks with technology use. Carl's mother describes how her son used online information to convince himself of not taking his medication:

At one point in the period of his illness he found some contacts online, or information, and he used that to show me, "Look here, this is the way it is, this is what they are putting me through." And it got worse from that.

Some stakeholders describe negative consequences like posting rants online during a psychosis for everyone to see, and assistant nurse Chris describes how one of his outpatients had their credit card emptied while playing an online game. This kind of naïve use, combined with being vulnerable to fraud and theft, can thus cause an increase of fear of digital technology, and reduce its use.

4.4   The Counteracting Improvement Behaviour

The results further indicate that people diagnosed with schizophrenia can behave in ways that counteract their improvement. The participants for instance describe avoiding strategies to cope with the illness. Jack's mother says about Jack:

He had this in himself that he runs- or he used to run away.

Frank also describes an avoiding behaviour. He found it easier to live on the streets than to be medically treated because there he could flee from his problems. He eventually realised that he could not run away from the voices.

Another behaviour that the participants describe is an isolating behaviour. Medical professional Alfred says that people with psychoses often tend to isolate themselves, and Dani's mother describes her daughter as exhibiting both avoiding and isolating behaviours:

*And it's not easy to help her, because she doesn't want to either. "I have to cancel," she says.
"I can't." /.../ She just isolates herself in the apartment.*

The stakeholders describe employment as particularly important for improvement.
Carl's mother believes her son's job to be one of the main reasons why he is better, and
psychiatric nurse Benjamin expresses that access to meaningful employment would be
key in treatment:

*... there are sometimes more medical solutions that there need to be. If you would have a
meaningful occupation and something that distracts you from the symptoms of your illness, I
think there would be a lessened need for medication compared to what is being prescribed
today.*

There is a constant struggle to maintain a balance in life. Having schizophrenia
means losing normality, and the illness is often described as going through periods.
David describes himself as currently going through a rough period:

*I am in a period when I don't think it's fun to do things and... /.../ I'm in a difficult period that is
maybe quite hard to get out of too.*

He describes his days as being spent mostly in bed. In contrast, he describes a
period when he felt better:

*I got out of bed at a normal time like... around 8 then... and then I had chores and stuff. I was
on my father's computer a lot... and downloaded music...*

In contrast, Angela has the opposite problem of tending to do too much:

*And then I worked out and went swimming on the same day, on Mondays, and Tuesdays, and
Wednesdays, and Fridays and Saturdays. /.../ But my body spoke up, because I did too much, so
I became ill instead.*

Alfred, one of the medical professionals, describes this lack of balance as being
common among people diagnosed with schizophrenia:

*Those basal functions are somehow affected in this. Either you fall behind or you sort of...
overdo it in some way. That you stodge and... things like that. The normal sort of goes away.*

Illness awareness also affects ability to cope and ability to maintain a meaningful
everyday life. Several of the stakeholders describe how their children or patients do not
want treatment simply because they do not think of themselves as ill. In order to
improve, it is important to maintain a balance. The avoiding coping strategies and
isolating behaviours that are exhibited by people diagnosed with schizophrenia thus
directly counteract the activities that would help them improve their lives.

5   Discussion

This paper has uncovered wickedness of the design context when designing digital
services for people diagnosed with schizophrenia. Four wicked problems in the design
context have been identified. Hereby, this paper demonstrates the viability of a
grounded approach to uncover wickedness of design contexts with the intent to gain

contextual awareness in complex and sensitive design contexts. In this section, the uncovered wickedness will be discussed along with the approach to uncover them.

The contextual wickedness that this paper has explored consists of struggles between dichotomies, or opposite forces, such as dependence versus independence. This is an important part in the discovery of how to design e-health services for people diagnosed with schizophrenia. As Buchanan [27] explains, wicked problems stem from the nature of the design subject; wicked problems are wicked because design implies discovery.

The wicked problems uncovered in this study are interrelated, and not mutually exclusive. As any wicked problems, they are indefinable, untestable, and unique to the context [15]. For example, the *struggle of dependence* and the *contradiction of trust* are related in that dependence causes a need to trust. If people diagnosed with schizophrenia had not been dependent on others, they would not be contradictorily trusting. However, it is equally possible that if the contradiction of trust had not existed, there would not be a struggle of dependence. As such, the wickedness of this context is not a single problem, but a chain of interrelated complexities that together make up the wickedness of the design context.

In this case, any designed artefact or outcome of a design process would have to deal with the contextual wickedness. Goldkuhl [40] argues that one part of a design theory is empirical grounding, which should answer whether the outcome is successful in practice and if it leads to its desired consequences. To answer this, we need to understand what would make an outcome successful, and its desired consequences; the first step in understanding this is to empirically study the context.

This paper shows that grounded theory is a viable approach for gaining understanding of wickedness in a design context. In this case, neither the interrelatedness of the nature of the wicked problems, nor their contradictory nature emerged from the literature. In IS, grounded theory is used to analyse phenomena from a process or context perspective [36, 41]. The rigidity of the method allowed for a structured analysis that led to uncovering the contradiction and complexities that cause the wickedness in this design context.

Furthermore, it was not only considered necessary to ground the study of the design context in empirical data from a theory-creating perspective, but also from an ethical perspective. Often people who are considered vulnerable, such as people with mental illness, are excluded from research due to the difficulties of involving them [42], yet they may still want to participate despite the challenges [43]. Similarly, both the stakeholders and the people who were diagnosed with schizophrenia who participated in this study expressed that their participation was important to them. The stakeholders further highlighted that there is a great need for anything that can help their children or patients. As a result, when a subject like this is not only rarely studied in IS research, but users are often excluded from the research, the ethical value of being grounded in the empirical data is high.

As a final reflection, the grounded approach used in this study was both helpful and led to the uncovering of many important insights that have expanded the understanding of the design context when designing digital services for people diagnosed with schizophrenia. The approach can be useful in contexts beyond this study; as the approach is grounded in the perspectives of the participants, and the methods for data collection primarily consists of dialogue, it is transferable to other complex and unexplored design contexts. It would seem particularly suitable in health-related contexts where sensitivity is high and contextual understanding is paramount.

The understanding of wickedness in design contexts that has been gained from this study can be used to support both the design process and design of e-health systems. For example, the *contradiction of trust* and the *contradiction of social interaction* indicate that the e-health service would need to enforce healthy social interaction and moderating the quality of the information, while at the same time creating the ability for the users to trust both the system and the other users. User participation in the design process is made more difficult by the *struggle of dependence* and the *contradiction of social interaction*, as users would have to both express their opinions and participate in the social process of designing with others.

6 Conclusion

This paper intended to answer the question: *how can the wickedness of the design context when designing digital services for people diagnosed with schizophrenia be understood?* From a grounded theory analysis of stakeholder interviews and focus group interviews with people diagnosed with schizophrenia the contexts is described as consisting of four wicked problems: the struggle of dependence, the contradiction of social interaction, the contradiction of trust and the counteracting improvement behaviour. These problems are not mutually exclusive, but together make up the complexity of the design context.

In addition to the description of the wickedness of the design context, this paper also contributes with a viable approach for studying complex design contexts of this kind. The grounded theory analysis that was used was valuable for capturing and describing the complexities of the context.

Since the context is particularly complex, there is a continuous need for research. In order to continue the design of e-health systems for people diagnosed with schizophrenia, it will be important to continuously include users throughout the design process. But there is also more research needed on how to involve people diagnosed with schizophrenia in design, and how to begin to tackle the wickedness that has been described here.

Acknowledgements. I would like to thank Henrika Jormfeldt and Magnus Bergquist for their contributions to the presented research. I would also like to thank the reviewers and all colleagues who have taken the time to comment on the paper. Last, but not least, I would like to thank the participants for their invaluable input, and for giving their time and energy to help.

References

1. Iivari, J., Isomäki, H., Pekkola, S.: The user—the great unknown of systems development: reasons, forms, challenges, experiences and intellectual contributions of user involvement. Inf. Syst. J. **20**, 109–117 (2010)

2. Tokar, O., Batoroev, K.: Identifying opportunities for future design research for mHealth for mental health. In: Proceedings of ECIS 2016, pp. Paper 65 (2016)
3. Aardoom, J.J., Dingemans, A.E., Van Furth, E.F.: E-health interventions for eating disorders: emerging findings, issues, and opportunities. Curr. Psychiatry Rep. 18, 1–8 (2016)
4. Kowatsch, T., Maass, W., Pletikosa Cvijikj, I., Büchter, D., Brogle, B., Dintheer, A., Wiegand, D., Durrer-Schutz, D., Xu, R., Schutz, Y.: Design of a health information system enhancing the performance of obesity expert and children teams. In: Proceedings of ECIS 2014 (2014)
5. Hevner, A.R., March, S.T., Park, J., Ram, S.: Design science in information systems research. MISQ 28, 75–105 (2004)
6. Arias, E., Eden, H., Fischer, G., Gorman, A., Scharff, E.: Transcending the individual human mind—creating shared understanding through collaborative design. ACM Trans. Comput. Hum. Interact. (TOCHI) 7, 84–113 (2000)
7. Gregor, S., Hevner, A.R.: Positioning and presenting design science research for maximum impact. MISQ 37, 337–356 (2013)
8. Mueser, K.T., McGurk, S.R.: Schizophrenia. Lancet 363, 2063–2072 (2004)
9. Frangou, S.: Schizophrenia. Medicine 36, 405–409 (2008)
10. Andreasen, N.C.: Schizophrenia: the fundamental questions. Brain Res. Rev. 31, 106–112 (2000)
11. Schuldberg, D.: Six subclinical spectrum traits in normal creativity. Creat. Res. J. 13, 5–16 (2001)
12. Couture, S.M., Penn, D.L., Roberts, D.L.: The functional significance of social cognition in schizophrenia: a review. Schizophr. Bull. 32, S44–S63 (2006)
13. Davidson, L., Shahar, G., Stayner, D.A., Chinman, M.J., Rakfeldt, J., Tebes, J.K.: Supported socialization for people with psychiatric disabilities: lessons from a randomized controlled trial. J. Commun. Psychol. 32, 453–477 (2004)
14. Campellone, T.R., Caponigro, J.M., Kring, A.M.: The power to resist: the relationship between power, stigma, and negative symptoms in schizophrenia. Psychiatry Res. 215, 280–285 (2014)
15. Rittel, H.W., Webber, M.M.: Dilemmas in a general theory of planning. Policy Sci. 4, 155–169 (1973)
16. Zimmerman, J., Forlizzi, J., Evenson, S.: Research through design as a method for interaction design research in HCI. In: Proceedings of CHI, pp. 493–502. ACM (2007)
17. Wilder-Willis, K.E., Shear, P.K., Steffen, J.J., Borkin, J.: The relationship between cognitive dysfunction and coping abilities in schizophrenia. Schizophr. Res. 55, 259–267 (2002)
18. Castelein, S., Bruggeman, R., Davidson, L., van der Gaag, M.: Creating a supportive environment: peer support groups for psychotic disorders. Schizophr. Bull. 41, 1211–1213 (2015)
19. Davidson, L., Chinman, M., Kloos, B., Weingarten, R., Stayner, D., Tebes, J.K.: Peer support among individuals with severe mental illness: a review of the evidence. Clin. Psychol. Sci. Pract. 6, 165–187 (1999)
20. Lloyd-Evans, B., Mayo-Wilson, E., Harrison, B., Istead, H., Brown, E., Pilling, S., Johnson, S., Kendall, T.: A systematic review and meta-analysis of randomised controlled trials of peer support for people with severe mental illness. BMC Psychiatry 14, 1 (2014)
21. Castelein, S., Bruggeman, R., Van Busschbach, J.T., Van Der Gaag, M., Stant, A., Knegtering, H., Wiersma, D.: The effectiveness of peer support groups in psychosis: a randomized controlled trial. Acta Psychiatr. Scand. 118, 64–72 (2008)
22. Chinman, M., George, P., Dougherty, R.H., Daniels, A.S., Ghose, S.S., Swift, A., Delphin-Rittmon, M.E.: Peer support services for individuals with serious mental illnesses: assessing the evidence. Psychiatr. Serv. 65, 429–441 (2014)

23. Naslund, J.A., Grande, S.W., Aschbrenner, K.A., Elwyn, G.: Naturally occurring peer support through social media: the experiences of individuals with severe mental illness using YouTube. PLoS ONE **9**, e110171 (2014)
24. Gowen, K., Deschaine, M., Gruttadara, D., Markey, D.: Young adults with mental health conditions and social networking websites: seeking tools to build community. Psychiatr. Rehabil. J. **35**, 245 (2012)
25. Farrell, R., Hooker, C.: Design, science and wicked problems. Des. Stud. **34**, 681–705 (2013)
26. Nelson, H.G., Stolterman, E.: The Design Way: Intentional Change in an Unpredictable World: Foundations and Fundamentals of Design Competence. Educational Technology, Englewood Cliffs (2003)
27. Buchanan, R.: Wicked problems in design thinking. Des. Issues **8**, 5–21 (1992)
28. Hawryszkiewycz, I.: Visualizations for addressing wicked problems using design thinking. In: Proceedings of European Conference on Information Systems 2014 (2014)
29. Alvesson, M., Kärreman, D.: Constructing mystery: empirical matters in theory development. Acad. Manag. Rev. **32**, 1265–1281 (2007)
30. Hong, W., Chan, F.K., Thong, J.Y., Chasalow, L.C., Dhillon, G.: A framework and guidelines for context-specific theorizing in information systems research. Inf. Syst. Res. **25**, 111–136 (2013)
31. Charmaz, K.: Constructing grounded theory: a practical guide through qualitative research. Sage Publications Ltd, London (2006)
32. Glaser, B.G., Strauss, A.L.: Discovery of grounded theory. Sociology Press, Mill Valley (1967)
33. Gregory, R.: Design science research and the grounded theory method: characteristics, differences, and complementary uses. In: Proceedings of ECIS 2010, pp. Paper 44 (2010)
34. Hughes, J., Jones, S.: Reflections on the use of grounded theory in interpretive information systems research. In: Proceedings of ECIS 2003, pp. Paper 62 (2003)
35. Urquhart, C., Fernandez, W.: Grounded theory method: the researcher as blank slate and other myths. In: Proceedings of ICIS 2006, pp. Paper 31 (2006)
36. Urquhart, C.: An encounter with grounded theory: tackling the practical and philosophical issues. In: Qualitative Research in IS: Issues and Trends, pp. 104–140 (2000)
37. Melling, B., Houguet-Pincham, T.: Online peer support for individuals with depression: A summary of current research and future considerations. Psychiatr. Rehabil. J. **34**, 252 (2011)
38. Webb, M., Burns, J., Collin, P.: Providing online support for young people with mental health difficulties: challenges and opportunities explored. Early Interv. Psychiatry **2**, 108–113 (2008)
39. Lederman, R., Wadley, G., Gleeson, J., Alvarez-Jimenez, M.: Using on-line technologies to identify and track early warning signs of psychosis. In: Proceedings of the 21st European Conference on Information Systems—Research in Progress, pp. Paper 1 (2013)
40. Goldkuhl, G.: Design theories in information systems—a need for multi-grounding. J. Inf. Technol. Theory Appl. **6**, 59 (2004)
41. Myers, M.D.: Qualitative research in information systems. Manag. Inf. Syst. Q **21**, 241–242 (1997)
42. Liamputtong, P.: Researching the vulnerable: a guide to sensitive research methods. Sage, London (2006)
43. Usher, K., Holmes, C.: Ethical aspects of phenomenological research with mentally ill people. Nurs. Ethics **4**, 49–56 (1997)

The 'Holy Grail' of Interoperability of Health Information Systems: Challenges and Implications

Line Silsand$^{(\boxtimes)}$

Norwegian Centre for E-Health Research, Tromsø, Norway
line.silsand@ehealthresearch.no

Abstract. Enabling integration between heterogeneous health information systems (IS) across different institutions is attracting growing interest from national and regional governments. "Interoperability of health information systems" is an overall goal to strive for. This empirical paper addresses the challenges of integrating heterogeneous health information systems with the goal of achieving semantic interoperability of patient information within and between all hospitals in a health region. The paper describes a complex development and integration process, and looks into a promising strategy of using openEHR archetypes as an architecture to reach the goal of interoperability.

Keywords: Health information systems · Integration · Interoperability · Healthcare processes

1 Introduction

Today, people have more mobility and longer lives, while healthcare services are increasingly shared between care providers and different jurisdictions. In addition, healthcare institutions tend to combine different information technologies, modules or subsystems, following a best-of-breed approach. Accordingly, integration of information systems (IS) is essential to support shared care and to provide consistent care to individuals [1–3].

Health IS and technologies have the potential to support a smart, sustainable and consistent healthcare service, in which accessibility, efficiency and effectiveness are key concepts. Enabling integration between heterogeneous health information systems (IS) across different institutions is attracting growing interest from national and regional governments; "interoperability of EPRs" is an overall goal to strive for [4, 5]. However, to integrate fragmented portfolios of health IS in such a way that communication and clinical information used for healthcare delivery will improve, address many different issues [9, 13, 20].

First, integration of health information systems involves complex processes due to diverging needs from healthcare practitioners, heterogeneous groups of patients, and diverse procedures and approaches to medical treatment and care. Accordingly, it is important to understand the characteristics of the healthcare processes the systems are

© Springer International Publishing AG 2017
S. Stigberg et al. (Eds.): SCIS 2017, LNBIP 294, pp. 140–154, 2017.
DOI: 10.1007/978-3-319-64695-4_11

going to support. Second, it is important to understand the concept of interoperability, in which smart and consistent healthcare services address a need for information shared by systems to be understood and processed by the receiving system (semantic interoperability). This is a premise for advanced process and decision support.

Prior studies have explored processes of IT integration in the context of healthcare and identified factors facilitating successful processes, for example, integration of new systems with existing work processes or necessary reorganization of clinical as well as organizational workflows when implementing a new EPR [6–8]. This paper addresses a different empirical situation: the challenges of integrating heterogeneous health ISs with a goal of achieving semantic interoperability of patient information within and between all hospitals in a region. Empirically, this study reports from a large-scale regional project to replace an existing, largely free-text-based electronic patient record (EPR) with a new semantically interoperable EPR base on the openEHR approach, and simultaneously integrating a new electronic charting and medication (ECM) system with the EPR in change. The project started in 2011, and took place in the Northern Norway Health Region.

Against this backdrop, the following research question is posed: *What are the key challenges when integrating heterogeneous health ISs to enable semantic interoperability?*

To conceptualize the dynamics of how various healthcare professionals, activities, stakeholders, and technology are interwoven during the integration process, the study draws on the notion of information infrastructure (II). II literature addresses the socio-technical challenges of realizing large-scale technological systems, and is relevant for analyzing the regional integration process [9–12]. In doing so, the study contributes with important empirical insights about introducing vendor-independent clinical information models [15], exemplified by the openEHR archetypes, as an approach to realizing the goal of semantic interoperability within and between heterogeneous health ISs on a regional scale.

The rest of the paper is organized as follows: Sect. 2 describes the theoretical framework for this paper. Section 3 briefly introduces the empirical setting and reflects on methodological issues. Section 4 presents the case and elaborates on important steps of the evolving development and integration process. In Sect. 5, the case is discussed in relation to the chosen theoretical framework, followed by Sect. 6, with the concluding remarks.

2 Theory

Integration of health ISs are complex processes due to the different needs of healthcare practitioners, different patients' needs, and diverse procedures and approaches to medical treatment and care. Integration of heterogeneous health ISs in such a way that communication and clinical information used to support these complex processes of healthcare delivery will be improved addresses various issues [9, 13, 20]. First, it is important to have a common understanding of what characterizes the healthcare processes the systems are going to support [13].

2.1   The Characteristics of Healthcare Processes

In Lenz and Reichert [13], healthcare processes are characterized as a cooperation of different organizational units and medical disciplines, which depend heavily on both information and knowledge management. They have identified different levels of process support in healthcare, and distinguished between organizational processes and the medical treatment process. In short, the organizational process patterns help to coordinate collaborating clinical personnel and organizational units (e.g., handling of a medical order and result reporting), and the medical treatment processes are linked to the patient.

In hospitals, organizational tasks often burden clinical personnel. For example, surgery planning procedures – like the empirical case – have to be planned and prepared, including scheduling appointments with different service providers, in-house transportation of patients, arranging visits of physicians from different departments, while reports need to be written, transmitted, and evaluated. If information is missing, the surgery planning procedure may become impossible to perform; preparations may be omitted, or a preparatory procedure may have to be postponed or canceled or may require latency time. Integrated process support, information management, and knowledge management on different levels are needed. The current situation of heterogeneous healthcare ISs, where patient information is often spread over different unintegrated applications, does not meet these requirements [13].

However, in recent years a number of integration and interoperability standards have emerged, which provide the basis for health ISs to support organizational and medical treatment processes in healthcare.

2.2   The Concept of Interoperability

Interoperability in health information systems is often referred to as the 'holy grail', in which the goal is to make clinical information available across different healthcare institution to provide a smart, sustainable and consistent healthcare service [1, 14]. Accordingly, it is important to understand the concept of interoperability, and in this paper, the review of HL7's EHR Interoperability Work Group is used to frame the concept [14].

Technical interoperability is the ability of two or more systems to exchange information so that it is readable by the receiver, but cannot be further processed into semantic equivalents by software.

Semantic interoperability is the ability to share information between two or several systems so that the meaning of the exchanged information is understood in exactly the same way by both systems and can be processed by the receiving system.

Process or social interoperability is a requirement for successful integration of computer systems into work settings. It describes the methods and strategies for optimal integration of computer-supported communication of clinical information into an actual work setting [14].

Successful process interoperability relies on successful technical and semantic interoperability because the preferred information must be successfully transmitted (technical interoperability) and properly understood (semantic interoperability).

A promising strategy for dealing with the challenges of supporting inter-organizational healthcare processes involves health ISs conforming to a vendor-independent health computing platform architecture, in this paper exemplified by the openEHR approach [15].

The openEHR approach separates the technical design of the system from detailed organizational and clinical issues. A standardized reference model represents the first level, which is a generic model for all kinds of health information. For example, a blood result from the laboratory would be stored in the same general-purpose data structure. The second level is represented by openEHR archetypes, in terms of reusable, formal definitions of domain level information. Archetypes are not part of the software or database of a system. An archetype represents a description of all the information a clinician might need about a clinical concept – a maximum definition. For instance, a blood pressure (BP) measurement is traditionally represented by systolic and diastolic pressure. As an archetype, the BP is accompanied by data describing the context of measurement such as who (who measured the BP), how (which type of equipment was used, did the patient rest/sit/stand, where on the patient's body (left/right arm or leg), and when (related to date and time of day). Accordingly, it is important that clinicians are involved in creating the knowledge inherent in archetypes, and a fundamental aim of the openEHR approach is to engage clinicians in the archetype design [16, 17]. The openEHR's approach offers a high degree of advanced semantic interoperability because the clinical and other domain semantics are defined above the software and database schema level, in which archetypes are an important means to achieve semantic interoperability between the different health ISs [17–19].

Accordingly, interoperability of health ISs is closely related to the healthcare context the systems are going to support. The goal of making clinical information available between different health ISs and across different healthcare institution addresses a need for a relationship between systems and human factors.

2.3   Information Infrastructures

To conceptualize the relationship between systems and human factors, the study draws on the notion of Information Infrastructures (II). II literature addresses the socio-technical challenges of realizing large-scale technological systems, and is relevant for analyzing the empirical case of integrating health ISs into a common health information infrastructure [9–12, 20].

The following characteristics describe an II [21–23]:

- Shared, by the members of a community, including vendors, users and staff
- Evolving, not "designed", but evolves continually, as growth and innovation expand it
- Open, based on the principle that there is no limit on the number of users
- Standardized, rests on standards, which allow scaling and interoperability

- Heterogeneous, consists of different elements such as technology, users, organizations, in large networks
- Installed base, such structures are seldom created from scratch, but grow from existing practices and infrastructures.

Accordingly, these systems are never seen as standalone entities, but are integrated with other information systems and communication technologies, and with non-technical elements [11, 20, 23]. With the rise in the fragmented portfolio of health ISs used in and between different hospitals across wide geographical distances, both the need for common standards and the need for situated, tailorable and flexible technologies grow stronger.

Star and Ruhleder [12] offer a socio-technical and relational understanding around the following dimensions of when an II emerges:

- Embeddedness; an II is "sunk" into, inside of, other structures, social arrangements and technologies.
- Transparency; II is transparent to use.
- Reach or scope; II has reach beyond a single event or one-site practice.
- Learned as part of membership.
- Links with conventions of practice.
- Embodiment of standards.
- Built on an installed base.
- Becomes visible upon breakdown.

Building II takes time, and all elements are connected – and in addition, the II has to adapt to new requirements as time passes. Accordingly, an II occurs when the tension between local customized use on the one hand and the need for standards and continuity (global) on the other hand is resolved.

Consequently, analyses of II need to take into account a broad range of socio-technical issues shaping the implementation or integration process, as the nature of an II is beyond a single event or one-site practice [11, 12, 20, 21, 23].

3   Method

3.1   Research Site

The paper reports from a large-scale ICT project initiated in 2011 in the Northern Norway Health Region, in which the Regional Health Authority decided to invest in new clinical ICT systems for all the 11 hospitals in the region. The Northern Norway Regional Health Authority is responsible for all 11 public hospitals, which have approximately 12,500 employees altogether. The FIKS program[1] was established with a budget of EUR 90 million for the period 2012–2016, and was one of the most ambitious healthcare-related ICT projects in Norway.

---

[1] A Norwegian acronym, in English "Common Deployment of Clinical Systems".

A key aim of the procurement was to replace an existing, largely free-text-based EPR with a semantically interoperable EPR enabling advanced process and decision support within and between the hospitals in the region. An additional aim was to integrate a new electronic charting and medication (ECM) system with the EPR in change. DIPS ASA was the vendor for the existing EPR, and was chosen as the principal vendor for the new EPR system as well. The vendor currently holds approximately 86% of the hospital-based EPR market in Norway. In 2011, the vendor decided to use the openEHR architecture for its future electronic medical system portfolio. This decision was in line with the reports from the Norwegian National ICT Health Trust[2], which explored the use of vendor-independent standardized clinical information models and the openEHR archetype as a starting point for national interoperability standards [24, 25].

The reports concluded that separating the clinical information models from the systems' internal data models was a preferred approach to enable sharing and reuse of clinical information within the healthcare domain independent of the current hetero-geneous portfolio of health ISs. The recommendation required development of national vendor-independent standardized clinical information models, but no official resolution was made concerning the openEHR archetypes as a preferred approach [1, 2].

3.2   Research Approach

The study is an interpretive case study positioned within the constructive paradigm, aimed to provide insight about the key mechanisms at play when developing and integrating heterogeneous health information systems [26, 27]. The epistemological belief in interpretive research emphasizes the understanding of social processes by getting involved inside the world of those generating them, and not by hypothetical deductions or predefined variables [28].

'Growing' an information infrastructure is a time-consuming process that tends to include many different phases in its evolution, and call for research approaches that encompass both short-time dynamics and longer-term evolutions [29]. The data have been collected from the initial start of the FIKS program in January 2012 and through different phases of the projects to January 2017. The author has collected the empirical data by becoming involved in the development process through different settings such as user-designer workshops, observing healthcare personnel, video-conference meet-ings, participant observation at the vendor's site, formal and informal discussions with project members, and formal semi-structured interviews. A digital voice recorder was used during the interviews, and the interviews were transcribed after recording. In addition, the author explored documents and studies of reports from the ongoing program, and reports from National ICT on ICT architecture and archetype strategy (Table 1).

---

[2] The National ICT Health Trust is responsible for coordinating ICT-related initiatives in the specialized health care services. It is a central agent in bringing about and realizing national efforts and strategies for ICT. The mandate is given by the Regional Health Authorities.

Table 1. Data collection.

Activities	Source and extent
Participatory observation	Informal meetings, workshops (EPR/ECM), observing healthcare personnel and developers (DIPS) at work, trials and pilot tests, seminars on archetype strategy. In total 470 h
Interviews	31 semi-structured interviews of healthcare personnel, developers and representatives from DIPS, archetype editors, project managers (FIKS). Each lasted 45–90 min
Document studies	Project documents (FIKS), official reports from National ICT on ICT architecture and archetype strategy, minutes from steering group and project meetings
Informal talks	FIKS management, vendor (EPR/ECM), regional ICT management, product manager at vendor (EPR), Healthcare personnel involved in the projects

The interpretive research approach calls for detailed case descriptions covering the development and integration process, which allow the readers to gain insight in the empirical field, followed by an analysis of the data for potential analytical themes guided by the chosen theoretical framework (Sect. 2). The analysis is presented as the four key challenges in Sect. 4 – discussion. However, the philosophical perspective implies considering the entire data collection in an iterative and interpretive process (the hermeneutic circle), and accordingly the analysis has been a back-and-forth process between collected data, case descriptions, and the use of relevant literature emphasizing the interoperability in complex healthcare processes and the concepts of information infrastructure. The author has discussed the data, case description, and analysis with other members of the IS research community in healthcare. To improve the understanding of the empirical case, the data were continuously presented and discussed in informal meetings with members of the FIKS program, the National Administration Office of Archetypes (NRUA), and healthcare personnel involved [4, 26].

The first author has worked as a nurse at a university hospital for several years. Accordingly, the empirical data is gathered from an "insider perspective" based on the knowledge of the healthcare field.

4   Case

4.1   The New EPR Required Standardized C

The overall goal of investing in a new semantic interoperable EPR was to improve the quality of treatment and care by improving the availability and accessibility of all relevant patient information regardless of where, when and by whom the information was created. This would form the basis for advanced process and decision support of clinical treatment processes in general and specific standardized patient pathways.

> *"The FIKS program is a major investment in the Northern Norway Health Region, and it's based on the paradigm shift where EPR systems primarily played a role as a tool for documentation of treatment, results, and clinical assessments, over to look at the systems as process*

supporting tools that maintain the clinical information process - which in turn will support the clinical workflow processes".
(Manager, the Northern Norway Health Region)

The first software module developed during the EPR project was made for supporting the surgery planning process. The idea was that easier access to relevant clinical information would improve the clinical decision-making and overall quality and safety for surgery patients. Moreover, the clinicians would spend less time looking up necessary information about the patient – and gain more time to do clinical work.

However, the new semantically interoperable EPR required standardized clinical information models – so-called archetypes, which were going to be developed by the user community, in accordance with the openEHR approach. As mentioned, the official resolution to use openEHR archetypes as standardized clinical information models on a regional or national level was not carried out, and the necessary repository of agreed-on archetypes was not established. Consequently, this situation was demanding for the vendor, but the Regional Health Authority also played a role in this situation because the openEHR framework encourages clinical communities to be in charge of modeling archetypes. However, the vendor was the principal EPR vendor in three of four health regions in Norway, and the responsibility to contribute to the archetype development process was in that sense beyond the scope of the Northern Norway Health Region. This was a complex situation, which culminated in establishing the national consensus-based repository of archetypes – the Norwegian Clinical Knowledge Manager (CKM) – but still, no official resolution was made to use the openEHR archetypes as national clinical information models.

4.2   National Repository of Standardized Clinical Information Models

In 2013 the National Administration Office of Archetypes (NRUA) was launched, aimed at coordinating the development of archetypes in Norway, both handling the national consensus process of reviewing and approving the clinical information models to ensure a high quality and a high degree of interoperability. To design optimal clinical information models, it was necessary to give the clinicians a key role in both developing and approving the archetypes. The clinicians should propose needs of clinical information to be modeled as archetypes and participate in the consensus process by using a web-based tool for distributed collaboration across the country. Nevertheless, the distributed collaboration also addressed a need for recruiting clinicians from different specialties and training them to use the web-based tool to participate in the consensus process. Even though the national repository of archetypes was established, filling the repository moved slowly due to challenges with recruiting the necessary clinicians, and NRUA had only three part-time employees to facilitate the work. In April 2017, the Norwegian CKM inherited 51 approved archetypes and approximately more than 90 were in process – but the slow progression of filling the repository during 2013-2014 influenced the progression of the semantic interoperable EPR system.

"Unless we get a repository of archetypes that we can process – making sharing and reuse of clinical information possible, the semantic interoperable EPRs are nothing but a good idea" (manager, DIPS).

4.3   Clinical Use - Transcending the Interdependency of Other Health Information Systems

In April 2016, a surgery planning module from the vendor's new EPR was ready for clinical use. The existing clinical workflow and the new surgery planning tool were adjusted to each other, and formalized into new routines. Accordingly, clinical roles and responsibilities cohered with filling in different documents (Fig. 1) - the surgery decision note (1), aesthetic pre-operative assessment (2) and the surgeon's assessment notes (3). The surgery planning process was initiated by a physician when assessing a patient in the out-patient clinic. If the assessment led to a decision on surgery, then the surgery decision note was filled in and completed, and became the trigger for the other two documents to be created as the next steps of the surgery planning process.

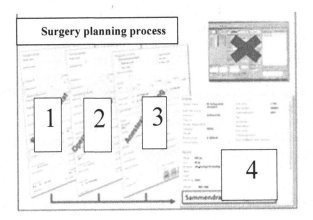

Fig. 1. Reuse of clinical information triggers follow-up activities

Parts of the clinical information within these documents were based on archetypes that could be extracted and reused between the documents, and compiled into a section of the summary document (4) to be used by surgery nurses in the surgery theatre. In addition, the surgery decision note gave instructions to the secretaries to allocate time for surgery to the patient. Nevertheless, to be able to fill in and complete the surgery decision note, the physician needed an overview of the patient's clinical condition. To obtain this, the physician collected clinical information from several different information systems e.g. radiology, laboratory, different specialized clinical subsystems, and the Medical Charting system. The latter was a paper-based system with information about the patient's medication and different clinical variables such as temperature, pulse, and blood pressure measurements.

The initial use of the surgery planning module revealed challenges related to the technical integrations between the existing free-text based EPR and the new archetype-based EPR. For example, if the physician needed information from documents recorded in the "old" EPR while filling in the surgery decision note – then the documents in the "old" system could not be uploaded on the screen while the physician was simultaneously filling in the surgery decision note in the new EPR. Moreover, filling in the surgery decision note depended on the necessity of clinical information from other health ISs as well – and, in particular, information from the existing paper-based Medical Charting system. In addition, there were unresolved issues related to the reuse of archetypes between the surgery planning documents. The challenges influenced the existing clinical workflow and did not optimize the overall quality of the surgery planning process. Two months after the initial implementation, the surgery planning module was "put on ice".

4.4 The New Electronic Charting and Medication Systems

As mentioned, the FIKS project embraced the development, customization, and implementation of a new Electronic Charting and Medication (ECM) system, which was going to be an integrated part of the new EPR. In December 2014, the procurement of the ECM was announced, and "MetaVision" was going to substitute the existing paper-based charting and medication system in all the hospitals. The new ECM system offered all necessary functionality to support all clinical settings, e.g. intensive care, out-patient consultations, and general in-patient wards. In addition, the ECM system offered automatic data capture, and accordingly clinical process and decision support based on the system's inherited clinical information models.

"The Electronic Charting and Medication system will be an integrated and comprehensive solution that can be applied across organizational and professional boundaries. The ECM will provide relevant documentation of a patient's clinical condition and treatment given, functionality for continuous medication within and between different wards as well as different hospitals – and accordingly provide advanced decision support to the clinicians"
(Project manager, ECM project)

The ECM project evolved fast and the implementation was planned to start during autumn 2017. The customization was arranged through workshops with engaged clinicians from different medical specialties and geographical locations in the region. During the customization process, a significant concern was raised by the clinicians involved:

"How to agree on which system to record the different clinical variables [Measurements, examinations, blood tests, medication, etc.] and descriptive information – should we use the ECM or the EPR, or are we supposed to record the same information in both systems, like we more or less do now [the paper-based charting and medication systems and the EPR]?"
(Group of clinicians, ECM project workshops).

Accordingly, the ECM addressed a new interdependency in reaching the goal of availability and accessibility of all relevant patient information because the two systems needed to share clinical data in a form that both systems could understand and process (Fig. 2).

4.5 Puzzling the Interdependencies

In January 2016, a new subproject "under the FIKS program's umbrella" was launched, the Regional Patient Pathway project. The goal of the new subproject was to form

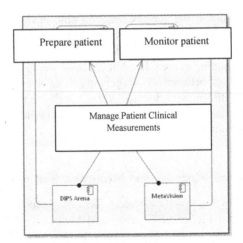

Fig. 2. Examples of clinical information necessary in EPR and/or ECM

appropriate interactions between the EPR and the ECM to enable the overall goal of availability and accessibility of all relevant patient information - regardless of where the information was created and recorded. The project manager stated:

"We (the Regional Patient Pathway project) are going to define the interaction between the Electronic Charting and Medication system and the Electronic Patient Record system in the Region. The interaction between these two systems will support the clinicians in making clinical decisions and planning treatment and care tailored for each patient. The point of departure for the interaction is the clinical workflow in the hospitals".

However, the Patient Pathway project was well aware that integrating the systems was not a straightforward process. First – the existing EPR was primarily a free-text based system, second – the new EPR was based on openEHR archetypes and their clinical information model, and third – the ECM system used standardized clinical information model hard-coded into its software and database model.

However, the first step of integrating the systems was done in close collaboration with the Regional Health Authority's ICT department. The project and the ICT department mapped the present clinical workflow and the interaction with different health information systems, both electronic and paper-based, to get hold of necessary clinical information during the different steps in the chosen patient pathway (Hip Prosthesis). The goal was to harmonize the different systems and overlapping func-tionalities, to avoid uncontrolled data redundancy and double documentation of similar information because of the heterogeneous health ISs. Nevertheless, with systems using different information models – the new EPR processing openEHR archetypes and the ECM system with clinical information hard-coded into its software and database model – the Regional goal of integrating the EPR and the ECM into a semantically inter-operable health information infrastructure supporting inter-organizational work pro-cesses was not solved.

5   Discussion

In this study, the characteristics of an II have been important when "catching" all the diverging issues of human, organizational and technical characters challenging the development of the new openEHR-based EPR system, and the integration between the existing and new EPR, in addition to the new ECM system. When analyzing the empirical case in light of the presented theoretical framework, it accumulated into four key challenges in the quest for semantic interoperability within and between heterogeneous health ISs.

First, in the empirical case, the first step of reaching interoperability seemed an easy target by replacing the existing highly free-text based EPR with the new innovative archetype-based EPR system. The replacement was supposed to make the goal of semantic interoperability within and between the hospitals' EPR systems reachable. In doing so, the vendor DIPS in cooperation with the Regional Project started the replacement as an evolution from the installed base, in terms of tailoring the new EPR to the existing EPR system in a specific clinical context of clinical routines and processes [11, 12, 20, 21, 23]. The integration was technically a success, but made the clinical work processes more cumbersome. For example, the physician needed to "jump" between the interfaces of the two systems when filling in the surgery decision note and this shift made the "clinical train of thoughts" more vulnerable to interruptions. Accordingly, the technical integration was not embedded into the clinicians' working routines because it did not rest on common standards allowing seamless scaling and interoperability [12, 21].

Second, the integration between the two EPRs was only an interim solution because the archetype-based EPR was going to replace the existing systems successively. As elaborated in the case, the vendor needed a repository of archetypes developed by the clinicians to speed up the development process of the new EPR. The "breakdown" of the vendor's development process brought in yet another perspective pointing at the need for common standards to make the new EPR evolve and replace the existing system – in comparison with an evolving II. The new angle addressed the necessary collaboration of clinicians to enroll, structure and standardize the clinical information (archetypes) supporting their healthcare processes [12, 14, 17]. In this sense, the evolving II had reach beyond the scope of the FIKS program's development process, in terms of beyond a single event and one-site practice [12]. This situation addressed an organizational interdependency, the establishment of NRUA, as well as a relational understanding because the archetype development process depended on the clinicians' engagement and collaboration. However, establishing NRUA with limited resources and the dependency of involvement from distributed clinicians was not a straightforward process. It is tempting to believe that the establishment would benefit from an overall resolution to use national or at least regional vendor-independent clinical information models as basis for a health information infrastructure [10, 12, 20, 22].

Third, in this empirical case – two best-of-breed systems are going to support the same healthcare process, the systems offer overlap in their functionality, partly providing the same or only slightly differing functionalities. This makes integration more difficult because archetypes represent maximum definition of clinical concepts, which is not applicable for traditional health ISs, such as the ECM, to receive and process. To solve this delicate situation, there will be a need for mapping clinical information e.g. a blood pressure measurement, between the two systems' different information models because much of the clinical information will be necessary for both systems to process. However, a consequence will be that the comprehensive information in archetypes will not be exchanged because the ECM does not use information models described as maximum definitions. On the contrary, exchanging clinical documentation recorded in the ECM to the new EPR will hamper the flexibility and possibility of contextualization inherent in archetypes as maximum definitions. Accordingly, the tension between local customized use and the need for standards and continuity (global) to support the same clinical process by two different systems in the same clinical context is not solved [12].

Fourth, successful integration of health ISs, in terms of a transparent II that supports clinicians with contextual clinical information necessary for instance in coordinating surgery planning processes, requires access to all relevant patient information regardless of where the information was created (the EPR or the ECM). However, comparing the new archetype-based EPR system with the new ECM (and the majority of today's health ISs), the latter was developed in such a way that the clinical information models are hard-coded directly into its software and database models. This situation challenges the transparency of the evolving II, and it was exactly the challenge that separating the clinical information models from the systems internal data models was trying to overcome. A platform of standardized vendor-independent clinical information models was meant to enable sharing and processing of clinical information, despite the situation of heterogeneous health ISs [15]. However, this brings to the surface that archetypes do not solve the goal of semantic interoperability by themselves. Even if there exists a repository of agreed-upon archetypes, the regional or national health authorities need to decide which clinical information models can act as interoperability standards and serve as a platform between heterogeneous health ISs [14, 15, 21–23].

6 Concluding Remarks

The overall goal of integrating health information systems is not a simple question of technical or semantic interoperability, or harmonizing the health ISs to the healthcare processes. The key challenges in integrating heterogeneous health ISs to enable sematic interoperability encompass a diversity of socio-technical issues and in particular political and policy barriers that need to be addressed.

To summarize the four explicit points discussed in the previous section, it is obvious that an archetype approach does not solve the holy grail of interoperability by itself. In light of the increased interest from national and regional governments to enable a smart, sustainable and consistent healthcare service, the potential within use of vendor-independent standardized clinical information models seems to be promising – but not solved. Vendor-independent standardized clinical information models, for example archetypes, are promising as an architecture to reach the goal of interoperability, but entail large structural changes if "interoperability standards" are going to form the foundation for integrating heterogeneous health ISs on a regional or national level. Moreover, this potential for deploying vendor-independent standardized clinical information models prepares the ground for further research.

References

1. Balka, E.S., Whitehouse, S., Coates, S.T., Andrusiek, D.: Ski hill injuries and ghost charts: socio-technical issues in achieving e-Health interoperability across jurisdictions. Inf. Syst. Front. **14**(1), 19–42 (2012)
2. Knaup, P., Bott, O., Kohl, C., Lovis, C., Garde, S.: Electronic patient records: moving from islands and bridges towards electronic health records for continuity of care. Yearb. Med. Inform. **1**, 34–46 (2007)
3. Gartner IT Glossary. http://www.gartner.com/it-glossary/
4. European Commission and Directorate-General for Health and Food: Safety, Disruptive Innovation: Considerations for Health and Health Care in Europe. Publications Office, Luxembourg (2015)
5. Singh, D.: How can Chronic Disease Management Programmes Operate Across Care Settings and Providers. World Health Organization Regional Office for Europe and European Observatory on Health Systems and Policies, Copenhagen (2008)
6. Berg, M.: Accumulating and coordinating: occasions for information technologies in medical work. Comput. Support. Coop. Work CSCW **8**(4), 373–401 (1999)
7. Ellingsen, G., Monteiro, E.: Mechanisms for producing a working knowledge: enacting, orchestrating and organizing. Inf. Organ. **13**(3), 203–229 (2003)
8. Grisot, M., Hanseth, O., Thorseng, A.A.: Innovation of, in, on infrastructures: articulating the role of architecture in information infrastructure evolution. J. Assoc. Inf. Syst. **15**(4), 2 (2014)
9. Ellingsen, G., Monteiro, E., Røed, K.: Integration as interdependent workaround. Int. J. Med. Inf. **82**(5), e161–e169 (2013)
10. Hanseth, O., Lyytinen, K.: Design theory for dynamic complexity in information infrastructures: the case of building internet. J. Inf. Technol. **25**(1), 1–19 (2010)
11. Monteiro, E., Pollock, N., Hanseth, O., Williams, R.: From artefacts to infrastructures. Comput. Support. Coop. Work CSCW **22**(4–6), 575–607 (2012)
12. Star, S.L., Ruhleder, K.: Steps toward an ecology of infrastructure: design and access for large information spaces. Inf. Syst. Res. **7**(1), 111–134 (1996)
13. Lenz, R., Reichert, M.: IT support for healthcare processes—premises, challenges, perspectives. Data Knowl. Eng. **61**(1), 39–58 (2007)
14. Gibbons, P., Arzt, N., Burke-Beebe, S., Chute, C., Dickinson, G., Flewelling, T., Jepsen, T., Kamens, D., Larson, J., Ritter, J., et al.: Coming to Terms: Scoping Interoperability for Health Care. Health Level Seven (2007). https://www.hln.com/assets/pdf/Coming-to-Terms-February-2007.pdf
15. Atalag, K., Beale, T., Chen, R., Gornik, T., Heard, S., McNicoll, I.: openEHR—a semantically enabled, vendor-independent health computing platform. http://www.openehr.org/resources/white_paper_docs/openEHR_vendor_independent_platform.pdf (2016)
16. Blobel, B., Goossen, W., Brochhausen, M.: Clinical modeling—a critical analysis. Int. J. Med. Inf. **83**(1), 57–69 (2014)
17. Beale, T.: Archetypes Constraint-Based Domain Models for Futureproof Information Systems (2000)

18. Duftschmid, G., Wrba, T., Rinner, C.: Extraction of standardized archetyped data from Electronic Health Record systems based on the Entity-Attribute-Value Model. Int. J. Med. Inf. **79**, 585–597 (2010)
19. Santos, M.R., Bax, M.P., Kalra, D.: Dealing with the archetypes development process for a regional EHR system. Appl. Clin. Inform. **3**(3), 258–275 (2012)
20. Aanestad, M., Jensen, T.B.: Building nation-wide information infrastructures in healthcare through modular implementation strategies. J. Strateg. Inf. Syst. **20**(2), 161–176 (2011)
21. Bowker, G.C., Star, S.L.: Sorting Things Out: Classification and Its Consequences. MIT, New Baskerville (1999)
22. Hanseth, O., Lundberg, N.: Designing work oriented infrastructures. Comput. Support. Coop. Work CSCW **10**(3–4), 347–372 (2001)
23. Hanseth, O., Monteiro, E.: Understanding Information Infrastructure (1998). http://heim.ifi.uio.no/~oleha/Publications/bok.pdf
24. National ICT. Service-based architecture for specialized health services (Action 12) (2008). www.nasjonalikt.no
25. National ICT, Use of archetype methodology for definingmaking available and using clinical information models in health information systems (Action 41) (2012). www.nasjonalikt.no
26. Klein, H.K., Myers, M.D.: A set of principles for conducting and evaluating interpretive field studies in information systems. MIS Q. **23**(1), 67–93 (1999)
27. Walsham, G.: Interpretive case studies in IS research: nature and method. Eur. J. Inf. Syst. **4**(2), 74–81 (1995)
28. Orlikowski, W.J., Baroudi, J.J.: Studying information technology in organizations: research approaches and assumptions. Inf. Syst. Res. **2**(1), 1–28 (1991)
29. Pollock, N., Williams, R.: Software and Organisations: The Biography of the Enterprise-Wide System or How SAP Conquered the World. Routledge, Abingdon (2008)

Erratum to: Nordic Contributions in IS Research

Susanne Stigberg$^{(\boxtimes)}$, Joakim Karlsen, Harald Holone,
and Cathrine Linnes

Østfold University College, Halden, Norway
susanne.k.stigberg@hiof.no

Erratum to:
S. Stigberg et al. (Eds.):
Nordic Contributions in IS Research, LNBIP 294,
DOI: 10.1007/978-3-319-64695-4

The name of the following editor Joakim Karlsen has been misspelled. The correct information is given below.

Joakim Karlsen

The updated online version of the book can be found at
http://dx.doi.org/10.1007/978-3-319-64695-4

© Springer International Publishing AG 2017
S. Stigberg et al. (Eds.): SCIS 2017, LNBIP 294, p. E1, 2017.
DOI: 10.1007/978-3-319-64695-4_12

Author Index

Printed in the United States
By Bookmasters